ECONOMIC
POVER

ECONOMICS OF POVERTY

R. Kothekar

CYBER TECH PUBLICATIONS
4264/3, Ansari Road, Daryaganj, New Delhi-110002 (India)
Ph.: 011-23244078. Fax: 011-23280028
E-Mail: cyberpublicationsdelhi@yahoo.com

ECONOMICS OF POVERTY

R. Kothekar

First Edition 2009

Published by :

G.S. Rawat for **Cyber Tech Publications**
4264/3, Ansari Road, Daryaganj, New Delhi-110002 (India)
Ph.: 011-23244078. Fax: 011-23280028
E-Mail: cyberpublicationsdelhi@yahoo.com

Printed at : Asian Offset Printers

Preface

In this world of plenty, almost half the world's six billion people live on two dollars a day or less. Between one third and one half suffer undernutrition due to insufficient intake of calories, protein or critical micronutrients such as vitamin A, iodine and iron. More than one child in five lives in acute poverty, an especially disturbing fact to thisfather of five. Why does such unnecessary injustice continue to disfigure a rich, technologically advanced world and what can be done to care for the poor and thereby to care for and honor God, as the Gospels instruct us?

We are called to feed the hungry, nurse the sick, and clothe the naked. The impulse to assist is obviously not unique to Christendom.Nor is it especially the comparative advantage of economics, for the instinct of economists is to look beyond the symptoms of poverty that indisputably demand prompt humanitarian response, and to seek instead the causal mechanisms that perpetuate poverty. In reflecting on the economics of poverty, my focus is therefore not on how best to run humanitarian operations but, rather, on the big picture mechanisms that necessitate the grim but honorable and too-necessary work of humanitarian relief agencies.

Most of this essay was composed during a two week trip to Madagascar, a fascinating country in which extraordinarily high species endemism rates fuel intense interest by conservationists and where the unique blend of Polynesian and Bantu cultures has long drawn the attention of cultural anthropologists. Such obvious unique qualities aside, Madagascar is nonetheless the quintessential poor economy.

— *Author*

CONTENTS

1

Introduction

POVERTY FACTS AND STATS

1. Half the world — nearly three billion people — live on less than two dollars a day.
2. More than 80 percent of the world's population lives in countries where income differentials are widening.
3. The poorest 40 percent of the world's population accounts for 5 percent of global income. The richest 20 percent accounts for three-quarters of world income.
4. According to UNICEF, 26,500-30,000 children die each day due to poverty. And they "die quietly in some of the poorest villages on earth, far removed from the scrutiny and the conscience of the world. Being meek and weak in life makes these dying multitudes even more invisible in death."
5. Around 27-28 percent of all children in developing countries are estimated to be underweight or stunted. The two regions that account for the bulk of the deficit are South Asia and sub-Saharan Africa.

   If current trends continue, the Millennium Development Goals target of halving the proportion of underweight children will be missed by 30 million children, largely because of slow progress in Southern Asia and sub-Saharan Africa.
6. Based on enrolment data, about 72 million children of primary school age in the developing world were not in

school in 2005; 57 per cent of them were girls. And these are regarded as optimisitic numbers.

7. Nearly a billion people entered the 21st century unable to read a book or sign their names.
8. Less than one per cent of what the world spent every year on weapons was needed to put every child into school by the year 2000 and yet it didn't happen.
9. Infectious diseases continue to blight the lives of the poor across the world. An estimated 40 million people are living with HIV/AIDS, with 3 million deaths in 2004. Every year there are 350–500 million cases of malaria, with 1 million fatalities: Africa accounts for 90 percent of malarial deaths and African children account for over 80 percent of malaria victims worldwide.
10. Water problems affect half of humanity:
    - Some 1.1 billion people in developing countries have inadequate access to water, and 2.6 billion lack basic sanitation.
    - Almost two in three people lacking access to clean water survive on less than $2 a day, with one in three living on less than $1 a day.
    - More than 660 million people without sanitation live on less than $2 a day, and more than 385 million on less than $1 a day.
    - Access to piped water into the household averages about 85% for the wealthiest 20% of the population, compared with 25% for the poorest 20%.
    - 1.8 billion people who have access to a water source within 1 kilometre, but not in their house or yard, consume around 20 litres per day. In the United Kingdom the average person uses more than 50 litres of water a day flushing toilets (where average daily water usage is about 150 liters a day. The highest average water use in the world is in the US, at 600 liters day.)

- Some 1.8 million child deaths each year as a result of diarrhoea
- The loss of 443 million school days each year from water-related illness.
- Close to half of all people in developing countries suffering at any given time from a health problem caused by water and sanitation deficits.
- Millions of women spending several hours a day collecting water.
- To these human costs can be added the massive economic waste associated with the water and sanitation deficit.... The costs associated with health spending, productivity losses and labour diversions ... are greatest in some of the poorest countries. Sub-Saharan Africa loses about 5% of GDP, or some $28.4 billion annually, a figure that exceeds total aid flows and debt relief to the region in 2003.

11. Number of children in the world

    2.2 billion

    Number in poverty

    1 billion (every second child)

    Shelter, safe water and health

    For the 1.9 billion children from the developing world, there are:

    - 640 million without adequate shelter (1 in 3)
    - 400 million with no access to safe water (1 in 5)
    - 270 million with no access to health services (1 in 7)

    Children out of education worldwide

    121 million

    Survival for children

    Worldwide,

    - 10.6 million died in 2003 before they reached the age of 5 (same as children population in France, Germany, Greece and Italy)

- 1.4 million die each year from lack of access to safe drinking water and adequate sanitation

Health of Children

Worldwide,

- 2.2 million children die each year because they are not immunized
- 15 million children orphaned due to HIV/AIDS (similar to the total children population in Germany or United Kingdom)

12. Rural areas account for three in every four people living on less than US$1 a day and a similar share of the world population suffering from malnutrition. However, urbanization is not synonymous with human progress. Urban slum growth is outpacing urban growth by a wide margin.
13. Approximately half the world's population now live in cities and towns. In 2005, one out of three urban dwellers (approximately 1 billion people) was living in slum conditions.
14. In developing countries some 2.5 billion people are forced to rely on biomass—fuelwood, charcoal and animal dung—to meet their energy needs for cooking. In sub-Saharan Africa, over 80 percent of the population depends on traditional biomass for cooking, as do over half of the populations of India and China.
15. Indoor air pollution resulting from the use of solid fuels [by poorer segments of society] is a major killer. It claims the lives of 1.5 million people each year, more than half of them below the age of five: that is 4000 deaths a day. To put this number in context, it exceeds total deaths from malaria and rivals the number of deaths from tuberculosis.
16. In the developing world, the national share of consumption for the poorest fifth of people was just 3.9% in 2004.

17. 1.6 billion people — a quarter of humanity — live without electricity:

Breaking that down further:

Number of people living without electricity

Region	Millions without electricity
South Asia	706
Sub-Saharan Africa	547
East Asia	224
Other	101

18. The GDP (Gross Domestic Product) of the 41 Heavily Indebted Poor Countries (567 million people) is less than the wealth of the world's 7 richest people combined.
19. World gross domestic product (world population approximately 6.5 billion) in 2006 was $48.2 trillion in 2006.
    - The world's wealthiest countries (approximately 1 billion people) accounted for $36.6 trillion dollars (76%).
    - The world's billionaires — just 497 people (approximately 0.000008% of the world's population) — were worth $3.5 trillion (over 7% of world GDP).
    - Low income countries (2.4 billion people) accounted for just $1.6 trillion of GDP (3.3%)
    - Middle income countries (3 billion people) made up the rest of GDP at just over $10 trillion (20.7%).
20. The world's low income countries (2.4 billion people) account for just 2.4% of world exports
21. The total wealth of the top 8.3 million people around the world "rose 8.2 percent to $30.8 trillion in 2004, giving them control of nearly a quarter of the world's financial assets."

    In other words, about 0.13% of the world's population controlled 25% of the world's financial assets in 2004.

22. For every $1 in aid a developing country receives, over $25 is spent on debt repayment.
23. 51 percent of the world's 100 hundred wealthiest bodies are corporations.
24. The wealthiest nation on Earth has the widest gap between rich and poor of any industrialized nation.
25. The poorer the country, the more likely it is that debt repayments are being extracted directly from people who neither contracted the loans nor received any of the money.
26. 20% of the population in the developed nations, consume 86% of the world's goods.
27. In 1960, the 20% of the world's people in the richest countries had 30 times the income of the poorest 20% — in 1997, 74 times as much.
28. An analysis of long-term trends shows the distance between the richest and poorest countries was about:
    - 3 to 1 in 1820
    - 11 to 1 in 1913
    - 35 to 1 in 1950
    - 44 to 1 in 1973
    - 72 to 1 in 1992
29. "Approximately 790 million people in the developing world are still chronically undernourished, almost two-thirds of whom reside in Asia and the Pacific."
30. For economic growth and almost all of the other indicators, the last 20 years [of the current form of globalization, from 1980 - 2000] have shown a very clear decline in progress as compared with the previous two decades [1960 - 1980]. For each indicator, countries were divided into five roughly equal groups, according to what level the countries had achieved by the start of the period (1960 or 1980). Among the findings:

- Growth: The fall in economic growth rates was most pronounced and across the board for all groups or countries.
- Life Expectancy: Progress in life expectancy was also reduced for 4 out of the 5 groups of countries, with the exception of the highest group (life expectancy 69-76 years).
- Infant and Child Mortality: Progress in reducing infant mortality was also considerably slower during the period of globalization (1980-1998) than over the previous two decades.
- Education and literacy: Progress in education also slowed during the period of globalization.

31. A mere 12 percent of the world's population uses 85 percent of its water, and these 12 percent do not live in the Third World.
32. Consider the global priorities in spending in 1998

Global Priority	$U.S. Billions
Cosmetics in the United States	8
Ice cream in Europe	11
Perfumes in Europe and the United States	12
Pet foods in Europe and the United States	17
Business entertainment in Japan	35
Cigarettes in Europe	50
Alcoholic drinks in Europe	105
Narcotics drugs in the world	400
Military spending in the world	780

33. And compare that to what was estimated as *additional* costs to achieve universal access to basic social services in all developing countries:

Global Priority	$U.S. Billions
Basic education for all	6
Water and sanitation for all	9
Reproductive health for all women	12
Basic health and nutrition	13

34. Notes and Sources

1. This figure is based on purchasing power parity (PPP), which basically suggests that prices of goods in countries tend to equate under floating exchange rates and therefore people would be able to purchase the same quantity of goods in any country for a given sum of money. That is, the notion that a dollar should buy the same amount in all countries. Hence if a poor person in a poor country living on a dollar a day moved to the U.S. with no changes to their income, they would still be living on a dollar a day. In addition, see the following:

   The 2007 Human Development Report (HDR) from the United Nations Development Program notes that, "There are still around 1 billion people living at the margins of survival on less than US$1 a day, with 2.6 billion—40 percent of the world's population—living on less than US$2 a day." (See page 25. The report also notes that the alleviation is limited mostly to parts of Asia.)

   For much of the 1990s and early 2000s, it was understood that roughly half of humanity had been living on about $2 a day.

   So, on initial read of the UN HDR report, this implies a reduction in recent years from half of humanity to 40 percent. However, the reduction may not be as much as previously thought. The previous link is to a Bretton Woods Project article noting that, "Preliminary recalculations of global economic output excluding differences in domestic prices and currencies, released by the World Bank in mid-December [2007], may undermine the much-trumpeted claims that globalisation has reduced the number of people living in extreme poverty.")

Also note that the use of $1 a day (and $2 a day) as poverty income measurements from the World Bank have been questioned and criticized as understating the level of poverty:

- o The World Bank has been criticized for almost arbitrarily coming up with a definition of a poverty line to mean one dollar per day.
- o In addition, as also stated in the previous link, in the United States for example, the poverty threshold for a family of four has been estimated to be around eleven dollars per day. The one dollar a day definition then misses out much of humanity to understand the impacts. Even the two dollars per day that I have pointed out here, while affecting half of humanity, also misses out the numbers under three or four, or eleven dollars per day. These statistics are harder to find, and as I come across them, I will post them here!
- o As an aside, Morgan Spurlock, the Oscar nominee for his documentary *Super Size Me* where he went 30 days on a diet of burgers only to see the effects, produced another documentary where for 30 days he tried to live on the minimum wage of $5.15 per hour. At times he was earning $50 to $70 a day and yet the tremendous hardships he faced was incredible (including a ludicrous $40 for a bandage in a hospital, and some $500 for just being seen to).
- o More fundamental than that though, for example, is a critique from Columbia University, called How not to count the poor. The report describes 3 main errors as being:
  1. An ill-defined poverty line;

2. A misleading and inaccurate measure of purchasing power equivalence; and
3. Incorrect extrapolation of limited data giving the false impression of precision while masking the high probably error of the estimates.

These errors are feared to lead to "a large understatement of the extent of global income poverty and to an incorrect inference that it has declined." (Emphasis added). This allows the World Bank to insist that the world is indeed "on the right track" in terms of poverty reduction strategy, attributing this "success" to the design and implementation of "good" or "better policies".

Nonetheless, the statistic has not been lost on some of the most prominent people in the world:

- o The *New York Times* in one of their email updates, in their Quote of the Day section, for July 18, 2001 provided the following quote: "A world where some live in comfort and plenty, while half of the human race lives on less than $2 a day, is neither just, nor stable." — President Bush
- o See also James Wolfenson, *The Other Crisis*, World Bank, October 1998 who said: "Today, across the world, 1.3 billion people live on less than one dollar a day; 3 billion live on under two dollars a day; 1.3 billion have no access to clean water; 3 billion have no access to sanitation; 2 billion have no access to electricity." (See also note 21 below.)
- o Koffi Anan, UN Secretary General, in a speech on the International Day for the Eradication of Poverty, 17 October 2000, said "Almost half the world's population lives on less than two dollars a day, yet even this statistic fails to capture the humiliation, powerlessness and brutal hardship that is the daily lot of the world's poor."

2

Poverty Around the World

INTRODUCTION

What does it mean to be poor? How is poverty measured? Third World countries are often described as "developing" while the First World, industrialized nations are often "developed". What does it mean to describe a nation as "developing"? A lack of material wealth does not necessarily mean that one is deprived. A strong economy in a developed nation doesn't mean much when a significant percentage (even a majority) of the population is struggling to survive.

Successful development can imply many things, such as (though not limited to):

- An improvement in living standards and access to all basic needs such that a person has enough food, water, shelter, clothing, health, education, etc;
- A stable political, social and economic environment, with associated political, social and economic freedoms, such as (though not limited to) equitable ownership of land and property;
- The ability to make free and informed choices that are not coerced;
- Be able to participate in a democratic environment with the ability to have a say in one's own future;
- To have the full potential for what the United Nations calls Human Development:

Human development is about much more than the rise or fall of national incomes. It is about creating an environment in which people can develop their full potential and lead productive, creative lives in accord with their needs and interests. People are the real wealth of nations. Development is thus about expanding the choices people have to lead lives that they value. And it is thus about much more than economic growth, which is only a means—if a very important one—of enlarging people's choices.

— *What is Human Development?, Human Development Reports, United Nations Development Program*

At household, community, societal, national and international levels, various aspects of the above need to be provided, as well as commitment to various democratic institutions that do not become corrupted by special interests and agendas. Yet, for a variety of reasons, these "full rights" are not available in many segments of various societies from the richest to the poorest. When political agendas deprive these possibilities in some nations, how can a nation develop? Is this progress?

Politics have led to dire conditions in many poorer nations. In many cases, international political interests have led to a diversion of available resources from domestic needs to western markets. (See the structural adjustment section to find out more about this.) This has resulted in a lack of basic access to food, water, health, education and other important social services. This is a major obstacle to equitable development.

Inequality

Inequality is not just bad for social justice, it is also bad for economic efficiency

— *Growth with equity is good for the poor, Oxfam, June 2000*

The Overseas Development Institute (ODI) describes poverty reduction as a *twin* function of:

1. The rate of growth, and

2. Changes in income distribution.

The ODI also adds that as well as increased growth, additional key factors to reducing poverty will be:

- The reduction in inequality
- The reduction in income differences

A few places around the world do see increasing rates of growth in a positive sense. But globally, there is also a negative change in income distribution. The reality unfortunately is that the gap between the rich and poor is widening. For example:

- About 0.13% of the world's population controlled 25% of the world's assets in 2004.
- 20% of the world's population consumes 86% of the world's goods while 80% of humanity gets just the remainder 14%.

(See poverty facts and stats on this site for more examples.)

Inequality and Health

A Canadian study also suggests that the wealthiest nations do not have the healthiest people; instead, it is countries with the smallest economic gap between the rich and poor.

Poverty has also been described as the number one health problem for many poor nations as they do not have the resources to meet the growing needs. Yet, it is not beyond humanity:

To satisfy all the world's sanitation and food requirements would cost only $13 billion, hardly as much as the people of the United States and the European Union spend each year on perfume.

— Ignacio Ramonet, The Politics of Hunger, Le Monde Diplomatique, November 1998 (see the article for many more statistics).

INEQUALITY FUELED BY MANY FACTORS

In some countries, a combination of successive military governments and/or corrupt leadership, as well as international economic policy have combined to create debt traps and wealth siphoning, affecting the poorer citizens the most (because the costs such as the debt gets "socialized").

Nigeria is one often-mentioned example, as Jubilee 2000 highlights. Indonesia is another example as part of this Noam Chomsky interview by *The Nation* magazine reveals. Latin America on the whole is another.

Latin America has the highest disparity rate in the world between the rich and the poor:

- Internal, regional and external geopolitics, various international economic factors and more, have all contributed to problems. For example, the foreign policy of the US in that region has often been criticized for failing to help tackle the various issues and only being involved to enhance US national interests and even interfering, affecting the course and direction of the nations in the region through overt and covert destabilization. This, combined with factors such as corruption, foreign debt, concentrated wealth and so on, has contributed to poverty there.
- Much of the above was written around early 1999. Unfortunately, well into 2003, the World Bank reported that the Latin American rich-poor gap is widening. There has been progress in closing the gender gap in income, and girls and young women had overtaken their male counterparts in education. However, inequality is very high. For example:
    - Income inequality in the region had worsened with the richest one tenth of the population earning 48% of its total income, while the poorest tenth earns only 1.6%
    - Race has also been a factor where "Indigenous and Afro-descended people are at considerable disadvantage with respect to whites, with the latter earning the highest wages in the region."

The U.S. itself also has the largest gap and inequality between rich and poor compared to all the other industrialized nations. For example, the top 1% receives more money than the bottom 40% and the gap is the widest in 70 years. Furthermore, in the last 20 years while the share of income going to the top 1% has increased, it has decreased for the poorest 40%.

INEQUALITY INCREASES SOCIAL TENSIONS

Andrew Simms, policy directory for the New Economics Foundation in U.K. (which spear-headed the Jubilee 2000 campaign to highlight the injustices of third world debt) makes an interesting suggestion in the British paper, *The Guardian* (August 6, 2003).

He suggests that as well as a minimum wage, for the sake of social cohesion there should perhaps be a maximum wage, too.

Amongst various things, Simms notes that tackling inequality from the other end is important because "the economic case for high executive pay in terms of company performance doesn't hold up, and because highly unequal societies have a habit of falling apart."

In addition: Crime and unhappiness stalk unequal societies. In the UK the bottom 50% of the population now owns only 1% of the wealth: in 1976 they owned 12%. Our economic system's incentive structure, instead of "trickle-down", is causing a "flood-up" of resources from the poor to the rich. Inequality leads to instability, the last thing the country or world needs right now.

Even the former hardline conservative head of the International Monetary Fund, Michel Camdessus, has come to the conclusion that "the widening gaps between rich and poor within nations" is "morally outrageous, economically wasteful and potentially socially explosive".

Above subsistence levels, what undermines our sense of well-being most is not our absolute income levels, but how big the gaps are between us and our peers. Allowing the super-rich to live apart from society is as damaging in its own way as the exclusion of the poorest.

— *Andrew Simms, Now for a maximum wage, The Guardian, August 6, 2003*

A prominent world leader does not think inequality is important.(This partial transcript of an interview with Britain's Prime Minister, Tony Blair, by the BBC prior to the June 2001 elections, reveals an example of that where Blair appeared to evade the question of the importance of reducing inequality, and kept suggesting that he wants to improve the lot of the poor, regardless of the levels of inequality between rich and poor.)

Britain's BBC aired a documentary on March 17, 2004, titled *IF*. It looked into a scenario of what would happen in a few years if the growing inequality in the United Kingdom continued to widen. While the predictions of what would happen are always tough to make, the documentary noted some important issues that are already present, and that also parallel many parts of the world today.

In summary, the documentary noted the increasing alienation and exclusion of people in society where inequality was high, but if government tried to do something about it, they would face a powerful obstacle: the rich. The remainder of this subsection provides more details:

"Gated communities", while providing an opportunity to develop otherwise derelict areas, also represents a sign of growing inequality, whereby those who can afford to do so live in areas where security is paid for and managed to ensure undesirables are kept out.

While individuals are making understandable decisions regarding their security, there is the additional effect of cutting off from the rest of society, leading to consequences such as:

- Resentment, fragmentation, and exclusion;
- A divided society (described as an "apartheid" of society);

- Further inequality of :
  - o Wealth;
  - o Opportunities;
  - o Space.

Side Note

While this phenomenon is rarely discussed in the U.K. for example, it is a common thing in many parts of the world, including the U.S., Latin America and many other parts of the Third World that exhibit high inequality.

These are times when the "welfare state" is failing people because it gives people a false sense of security and uses an element of coercion (payment of taxes to pay for the services). Yet, at the same time, the documentary noted, what is making this situation more complicated is that the super rich are taking advantage of globalization and all the loop holes it provides, such as off-shore tax havens. As a result, there is less the state is able to do, leading to further frustrations.

In the U.K., it was noted that inequality has been increasing to levels not seen since around the Second World War.

At the same time, in U.K. (as elsewhere) private security services are increasing, providing a quasi-policing role. This is in response to the increase in crime, an effect of inequality. But this has important implications. For example:

- Such services are good at protecting everything that is a commodity and has a price. This typically implies possessions of individuals.
- The wealthy, the documentary also noted, can afford more private security than the poor. When a fear of crime exists then it is understandable that people will want security services that can protect their property. Furthermore, one would not expect an individual concerned with their own well-being to appear to sacrifice that for the sake of society. The concerns for their immediate family, children naturally take precedence.

- Regrettably though, a downward spiral potentially emerges that seems hard to get out of, because of the increasing fragmentation and exclusion that this results it.

However, policing is meant to be more than protecting things of material value; the police are supposed to have social and human concerns for society as well, something a private security firm neither is mandated to have, nor is usually created for. Due to the different roles, the costs, structures and accountability are also different.

If crime is perceived to be increasing and the police are not seen as trusted, people can, and do take actions into their own hands. Wealthier people of course can afford to take more measures.

In theory then, one of the many things that makes up a functioning, stable and democratic society is an uncorrupted judicial system and law enforcement.

Addressing the root causes of inequality would therefore seem to be where the challenge lies. The political costs of inequality are recognized and accepted as being too high. The economic costs of fighting effects are also high. Citing some research, the BBC also noted that for each dollar spent on poverty causes, seven dollars was saved on consequences.

Unfortunately, governments are in a difficult situation, because they "can try to address inequality, but they will anger the rich".

Fragile Democracies, Inequality "turn good people to evil"

Earlier in May 2002, the BBC aired another documentary related to inequality, called *The Experiment*, where they showed in detail how inequality can "turn good people to evil".

- The experiment involved a system of guards and prisoners.
- The prisoners eventually revolted against the initial inequality.

- However, some of the former prisoners themselves instituted what was becoming an almost fascist regime before the experiment was eventually stopped.
- The documentary concluded that on a more general sense,
  - o Our democracies are more fragile than we realize;
  - o In addition, any power vacuums, which inequality can create and exacerbate, can seriously threaten to undermine democracy.

Inequality is also characterized by a concentration of wealth, which means a concentration of political power. Historically, one of the main reasons for continued poverty has been in order to maintain this power.

THE WEALTHY AND THE POOR

There is a pattern of inequality caused by the powerful subjugating the poor and keeping them dependent. Outside influence is often a large factor and access to trade and resources is the usual cause. It is often asked why the people of these countries do not stand up for themselves. In most cases when they do, they face incredible and often violent oppression from their ruling elites and from outsiders who see their national interests threatened.

Consider the following from the United Nations: Everyone has the right to work, to just and favourable conditions of work and to protection for himself and his family [and] an existence worthy of human dignity ... Everyone has the right to a standard of living adequate for the health and well being of himself and his family, including food, clothing, housing and medical care.

— *Universal Declaration of Human Rights, 1948*

And contrast that with the following around the same time, from a key superpower that helped create the United Nations. It is from George Kennan, head of the US State Department planning staff until 1950, and his comments on US relations with Far East: we have about 50% of the world's wealth, but only 6.3% of its population....In this situation, we cannot fail to be the object of envy and resentment. Our real task in the coming period is to devise a pattern of relationships which will permit us to maintain this position of disparity....To do so, we will have to dispense with all sentimentality and day-dreaming; and our attention will have to be concentrated everywhere on our immediate national objectives....We should cease to talk about vague and... unreal objectives such as human rights, the raising of the living standards, and democratization. The day is not far off when we are going to have to deal in straight power concepts. The less we are then hampered by idealistic slogans, the better.

... We should recognize that our influence in the Far Eastern area in the coming period is going to be primarily military and economic. We should make a careful study to see what parts of the Pacific and Far Eastern world are absolutely vital to our security, and we should concentrate our policy on seeing to it that those areas remain in hands which we can control or rely on.

— *George Kennan, U.S. State Department Policy Planning, Study #23, February 24, 1948. (See also Foreign Relations of the United States 1948, Vol. 1, No. 2, 1976 for the full text where this was first published; The text to the part on realism of US relations in the Far East; David McGowan, Derailing Democracy, (Common Courage Press, 2000), p.169; Noam Chomsky, What Uncle Sam Really Wants, (Odian Press, 1993), Chapter 2.*

While it is recognized that strong institutions, a functioning and non-corrupt democracy, an impartial media, equitable distribution of land and a well structured judicial system (and other such factors), etc. all help in realizing a successful nation and society, a lack of any of these things can lead to a marginalization of a sector of people. Often, it can be a very large sector.

For example, those likely to lose out in such an equalizing effect are the rich, elite power holders.

As a result of their ability to own and/or influence one of these above-mentioned things, they affect the lives of millions. This is a pattern seen throughout history. Take for example the medieval days of Europe where the wealthy of the time controlled land via a feudal ruling system and hence impoverished the common people intentionally.

- The rulers (Kings etc), would proclaim their "Divine Right" to rule over their subjects.
- They had an army of Lords and Bishops to advise on policies that benefited these groups (religion was used—and still is—to control and influence people, while Lords and Knights were an extension to the ruling family that would carry out the wishes.)
- They would heavily tax the people of their land.
- Not allowing the peasants to own the land upon which they lived meant that they would be stuck in poverty and dependency.
- When the elite.could no longer tax the poor, they started to tax the wealthy nobility.
    - o It was only at that point did the revolutions such as the French Revolution take hold (because now the nobility had their wealth affected and were able to influence the peasants to fight for their cause.)
    - o While this helped bring more rights, once the "people" won, there were concessions made that allowed the elite to retain their power, but to share it a bit more.

In the same way, today, certain rich multinational corporations influence the media, politicians and various institutions to foster an environment that benefits these few people. Dressed in rhetoric about how this is good for "everyone" it becomes difficult to break from this pattern.

Today's "corporate globalization", is another example (in a more international context) where the wealthier are able to determine the rules, shape the international institutions and influence the communication mechanisms that disseminate information to people.

Geopolitically, the elite in the United States of America then, follows the same pattern seen throughout history. As the world tried to break free from their imperial rulers (i.e as seen by the wealthy nations fighting over themselves in World War I and II and the subsequent fights for freedom in the colonial nations), the United States emerged as the intact wealthy nation to continue the same process.

Trading superiority was maintained by raiding and plundering areas deemed as a threat. Summarizing from the works of the Institute for Economic Democracy:

- The old European city states, which were centers of wealth, would control their countryside as the source of their resources and production, and hence, the source of their wealth. If the countryside became more efficient and produced better, or threatened to trade with other neighboring cities, this would be seen as a threat to the wealth, power and influence of the city. These peripheries would therefore be raided and their means of production would be destroyed.
- The cities would fight over each other for similar reasons.
- For continual support, those rulers would proclaim various reasons to their people, of maintaining security and so on (not unlike what we hear today about national security). Even some laws were established that basically allow these practices.
- A strong military was therefore necessary (just as it is today) to ensure those trade advantages were unfairly maintained.
- Those European city states evolved into nation states and imperial powers, and the countryside expanded to include today's "third world", which was much of the rest of the world. The discovery of the Americas,

expansion of trade routes etc brought much wealth to these "centers of empire" which helped fuel the industrial revolution, which required even more resources and wealth to be appropriated, to continue this growth. Mass "luxury" consumption in Europe expanded as well as a result of the increased production from the industrial revolution. But this had a further negative impact on the colonized nations, the "country side", or the resource-providers. (See the behind consumption and consumerism section on this site, for more about how this impacted much of the world in different ways as mass consumerism also resulted from the industrial revolution.)

- As with the previous wars throughout Europe's rise, World War I and II were also battles amongst the various European empires who struggled over each other to control more of the world's resources and who would "decide the rules of unequal trade".

Except for religious conflicts and the petty wars of feudal lords, wars are primarily fought over resources and trade. President Woodrow Wilson recognized that this was the cause of World War I: "Is there any man, is there any woman, let me say any child here that does not know that the seed of war in the modern world is industrial and commercial rivalry?"

— *J.W. Smith, Economic Democracy: The Political Struggle for the Twenty-First Century, (M.E. Sharpe. 2000, 1st Edition), p.58*

Plundering the "countryside" to maintain dominance and control of the wealth-producing process has been an age-old process.

These mercantilist processes continue today. Those policies of "plunder by raid" have continued, but include a more sophisticated "plunder by trade":

The powerful and cunning had learned to plunder by trade centuries ago and societies ever since have been caught in the trap of those unequal trades. Once unequal trades were in place, restructuring to equal trade would mean the severing of arteries of commerce which provide the higher standard of living for the dominant society and collapse of those living standards would almost certainly trigger open revolt. The world is trapped in that pattern of unequal trades yet today.

— J. W. Smith, Economic Democracy: The Political Struggle for the Twenty-First Century, (1st Books, 2002, 2nd Edition), Chapter 2

While Europe is now more cooperative, (in comparison to the horrors of World War II) and the U.S. has taken the lead, for the rest of the world, international trade arrangements and various economic policies still lead to the same result. Prosperity for a few has increased, as has poverty for the majority.

The geopolitical events of the post World War II era have been crucial for their impacts on poverty and most other issues. J.W. Smith summarizes this: Virtually the entire colonial world was breaking free, its resources would be turned to the care of its own people, and those resources could no longer be siphoned to the old imperial-centers-of-capital for a fraction of their value.

... If India and the rest of the world's former colonies continued to take the rhetoric of democracy seriously and form the nonaligned bloc as they were planning, over 80 percent of the world's population would be independent or on the other side of the ideological battle. And, if Japan, Germany, Italy, and France could not be held (it was far from sure they could be), that would leave only the United States, Britain, Canada, and Australia, about 10 percent of the world's population, still under the old belief system, and even there the ideological hold would be tenuous at best. After all, if there were no countryside under the firm control of an imperial center, the entire neo-liberal/neo-mercantilist belief system will have disappeared.

What Western nations were observing, of course, was the same potential loss of the resources and markets of their "countryside" as the cities of Europe had experienced centuries earlier. "National security" and "security interests," which citizens were coached (propagandized) to believe meant fear of a military attack, really meant maintaining access to the weak, impoverished world's valuable resources. The "domestic prosperity" worried about was only their own and the "constantly expanding trade" were unequal trades maintaining the prosperity of the developed world and the impoverishment of the undeveloped world as the imperial-centers-of-capital siphoned the natural wealth of their "countryside" to themselves.

... Those crucial natural resources are in the Third World and developed world capital could never compete if those people had their own industrial capital and processed their own resources into consumer products. With their own industrial capital, and assuming political and economic freedom as opposed to world neo-liberal/neo-mercantilist law dictated by military power, they could demand full value for their natural resources while simultaneously underselling the current developed world on manufactured product markets. The managers-of-state had to avert that crisis. The world's break for freedom must be contained.

— J.W. Smith, The World Breaking Free Frightened the Security Councils of Every Western Nation, Economic Democracy; The Political Struggle for the 21st Century (1st Books, Second Edition, 2002), Chapter 7

In this backdrop, how do developing nations contend with poverty?

- Often, if governments try to improve situations for their people, they may face pressure or even military intervention by the powerful nations. (Ironic then, that the foremost backers of free trade point out that it will help reduce conflicts. It probably would, if there was truly free but fair and possibly managed to avoid problems related to power and undue influence. Today's international trade is influenced by the wealthy.)
- The powerful nations of course claim this is to save the other country, but it is usually to do with protecting

"their" national interests; namely a constant supply of cheap resources or some other reason related ultimately to maintaining influence and power.

- Dictators and other corrupt rulers have often been placed/supported in power by the wealthier nations to help fulfill those "national interests" in a similar way the old rulers of Europe used the Lords and Knights to control the peripheries and direct resources to the centers of capital. (Although, now, increasingly, "democracies" are supported, but ones where the economic choices are so limited, that the "democracy" provides a similar environment that a dictatorship did, for foreign investors, but without the overt violence and oppression.)
- This means that it is hard to break out from poverty, or to reduce dependency from the US/IMF/World Bank etc. Structural Adjustment, as described in a previous section on this web site, is an example of that dependency.

Hence, many back the economic neoliberal policies without realizing the background to it. It is another example that while international trade and globalization is what probably most would like to see, the reality of it is that it is not matching the rhetoric that is broadcast.

J.W. Smith has researched this in depth and the following offers a relevant summary:

The Third World remains poor because the powerful strive to dominate every choke-point of commerce. One key choke-point is political control through the "co-respective" support of local elites. Where loyalty is lacking, money will be spent to purchase it. If a government cannot be bought or otherwise controlled, corrupt groups will be financed and armed to overthrow that government and, in extreme cases, another country will be financed to attack and defeat it.... The pattern has been well established repeatedly throughout history and throughout the world, as noted by the well-known philosopher Bertrand Russell,

An enormous proportion of the income of nations and individuals, nowadays, is blood money: payment exacted by the threat of death. Therefore the most prudent nation is the nation which is in the best position to levy blackmail....Modern nations are highwaymen, saying to each other "your money or your life," and generally taking both.

— J.W. Smith, The World's Wasted Wealth 2, (Institute for Economic Democracy, 1994), p. 134.

(To find out more about the political dimensions of the economy of the world and to see the detailed links between history (how it is both told and repeated), politics that are always at play and the effects on the economy the world over, visit the Institute for Economic Democracy web site. It provides much more in-depth research into these backgrounds and in far more detail than what I have summarized above.)

With this in mind, why would so many people not oppose such things? There are many reasons, including:

- Most people don't know—this is not an accident. It is in the interest of power-holders to ensure as little is questioned by outsiders as possible. Whether it be via an aristocracy or by simple distortion of information, educational systems, or whatever, different nations have had various means to handle this.

The smart way to keep people passive and obedient is to strictly limit the spectrum of acceptable opinion, but allow very lively debate within that spectrum—even encourage the more critical and dissident views. That gives people the sense that there's free thinking going on, while all the time the presuppositions of the system are being reinforced by the limits put on the range of the debate.

— Noam Chomsky, The Common Good, Odonian Press, 1998

- Those that have opposed such things in the past may have been persecuted in some way. In some societies those who try to say something may just face ridicule due to the embedded belief systems which are being questioned, while in other societies, people may even face violent oppositions.

- Some dare not entertain the thought that the work they may be doing could be at the expense and exploitation of someone else. The following summarizes this aspect quite well:

[W]e should be familiar with the sincerity with which people will protect the economic territory that provides them their livelihood and wealth. Besides the necessity of a job or other source of income for survival, people need to feel that they are good and useful to society. Few even admit, even to themselves, that their hard work may not be fully productive. This emotional shield requires most people to say with equal sincerity that those on welfare are "lazy, ignorant, and nonfunctional."

Those above the poverty level vigorously insist that they are honest and productive and fulfill a social need. It is important to their emotional well-being that they believe this. They dare not acknowledge that their segment of the economy may have 30 to 70 percent more workers than necessary or that the displaced should have a relatively equal share of jobs and income. This would expose their redundancy and, under current social rules, undermine their moral claim to their share. Such an admission could lead to the loss of their economic niche in society. They would then have to find another territory within the economy or drop into poverty themselves.

— J.W. Smith, The World's Wasted Wealth 2, (Institute for Economic Democracy, 1994), p. 90.

J.W. Smith, quoted above, also points out (and details in his work) how we have moved from "plunder by raid to plunder by trade" in recent centuries. The complexities of some of today's economics and trading systems also make it harder to address root causes of poverty: Although in [the] early years the power brokers knew they were destroying others' tools of production (industrial capital) in the ongoing battle for economic territory, trade has now become so complex that few of today's powerful are aware of the waste and destruction created by the continuation of this neo-mercantilist struggle for markets. Instead, they feel that it is they who are responsible for the world's improving standards of living and that they are defending not only their rights but everybody's rights.

This illusion is possible because in the battle to monopolize society's productive tools and the wealth they produce, industrial capital has become so productive that—even as capital, resources, and labor are indiscriminately consumed—living standards in the over-capitalized nations have continued to improve. And societies are so accustomed to long struggles for improved living standards that to think it could be done much faster seems irrational.

— J.W. Smith, The World's Wasted Wealth 2, (Institute for Economic Democracy, 1994), p. 158.

And when considering how today's global economic model promotes the liberalization of capital more and more, the effects of rapid flows of capital and other impacts of over-liberalization is borne largely by the poorer members of society:

A French humorist once wrote, "When it's money you're after, look for it where it is most abundant, among the poor." Governments now do this more than ever because the poor are rooted, stationary, "slow"; whereas the big money is nomadic and travels at the speed of bytes. Stationary money (of local businesses, professionals, wage and salary earners) will be taxed to the limit for the simple reason that it can be got at.

— Susan George, The Lugano Report, (Pluto Press, 1999), p. 186

THE WORLD BANK AND POVERTY

The World Bank, being a major international institution, is worth looking at to see how its policies help or impact poverty and development around the world. The World Bank produces an annual report, called the World Development Report. The

Bank regards this as its flagship report. Most mainstream economists use this report in some way or form, and it is one of the few reports on development that the US mainstream media reports on (because it usually shows the US, and its policies that it prescribes to the rest of the world, in a favorable light.)

The way the 2000 report was released highlighted another problem with the World Bank, and how it doesn't like to accept criticism on the current forms of globalization and neoliberalism. For the 2000 report, Ravi Kanbur, a professor from Cornell University had been asked to lead up the report team.

Kanbur won respect from NGO circles as he tried to be inclusive and take in a wide range of views, something the Bank has been criticized for not doing (which is a problem in itself!).

However, as the report was to be published, he resigned because he was unreasonably pressured by the Bank to tone down sections on globalization, which, amongst other things called for developing nations to accept market neoliberalism cautiously.

The World Bank was apparently influenced itself by the US Treasury on this—this is not new though; critics have long pointed out that the Bank is very much influenced by the US, thus affecting the chance of real progress being made on poverty issues around the world.

The following quotes collected from the Bretton Woods Project, reveal some interesting insights:

The Washington Consensus has emerged from the Asia Crisis with its faith in free markets only slightly shaken. Poverty eradication is now the menu, but the main dish is still growth and market liberalisation, with social safety nets added as a side dish, and social capital scattered over it as a relish. The overall implication of the resignation is fairly clear. The US does not want the World Bank to stray too far from its agenda of economic growth and market liberalisation. Ravi Kanbur's draft has raised a few too many doubts about this agenda, and strayed too much towards politics.

— *The Nation, Bangkok, 5 July, 2000*

To keep the Bank afloat Wolfensohn has to steer between two major constituencies. The first are the critics, the second is the US Treasury. You don't need to be a World Bank economist to do the cost benefit analysis. To save the Bank, and his own reputation, it is essential that the Bank's policies and public pronouncements do not err too far from its main shareholder and political protector, the US Treasury.

— *Focus on Trade, Issue Number 51, Focus on the Global South, June 2000*

The World Bank has often come under criticism for its development projects not actually helping the societies that they claimed they will. One such example is the numerous dam projects that have seen lives devastated, where millions have been displaced and people have not seen the benefits promised, while at the same time, the environment has degraded and crucial arable land has been flooded. This is discussed further on this site's hunger and poverty causes section.

Another example is the devastating Structural Adjustment Policies pressured upon poor countries by the First World, The World Bank and the IMF. These have had devastating consequences for much of the third world, though benefiting the First World.

Another example involves a recent Chad-Cameroon oil pipeline project, which started construction in 2000. The World Bank had also stressed commitments to ensure policies were observed that would protect society and the environment, while helping millions of poor in Chad out of extreme poverty (Chad is the fifth poorest country in the world) and also providing land-locked Cameroon with much needed revenue.

The World Bank's actual monetary investment amount was just four percent of the cost. However their participation and stated commitment to poverty-combating development gave political backing that allowed multinational oil companies (who were the main investors) to raise sufficient capital on the international capital markets, which they would not have been able to otherwise do.

The World Bank had therefore highlighted this project as a prototype for the extractive industry, designed to carry oil wealth not to a few but to the mass of the poor.

AfricaFiles is an organization about African issues from the perspective of human rights, economic justice, and African perspective and alternative analysis. Given the World Bank's claims and presenting this project as a flagship of sorts, AfricaFiles issued a report looking to see how the World Bank's claims held up.

They concluded that:

1. "Oil corporations cannot be transformed into development agencies even with the best intentions and monitoring mechanisms" referring to the sidelining of time-intensive parts of the project such as capacity building and taking social and environmental issues into consideration.
2. As a result, "global levers of development outcomes like the World Bank cannot exercise sufficient clout on oil multinationals' penchant for profits"
3. "The World Bank is incapable of respecting its own weakening safeguard policies, which are premised on controlling damage rather than avoiding harm. This is particularly significant as Africa banks on the increasing trend in Foreign Direct Investments (FDIs)."
4. "The embryonic neo-liberal governance structures in Africa are incapable of forcing FDIs, which are principally attracted by ground mineral resources, to respect ecological and social principles. This cannot be over-stressed, especially as the World Bank prepares to engage in what it calls high risk/high reward projects in developing countries."

5. "The flawed contention of the World Bank is 'you cannot eat omelettes without breaking some eggs.' As this paper has demonstrated, the eggs most often broken are those of the poor who are left with no alternative livelihood." The paper has also noted the high level of corruption, implying that those who would "eat the omelette" so to speak, would be the wealthy elite and multinationals.
6. "Public Private Partnership [PPP], the buzz paradigm of sustainable development, is fundamentally incapable of addressing the unequal power relation between fattening multinationals, weakening states and the World Bank, in this era of globalisation."

AfricaFiles also, interestingly, suggested the World Bank use its precious resources to support more renewable energy sources development rather than oil, which has had so much political, economic and environmental problems associated with it. This was also a recommendation from a report commissioned by the World Bank itself, which has not been followed.

In mid-2004, the committee set up to oversee transparency in the oil revenues in Chad has protested about the lack of resources from both the government and the oil company involved, and that people in Chad were becoming disillusioned at the project.

In September 2005, the human rights organization, *Amnesty International* criticized the project investment agreements for undermining human rights, noting that, "The investment agreements governing the project risk seriously undermining the ability and willingness of Chad and Cameroon to protect their citizens' human rights, making the oil companies de facto unaccountable in the pipeline zone." Nearby fisherman and farmers have also been denied access to water and land, and that "there is a prevailing climate of fear and intimidation around the pipeline, some of whose critics have already been arrested and intimidated."

In mid-January, 2006, the *BBC* reports that the World Bank shut down the Chad oil account which was to keep 10%

of the oil revenue for future generations of people in Chad. The Chad government argued it needed to fight against poverty now and had a right to that revenue and signed a law allowing access to that account early.

Earlier, the World Bank had suspended some loans, too. Some will raise concern of possible intention for corrupt practices by the Chad government, while others will see the World Bank's influence at play here, preventing another African country to determine its own policies and be accountable to its own people.

POVERTY IN INDUSTRIALIZED COUNTRIES

But poverty is not restricted just to developing countries. Industrialized nations are also seeing a sharp increase in poverty. While the current form of globalization is resulting in additional wealth, the disparities are sharp. Less people are turning out to be benefiting while an increasing number are left behind.

Even in places such as Europe and USA, poor people still do not seem to get enough attention or resources to help alleviate their problems. For example, consider Britain:

- Even though Britain is one of the most affluent members of the European Union (EU), a report shows that UK is the worst place in Europe to be growing up if you are poor, as more children are likely to be born in to poverty there, compared to elsewhere in the EU.
- The UK National Office of Statistics also shows that disparities between rich and poor continue to grow in UK, as reported by a UK newspaper, *The Independent*, April 2000.
- Priorities of the Labour Party government have often been questioned (as with priorities of any party) but highlighted by how at the turn of the century, some 150,000 people were homeless in Britain, yet the government helped build the Millennium Dome, that cost over a billion US dollars.

- Andrew Simms, policy director of the New Economics Foundation in an article mentioned further above about inequality notes that

Crime and unhappiness stalk unequal societies. In the UK the bottom 50% of the population now owns only 1% of the wealth: in 1976 they owned 12%. Our economic system's incentive structure, instead of "trickle-down", is causing a "flood-up" of resources from the poor to the rich. Inequality leads to instability, the last thing the country or world needs right now.

Even the former hardline conservative head of the International Monetary Fund, Michel Camdessus, has come to the conclusion that "the widening gaps between rich and poor within nations" is "morally outrageous, economically wasteful and potentially socially explosive".

— *Andrew Simms, Now for a maximum wage, The Guardian, August 6, 2003*

- A UNICEF report in February 2007 finds that UK is failing its children as it comes bottom of all industrialized nations in terms of child well being. UK child poverty has doubled since 1979, for example.

As another example, the U.S. is worth looking at as well.

- It may be surprising to most people to realize that USA, the wealthiest nation on Earth, has the widest gap between rich and poor of any industrialized nation, and disparities continue to grow (See also this article and this article about how the media deals with such issues.)
- United For a Fair Economy reported that for 1998 almost 70% of the wealth was in the hand of the top 10%. In another report, they mention that the gap has widened in recent decades. "In 1989, the United States had 66 billionaires and 31.5 million people living below the official poverty line. A decade later, the United States has 268 billionaires and 34.5 million people living below the poverty line-about $13,000 for a three-person family."

- Even during the "booming economy" (for some in society, not all) in the late 1990s and early 2000, there was an increasing gap between the rich and poor. Even into 2002, fighting poverty appears not to have been a major election campaign issue as with recent previous election campaigns.
- Then chairman of the Federal Reserve, Allan Greenspan, revealed concerns in mid-2005 that the increasing and widening income gap might eventually threaten the stability of democratic capitalism itself in the US.
- While health and education are key to any economy or nation to grow and be strong, both of these suffer issues of access, equality and pressure to cut back (including elsewhere around the world as discussed in the structural adjustment part of this site).
  - For example, as a summary of a report titled *Economic Apartheid in America* mentions, "that the United States is the only industrialised nation that 'views health care as a privilege, not a basic human right.'". (Unfortunately the report itself not available on the Internet, but is produced by United for a Fair Economy where you can see many extracts and similar reports.)
  - In addition, as good education is linked to a strong economy, *Business Week* reports (February 14, 2002) on a study that analyses OECD data from 1994 to 1998, and summarizes that "the literacy of American adults ranks 10th out of 17 industrialized countries." In addition, the issue of inequality was highlighted: "More troubling, the U.S. has the largest gap between highly and poorly educated adults, with immigrants and minorities making up the largest chunk of those at the bottom." While *Business Week* concentrates on the U.S. they also point out that "Despite the mediocre U.S. ranking, it still beat out most of its major trading partners except Germany, including

France, Britain, and Italy. (Japan didn't participate [in the study].)"

- The above-mentioned UNICEF report on child health found that as well as the UK being ranked bottom of all rich countries, the US ranked second to last. The report suggests that absolute wealth isn't necessarily a guarantor of poverty alleviation or a measure for indicators such as child well-being, and factors such as inequality are also important.

And it isn't in just these two industrialized nations that these problems persist. A *Guardian* news report, for example, shows that certain types of poverty in various European cities can be regarded as worse than in some other parts of the world which one would not normally think would compare with Europe, such as India.

3

Structural Adjustment—a Major Cause of Poverty

Debt is an efficient tool. It ensures access to other peoples' raw materials and infrastructure on the cheapest possible terms. Dozens of countries must compete for shrinking export markets and can export only a limited range of products because of Northern protectionism and their lack of cash to invest in diversification. Market saturation ensues, reducing exporters' income to a bare minimum while the North enjoys huge savings. The IMF cannot seem to understand that investing in ... [a] healthy, well-fed, literate population ... is the most intelligent economic choice a country can make.

— Susan George, A Fate Worse Than Debt, (New York: Grove Weidenfeld, 1990), pp. 143, 187, 235

Many developing nations are in debt and poverty partly due to the policies of international institutions such as the International Monetary Fund (IMF) and the World Bank.

Their programs have been heavily criticized for many years for resulting in poverty. In addition, for developing or third world countries, there has been an increased dependency on the richer nations. This is despite the IMF and World Bank's claim that they will reduce poverty.

Following an ideology known as neoliberalism, and spearheaded by these and other institutions known as the "Washington Consensus" (for being based in Washington D.C.),

Structural Adjustment Policies (SAPs) have been imposed to ensure debt repayment and economic restructuring. But the way it has happened has required poor countries to reduce spending on things like health, education and development, while debt repayment and other economic policies have been made the priority. In effect, the IMF and World Bank have demanded that poor nations lower the standard of living of their people.

A Spiraling Race to the Bottom

As detailed further below, the IMF and World Bank provide financial assistance to countries seeking it, but apply a neoliberal economic ideology or agenda as a precondition to receiving the money. For example:

- They prescribe cutbacks, "liberalization" of the economy and resource extraction/export-oriented open markets as part of their structural adjustment.
- The role of the state is minimized.
- Privatization is encouraged as well as reduced protection of domestic industries.
- Other adjustment policies also include currency devaluation, increased interest rates, "flexibility" of the labor market, and the elimination of subsidies such as food subsidies.
- To be attractive to foreign investors various regulations and standards are reduced or removed.

The impact of these preconditions on poorer countries can be devastating. Factors such as the following lead to further misery for the developing nations and keep them dependent on developed nations:

- Poor countries must export more in order to raise enough money to pay off their debts in a timely manner.
- Because there are so many nations being asked or forced into the global market place—before they are economically and socially stable and ready—and told to

concentrate on similar cash crops and commodities as others, the situation resembles a large-scale price war.

- Then, the resources from the poorer regions become even cheaper, which favors consumers in the West.
- Governments then need to increase exports just to keep their currencies stable (which may not be sustainable, either) and earn foreign exchange with which to help pay off debts.
- Governments therefore must:
  - o spend less
  - o reduce consumption
  - o remove or decrease financial regulations
  - o and so on.
- Over time then:
  - o the value of labor decreases
  - o capital flows become more volatile
  - o a spiraling race to the bottom then begins, which generates
  - o social unrest, which in turn leads to "IMF riots" and protests around the world
- These nations are then told to peg their currencies to the dollar. But keeping the exchange rate stable is costly due to measures such as increased interest rates.
- Investors obviously concerned about their assets and interests can then pull out very easily if things get tough
  - o In the worst cases, capital flight can lead to economic collapse, such as we saw in the Asian/global finacial crises of 1997/98/99, or in Mexico, Brazil, and many other places. During and after a crisis, the mainstream media and free trade economists lay the blame on emerging markets and their governments' restrictive or inefficient policies, crony capitalism, etc., which is a cruel irony.

- When IMF donors keep the exchange rates in their favor, it often means that the poor nations remain poor, or get even poorer. Even the 1997/98/99 global financial crisis cam be partly blamed on structural adjustment and early, overly aggressive deregulation for emerging economies.
- Millions of children end up dying each year.

Competition between companies involved in manufacturing in developing countries is often ruthless. We are seeing what Korten described as "a race to the bottom. With each passing day it becomes more difficult to obtain contracts from one of the mega-retailers without hiring child labor, cheating workers on overtime pay, imposing merciless quotas, and operating unsafe practices."

— *John Madeley, Big Business Poor Peoples; The Impact of Transnational Corporations on the World's Poor, (Zed Books, 1999) p. 103*

This is one of the backbones to today's so-called "free" trade. In this form, as a result, it is seen by some as unfair and one-way, or extractionalist. It also serves to maintain unequal free trade as pointed out by J.W. Smith.

As a result, policies such as Structural Adjustments have, as described by Smith, contributed to "the greatest peacetime transfer of wealth from the periphery to the imperial center in history", to which we could add, without much media attention.

Maintaining Dependency and Poverty

One of the many things that the powerful nations (through the IMF, World Bank, etc.) prescribe is that the developing nation should open up to allow more imports in and export more of their commodities. However, this is precisely what contributes to poverty and dependency.

[I]f a society spends one hundred dollars to manufacture a product within its borders, the money that is used to pay for materials, labor and, other costs moves through the economy as each recipient spends it. Due to this multiplier effect, a hundred dollars worth of primary production can add several hundred dollars to the Gross National Product (GNP) of that country. If money is spent in another country, circulation of that money is within the exporting country. This is the reason an industrialized product-exporting/commodity-importing country is wealthy and an undeveloped product-importing/commodity-exporting country is poor. [Emphasis Added]

...Developed countries grow rich by selling capital-intensive (thus cheap) products for a high price and buying labor-intensive (thus expensive) products for a low price. This imbalance of trade expands the gap between rich and poor. The wealthy sell products to be consumed, not tools to produce. This maintains the monopolization of the tools of production, and assures a continued market for the product. [Such control of tools of production is a strategy of a mercantilist process. That control often requires military might.]

— J.W. Smith, The World's Wasted Wealth 2, (Institute for Economic Democracy, 1994), pp. 127, 139.

As seen above as well, one of the effects of structural adjustment is that developing countries must increase their exports. Usually commodities and raw materials are exported. But as Smith noted above, poor countries lose out when they

- export commodities (which are cheaper than finished products)
- are denied or effectively blocked from industrial capital and real technology transfer, and
- import finished products (which are more expensive due to the added labor to make the product from those commodities and other resources)

This leads to less circulation of money in their own economy and a smaller multiplier effect. Yet, this is not new. Historically this has been a partial reason for dependent economies and poor nations. This was also the role enforced upon former countries under imperial or colonial rule. Those same third world countries find themselves in a similar situation. This can also be described as *unequal* trade:

> At first glance it may seem that the growth in development of export goods such as coffee, cotton, sugar, and lumber, would be beneficial to the exporting country, since it brings in revenue. In fact, it represents a type of exploitation called *unequal exchange*. A country that exports raw or unprocessed materials may gain currency for their sale, but they lose it if they import processed goods. The reason is that processed goods—goods that require additional labor—are more costly. Thus a country that exports lumber but does not have the capacity to process it must then re-import it in the form of finished lumber products, at a cost that is greater than the price it received for the raw product. The country that processes the materials gets the added revenue contributed by its laborers. (Emphasis is original)
>
> — *Richard Robbins, Global Problems and the Culture of Capitalism, (Allyn and Bacon, 1999), p. 95*

Exporting commodities and resources is seen as favorable to help earn foreign exchange with which to pay off debts and keep currencies stable. However, partly due to the price war scenario mentioned above, commodity prices have also dropped. Furthermore, reliance on just a few commodities makes countries even more vulnerable to global market conditions and other political and economic influences. As *Gemini News Service* also reports, talking to the World Bank:

> More than 50 developing countries depend on three or fewer commodities for over half of their export earnings. Twenty countries are dependent on commodities for over 90 percent of their total foreign exchange earnings, says the World Bank.
>
> — *Ken Laidlaw, Market Cure Proposed For Third World's Battered Farmers, Gemini News Service, December 4, 2001 (Link is to reposted version on this web site)*

Almost four years after the above was written, *Oxfam* reveals that things have not changed for the better: more than

50 per cent of Africa's export earnings is derived from a single commodity; numerous countries are dependent on two commodities for the vast majority of their export earnings; and there are a number of other countries in Africa heavily dependent on very few commodities.

In addition, as Celine Tan of the *Third World Network* explains:

> Falling [commodity] prices have meant that large increases in export volume by commodity producers have not translated into greater export revenues, leading to severely declining terms of trade for many commodity producing countries. When the purchasing power of a country's exports declines, a country is unable to purchase imported goods and services necessary for its sustenance, as well as generating income for the implementation of sustainable development programs.
>
> A vast majority of developing countries depend on commodities as a main source of revenue. Primary commodities account for about half of the export revenues of developing countries and many developing countries continue to rely heavily on one or two primary commodities for the bulk of their export earnings.
>
> — *Celine Tan, Tackling the Commodity Price Crisis Should Be WSSD's Priority, TWN Briefings for WSSD No.14, Third World Network, August 2002*

Tan also highlights in the above article that "a fall in commodity prices have [sic] also led to a build-up of unsustainable debt." The lack of greater revenues from exports has knock-on effects, as described further above. The irony is that structural adjustments were prescribed by the IMF and the World Bank due to debt repayment concerns in the first place.

As debt-relief and trade became major topics of discussion during the G8 Summit 2005, Yaya Orou-Guidou, an economist from Benin (a small African country), also noted that exporting raw materials and agricultural products would not help fight poverty. Those raw materials have to be processed in the same poor country to help create a multiplier effect:

Orou-Guidou believes Benin will need to start processing the raw materials it produces if it is to escape the poverty trap.

"A prime material kept in Africa for processing in our factories is one less thing for Western factories to earn money on," he notes. But, if "we content ourselves with selling our agricultural or mining products in their raw states, they will always feed Western factories which provide jobs for (the West's) own people."

— Ali Idrissou-Toure, Debt Cancellation No Panacea for Benin, Inter Press Service, July 7, 2005

Political economist Adam Smith also provided some insights in his 1776 classic, *The Wealth of Nations*, which is regarded as the Bible of capitalism. He was highly critical of the mercantilist practices of the wealthy nations, while he recognized the value of local industry and the impact of imported manufactured products on local industries:

Though the encouragement of exportation and the discouragement of importation are the two great engines by which the mercantile system proposes to enrich every country, yet with regard to some particular commodities it seems to follow an opposite plan: to discourage exportation and to encourage importation.

Its ultimate object, however, it pretends, is always the same, to enrich the country by the advantageous balance of trade. It discourages the exportation of the materials of manufacture, and of the instruments of trade, in order to give our own workmen an advantage, and to enable them to undersell those of other nations in all foreign markets; and by restraining, in this manner, the exportation of a few commodities of no great price, it proposes to occasion a much greater and more valuable exportation of others.

It encourages the importation of the materials of manufacture in order that our own people may be enabled to work them up more cheaply, and thereby prevent a greater and more valuable importation of the manufactured commodities. (Emphasis Added)

— Adam Smith, Wealth of Nations, Book IV, Chapter VIII, (Everyman's Library, Sixth Printing, 1991), p.577

Reading the above, we can say that structural adjustment policies are also mercantilist. We are constantly told that we live in a world of global capitalism, and yet we see that while free markets are preached (in Adam Smith's name), mercantilism is still practiced!

Of course, today it is a bit more complicated too. We do have, for example, products being exported from the poorer countries (albeit some facing high barriers in the rich nations). But exporting rather than first creating and developing local industry and economy, means the "developing" country loses out in the long run, (hardly "developing") because there is little multiplier effect of money circulating within the country, as mentioned above. Furthermore, with labor being paid less than their fair wages in the poorer nations, wealth is still accumulated by—and concentrated in—the richer nations.

The Luckiest Nut In The World is an 8 minute video (sorry, no transcript available, as far as I know), produced by Emily James. It is a cartoon animation explaining the effects of loans, structural adjustment and cashcrops, and their impacts on poorer countries. It traces how Senegal was encouraged to grow nuts for export. In summary,

- As a poor nation without many resources, it took out loans to help develop the industry.
- Other nations saw this was going well, so they followed suit.
- The price of nuts started to drop and Senegal faced debt repayment problems.
- Structural adjustment policies were put in place, cutting spending and reducing government involvement in the nut industry and elsewhere.

- However, things got worse.
- At the same time rich countries, such as the US, were subsidizing their own nut (and other) industries, allowing them to gain in market share around the world.
- Rich countries have tools such as trade tariffs and the threat of sanctions at their disposal to help their industries, if needed.

Thus we are in a situation where the rich promote a system of free trade for everyone else to follow, while mercantilism is often practiced for themselves.

- "Free trade" is promoted by the rich and influential as the means for all nations to achieve prosperity and development.
- The wealth accumulated by the richer countries in the past is attributed to this policy to strengthen this idea.
- That such immense wealth was accumulated not so much from "free" trade but from the violent and age-old mercantilism or "monopoly capitalism" is ignored.
- Such systems are being practiced again today, and even tough they are claimed to be Adam-Smith-style free trade, they are the very systems that Adam Smith himself criticized and attacked.

In 1991 Larry Summers, then Chief Economist for the World Bank (and US Treasury Secretary, in the Clinton Administration, until George Bush and the Republican party came into power), had been a strong backer of structural adjustment policies. He wrote in an internal memo:

Just between you and me, shouldn't the World Bank be encouraging more migration of dirty industries to the LDCs [less developed countries]?... The economic logic behind dumping a load of toxic waste in the lowest wage country is impeccable, and we should face up to that... Under-populated countries in Africa are vastly under-polluted; their air quality is probably vastly inefficiently low compared to Los Angeles or Mexico City... The concern over an agent that causes a one in a million change in the odds of prostate cancer is obviously going to be much higher in a country where people survive to get prostate cancer than in a country where under-five mortality is 200 per thousand.

> *— Lawrence Summers, Let them eat pollution, The Economist, February 8, 1992. Quoted from Vandana Shiva, Stolen Harvest, (South End Press, 2000) p.65; See also Richard Robbins, Global Problems and the Culture of Capitalism (Allyn and Bacon, 1999), pp. 233-236 for a detailed look at this.*

When looked at in this light, poverty is more than simple economic issues; it is also an ideological construct.

Earn More, Eat Less

Half a world away [from Zambia] in Washington, the architects of this human disaster dine in comfort and seclusion, spending more on one meal than Masauso Phiri's wife makes in a year of selling buns in their shantytown. Although most World Bank staff work at its Washington headquarters, those unlucky enough to be posted in the Third World receive ample compensation for their misfortune.

This includes subsidized housing (complete with free furnishings), an extended "assignment grant" of $25,000 and a "mobility premium" to defray the cost of child education. Salaries are tax-free and averaged $86,000 in 1995, according to a General Accounting Office report to Congress. No "structural adjustment," then, for this privileged coterie of bankers and policy analysts. Meanwhile, in Africa a hidden genocide lays waste the continent.

"It's not right for a bank to run the whole world," says Fred M'membe, editor of the Zambia Post. "They do not represent anybody other than the countries that control them.

What this means in practice is that the United States runs our countries." He continues: "Look at any African country today, and you'll find that the figures are swinging down.

Education standards are going down, health standards going down and infrastructure is literally breaking up."

— *Mark Lynas, Letter from Zambia, The Nation, February 14, 2000*

In some countries, more is spent on debt servicing than education. For example, even in the former communist countries that are trying to undergo rapid economic "reform", education is given a back seat. In fact, the UK-based development and relief organization, Oxfam, goes as far as saying that the IMF policies deny children an education.

Since the end of the Cold War, even wealthier nations have seen government rollback on some functions, in a similar style to structural adjustment. John McMurtry captures this well, being very critical on the impact of such adjustments on "life requirements":

Such systematic overriding of life requirements is now clearly evident from the most undeveloped to the most advanced societies of the world.

In the case of Canada, again, infant mortality rates, the quintessential indicator of social health, rose an astonishing 43 per cent in the 1995 Statistics Canada figures, the first recorded rise in over thirty-one years, while child poverty had increased by 46 per cent since 1989. In Africa an estimated 500,000 more children died from the imposed restructuring of their countries' economies to ensure increased flows of money to external banks, while spending on health care declined by 50 per cent and on education by 25 per cent since these structural adjustment programs began.

— *John McMurtry, Unequal Freedoms; The Global Market as an Ethical System, (Kumarian Press, 1998), p.305.*

And as the crisis of AIDS gets worse in Africa, measures that reduce health budgets in already poor countries contribute to the problems. (See this site's section on AIDS in Africa for more on that issue.)

What is the IMF/World Bank Prescription?

As economist Robin Hanhel summarizes:

The IMF has prescribed the same medicine for troubled third world economies for over two decades:

- *Monetary austerity.* Tighten up the money supply to increase internal interest rates to whatever heights needed to stabilize the value of the local currency.
- *Fiscal austerity.* Increase tax collections and reduce government spending dramatically.
- *Privatization.* Sell off public enterprises to the private sector.
- *Financial Liberalization.* Remove restrictions on the inflow and outflow of international capital as well as restrictions on what foreign businesses and banks are allowed to buy, own, and operate.

Only when governments sign this "structural adjustment agreement" does the IMF agree to:

- Lend enough itself to prevent default on international loans that are about to come due and otherwise would be unpayable.
- Arrange a restructuring of the country's debt among private international lenders that includes a pledge of new loans.

—Robin Hanhel, Panic Rules!, (South End Press, 1999) p. 52.

Joseph Stiglitz, former head of World Bank, "resigned" under pressure from criticisms he made of the IMF and World Bank. He was also a member of Bill Clinton's cabinet and chairman of the U.S. President's Council of Economic Advisers. His insights and criticisms are worth paying attention to. He notes that:

The IMF likes to go about its business without outsiders asking too many questions. In theory, the fund supports democratic institutions in the nations it assists. In practice, it undermines the democratic process by imposing policies. Officially, of course, the IMF doesn't "impose" anything. It "negotiates" the conditions for receiving aid. But all the power in the negotiations is on one side—the IMF's—and the fund rarely allows sufficient time for broad consensus-building or even widespread consultations with either parliaments or civil society. Sometimes the IMF dispenses with the pretense of openness altogether and negotiates secret covenants.

— Joseph Stiglitz, What I learned at the world economic crisis. The Insider, The New Republic, April 17, 2000

In April 2001, Greg Palast conducted an interview with Joseph Stiglitz which was published in the British newspaper *Observer and Guardian*.

The World Bank talks of "assistance strategies" for every poor nation using careful country by country investigations. However, as reported in the article, "according to insider Stiglitz, the Bank's 'investigation' involves little more than close inspection of five-star hotels. It concludes with a meeting with a begging finance minister, who is handed a 'restructuring agreement' pre-drafted for 'voluntary' signature."

Stiglitz then tells Palast that after each nation's economy is analyzed, the World Bank "hands every minister the *same* four-step program" (emphasis added), described in the article as follows:

1. Privatization. Stiglitz tells Palast that some politicians were corrupt enough to go ahead with some state sell-offs: "Rather than object to the sell-offs of state industries, he said national leaders—using the World Bank's demands to silence local critics—happily flogged their electricity and water companies. 'You could see their eyes widen' at the prospect of 10% commissions paid to Swiss bank accounts for simply shaving a few billion off the sale price of national assets." According to Palast, Stiglitz asserts that the US government knew about, at least in one case: the 1995 Russian sell-off: "'The US Treasury view was this was great as we wanted Yeltsin

re-elected. We don't care if it's a corrupt election.'" (Emphasis added)

2. Capital market liberalization. According to Palast, Stiglitz describes the disastrous capital flows that can ruin economies as being "predictable," and says that "when [the outflow of capital] happens, to seduce speculators into returning a nation's own capital funds, the IMF demands these nations raise interest rates to 30%, 50% and 80%."
3. Market-based pricing. Palast writes that it is at this point that the IMF "drags the gasping nation" to this third points, described as "a fancy term for raising prices on food, water and cooking gas" which, Palast continues, "leads, predictably, to Step-Three-and-a-Half: what Stiglitz calls, 'The IMF riot.'" These riots, which the article clarifies are "peaceful demonstrations dispersed by bullets, tanks and teargas[sic]," cause further capital outflows, a situation which, as Palast points out, is not without a "bright" side: "foreign corporations ... can then pick off remaining assets, such as the odd mining concession or port, at fire sale prices."
4. Free trade. But a version dominated by "rules of the World Trade Organization and the World Bank," which according to Palast, Stiglitz likens to the Opium Wars: "That too was about 'opening markets'," he said. Palast writes that "As in the nineteenth century, Europeans and Americans today are kicking down barriers to sales in Asia, Latin American and Africa while barricading our own markets against the Third World's agriculture." (Note that while even President Bush will claim that we want rules based global mechanisms, the mainstream media often does not ask what the rules themselves are, and whether they are most appropriate.) Palast highlights Stiglitz's problems with the IMF/World Bank plans, plans that the article describes as "devised in secrecy and driven by an absolutist ideology": first, they are not open to discourse and dissent, and second, that

> they don't work. Palast writes that "Under the guiding hand of IMF structural 'assistance' Africa's income dropped by 23%."

In a 5 minute video clip (available in transcript), the well-respected Martin Khor, director of the Third World Network notes similar concerns to Stiglitz and adds that rich countries are being hypocritical and aggressive by

- Protecting their own industries while attempting to force open markets of poor countries
- Selling artificially cheaper products in poor countries, undermining local producers
- Promising more aid while real economic development suffers:

As part of a wider process of globalization, these policies, he argues in another clip (2 minutes, transcript), creates a "straight jacket" for poor countries in terms of policy space to make their own decisions:

Africa Action, an organization working for political, economic and social justice in Africa is highly critical of SAPS noting that, "The basic assumption behind structural adjustment was that an increased role for the market would bring benefits to both poor and rich. In the Darwinian world of international markets, the strongest would win out. This would encourage others to follow their example. The development of a market economy with a greater role for the private sector was therefore seen as the key to stimulating economic growth."

Focusing on Africa, the article continues that it wasn't that African countries did not need corrective reforms, but whether SAPs were the appropriate answers. "The key issue with adjustments of this kind, however, is whether they build the capacity to recover and whether they promote long-term development. The adjustments dictated by the World Bank and IMF did neither."

In these ways then, the IMF and World Bank's encouragement of poor countries to open up for foreign trade is too aggressive for putting poor countries on "level playing field" with rich countries is an oxy-moron. The aggressiveness comes from too much privatization and deregulation with fewer safety nets for poorer governments to provide (which would be there for the benefit of the people of that nation).

Oxfam International estimates that, in the Philippines alone, IMF-imposed cuts in preventative medicine will result in 29,000 deaths from malaria and an increase of 90,000 in the number of untreated tuberculosis cases. Tribunals investigating "crimes against humanity" take note!

— *Jeremy Brecher, Panic Rules: Everything you want to know about the Global Economy, by Robin Hahnel (South End Press, 1999).*

Perhaps one of the most serious effects is that these external policies indirectly undermine democracy and democratic accountability, of both the IMF and World Bank (after all, if their policies fail, who are they accountable to?) and the poor country government themselves (they have less ability to make important decisions for their people. In some cases, the more corrupt governments can use structural adjustment as an excuse not to cater for all their people). That some of the poor nations may not be as aggressive as the IMF or World Bank would like, in privatization and other conditionalities, is also one of the reasons in the continual delay of debt relief.

This model of development, whereby the North (or the developed Nations) impose their conditions on the South (the developing Nations) has come under criticism by many NGOs and other groups/individuals. Perhaps the model needs to be revised and approached from different angles, as this Oxfam paper suggests.

True, in some cases corrupt governments have borrowed money from these institutions and/or directly from various donor nations and ended up using that money to pursue conflicts, arms deals and divert resources away from their people. However, in most cases that has been done knowingly, with the support of various rich nations due to their own "national interests", especially during the Cold War. As Oxfam says, "it would be wrong to hold civilians to ransom by placing stringent conditions on humanitarian relief because of the way their government spends its money."

Furthermore, it has been argued that Structural Adjustments encourage corruption and undermines democracy. As Ann Pettifor and Jospeh Hanlon note, top-down "conditionality has undermined democracy by making elected governments accountable to Washington-based institutions instead of to their own people." The potential for unaccountability and corruption therefore increases as well.

As the article from Africa Action above also mentions, "African countries require essential investments in health, education and infrastructure before they can compete internationally. The World Bank and IMF instead required countries to reduce state support and protection for social and economic sectors. They insisted on pushing weak African economies into markets where they were unable to compete with the might of the international private sector. These policies further undermined the economic development of African countries."Also note that the illegal drug trade, has increased in countries that are in debt (because of the hard cash that is earned), as Jubilee 2000 points out. Moving towards growing such crops also means land is diverted away from meeting local and immediate needs, which also leads to more hunger. Debt's chain reactions and related effects are enormous. (For more information on debt in general, see this web site's section on debt related issues.)

These policies may be described as "reforms", "adjustments", "restructuring" or some other benign-sounding term, but the effects on the poor are the same nonetheless. Some even describe this as leading to economic apartheid.

- The U.S. uses its dominant role in the global economy and in the IFIs [International Financial Institutions] to impose SAPs on developing countries and open up their markets to competition from U.S. companies.

- SAPs are based on a narrow economic model that perpetuates poverty, inequality, and environmental degradation.
- The growing civil society critique of structural adjustment is forcing the IFIs and Washington to offer new mitigation measures regarding SAPs, including national debates on economic policy.

— *Carol Welch, Structural Adjustment Programs & Poverty Reduction Strategy, Foreign Policy in Focus, Vol 5, Number 14, April 2000*

In a more cynical or harsher description, structural adjustments and other trade related policies could also be seen as a "weapon of mass destruction" as Raj Patel hints, (commenting on the Doha WTO conference in November, 2001. Although this is a different context, the overall aspect remains the same): A fertilizer bomb that kills hundreds in Oklahoma. Fuel-laden civil jets that kill 4000 in New York. A sanctions policy that kills one and a half million in Iraq. A trade policy that immiserates continents. You can make a bomb out of anything. The ones on paper hurt the most.

— *Raj Patel, They also make bombs out of paper, ZNet, November 28, 2001*

Indeed, consider the following:

According to UNICEF, over 500,000 children under the age of five died each year in Africa and Latin America in the late 1980s as a direct result of the debt crisis and its management under the International Monetary Fund's structural adjustment programs. These programs required the abolition of price supports on essential food-stuffs, steep reductions in spending on health, education, and other social services, and increases in taxes. The debt crisis has never been resolved for much of sub-Saharan Africa. Extrapolating from the UNICEF data, as many as 5,000,000 children and vulnerable adults may have lost their lives in this blighted continent as a result of the debt crunch.

— *Ross P. Buckley, The Rich Borrow and the Poor Repay: The Fatal Flaw in International Finance, World Policy Journal, Volume XIX, No 4, Winter 2002/03 (Emphasis Added)*

THE "WELFARE" STATE HAS HELPED TODAY'S RICH COUNTRIES TO DEVELOP

The era of globalization can be contrasted with the development path pursued in prior decades, which was generally more inward-looking. Prior to 1980, many countries quite deliberately adopted policies that were designed to insulate their economies from the world market in order to give their domestic industries an opportunity to advance to the point where they could be competitive. The policy of development via import substitution, for example, was often associated with protective tariffs and subsidies for key industries. Performance requirements on foreign investment were also common. These measures often required foreign investors to employ native workers in skilled positions, and to purchase inputs from domestic producers, as ways of ensuring technology transfers. It was also common for developing countries to sharply restrict capital flows. This was done for a number of purposes: to increase the stability of currencies, to encourage both foreign corporations and citizens holding large amounts of domestic currency to invest within the country, and to use the allocation and price of foreign exchange as part of an industrial or development policy.

— *Mark Weisbrot, Dean Baker, Egor Kraev and Judy Chen, The Scorecard on Globalization 1980-2000: Twenty Years of Diminished Progress, Center for Economic Policy and Research, July 11, 2001*

As J.W. Smith notes, every rich nation today has developed because in the past their governments took major responsibility to promote economic growth. There was also a lot of protectionism and intervention in technology transfer. There was an attempt to provide some sort of equality, education, health, and other services to help enhance the nation.

The industrialized nations have understood that some forms of protection allows capital to remain within the economy, and hence via a multiplier effect, help enhance the economy.

Yet, as seen in the structural adjustment initiatives and other western-imposed policies, the developing nations are effectively being forced to cut back these very same provisions that have helped the developed countries to prosper in the past.

The extent of the devastation caused has led many to ask if development is really the objective of the IMF, World Bank, and their ideological backers. Focusing on Africa as an example:

The past two decades of World Bank and IMF structural adjustment in Africa have led to greater social and economic deprivation, and an increased dependence of African countries on external loans.

The failure of structural adjustment has been so dramatic that some critics of the World Bank and IMF argue that the policies imposed on African countries were never intended to promote development. On the contrary, they claim that their intention was to keep these countries economically weak and dependent.

The most industrialized countries in the world have actually developed under conditions opposite to those imposed by the World Bank and IMF on African governments. The U.S. and the countries of Western Europe accorded a central role to the state in economic activity, and practiced strong protectionism, with subsidies for domestic industries.

Under World Bank and IMF programs, African countries have been forced to cut back or abandon the very provisions which helped rich countries to grow and prosper in the past.

Even more significantly, the policies of the World Bank and IMF have impeded Africa's development by undermining Africa's health. Their free market perspective has failed to consider health an integral component of an economic growth and human development strategy. Instead, the policies of these institutions have caused a deterioration in health and in health care services across the African continent.

—*Ann-Louise Colgan, Hazardous to Health: The World Bank and IMF in Africa, Africa Action, April 18, 2002*

While the phrase "Welfare State" often conjures up negative images, with regards to globalization, most European countries feel that protecting their people when developing helps society as well as the economy.

It may be that for real free trade to be effective countries with similar strength economies can reduce such protective measures when trading with one another. However, for developing countries to try to compete in the global market place at the same level as the more established and industrialized nations—and before their own foundations and institutions are stable enough—is almost economic suicide.

An example of this can be seen with the global economic crisis of 1997/98/99 that affected Asia in particular. A UN report looking into this suggested that such nations should rely on domestic roots for growth, diversifying exports and deepening social safety nets. For more about this economic crisis and this UN report, go to this web site's section on debt and the economic crisis.

The *type* of trade is important. As the UN report also suggested, diversification is important. Just as biodiversity is important to ensure resilience to whatever nature can throw at a given ecosystem, diverse economies can help countries weather economic storms. Matthew Lockwood is worth quoting in regards to Africa:

What Africa needs is to shake off its dependence on primary commodity exports, a problem underlying not only its marginalization from world trade but also its chronic debt problems. Many countries rely today on as narrow a range of agricultural and mineral products as they did 30 years ago, and suffer the consequences of inexorably declining export earnings.

Again, the campaigners' remedy—to improve market access for African exports to Europe and America—is wide of the mark.

— *Matthew Lockwood, We must breed tigers in Africa, The Guardian, June 24, 2005*

Asia too has seen development where policies counter to neoliberalism have been followed, as Lockwood also notes.

To see more about the relationship of protectionism with free trade, check out this site's section on Free Trade, which also discusses protectionism, it's negatives and positives.

IMF and World Bank

The IMF and World Bank's policies are very different now from their original intent, as summarized here by the John F. Henning Center for International Labor Relations:

The International Monetary Fund and the World Bank were conceived by 44 nations at the Bretton Woods Conference in 1944 with the goal of creating a stable framework for post-war global economy. The IMF was originally envisioned to promote steady growth and full employment by offering unconditional loans to economies in crisis and establishing mechanisms to stabilize exchange rates and facilitate currency exchange. Much of that vision, however, was never born out. Instead, pressured by US representatives, the IMF took to offering loans based on strict conditions, later to be known as structural adjustment or austerity measures, dictated largely by the most powerful member nations. Critics charge that these policies have decimated social safety nets and worsened lax labor and environmental standards in developing countries.

The World Bank (The International Bank for Reconstruction and Development) was created to fund the rebuilding of infrastructure in nations ravaged by World War Two. Its vision too, however, soon changed.

In the mid 1950's, the Bank turned its attention away from Europe to the Third World, and began funding massive industrial development projects in Latin American, Asia, and Africa. Many scholars and activists contend that the Bank's aggressive dealings with developing nations, which were often ruled by dictatorial regimes, exacerbated the developing world's growing debt crisis and devastated local ecologies and indigenous communities. Both IMF and World Bank policies remain a source of heated debate.

— *John F. Henning Center for International Labor Relations, Institute for Industrial Relations, University of California, Berkeley*

While their goals are slightly different then, the IMF and World Bank policies compliment each other:

World Bank and IMF adjustment programs differ according to the role of each institution. In general, IMF loan conditions focus on monetary and fiscal issues. They emphasize programs to address inflation and balance of payments problems, often requiring specific levels of cutbacks in total government spending. The adjustment programs of the World Bank are wider in scope, with a more long-term development focus. They highlight market liberalization and public sector reforms, seen as promoting growth through expanding exports, particularly of cash crops.

Despite these differences, World Bank and IMF adjustment programs reinforce each other. One way is called "cross-conditionality." This means that a government generally must first be approved by the IMF, before qualifying for an adjustment loan from the World Bank. Their agendas also overlap in the financial sector in particular. Both work to impose fiscal austerity and to eliminate subsidies for workers, for example. The market-oriented perspective of both institutions makes their policy prescriptions complementary.

—*Ann-Louise Colgan, Hazardous to Health: The World Bank and IMF in Africa, Africa Action, April 18, 2002*

But economics is often driven by politics. As a result of policies by the IMF, World Bank and various powerful nations, basic human rights have been severely undermined in many countries, as also noted sharply by Global Exchange:

By insisting that national leaders place the interests of international financial investors above the needs of their own citizens, the IMF and the World Bank have short circuited the accountability at the heart of self-governance, thereby corrupting the democratic process.

The subordination of social needs to the concerns of financial markets has, in turn, made it more difficult for national governments to ensure that their people receive food, health care, and education—basic human rights as defined by the Universal Declaration of Human Rights. The Bank's and the Fund's erosion of basic human rights and their perversion of the democratic process have made the institutions a clear and present threat to the well being of hundreds of millions of people worldwide.

— How the International Monetary Fund and the World Bank Undermine Democracy and Erode Human Rights, Global Exchange, September 2001

The IMF and World Bank are largely controlled and "owned" by the developed nations such as USA, Germany, UK, Japan etc. (The IMF web site has a breakdown of the quotas and voting powers.) The US, for example, controls 17 to 18% of the voting power at the IMF. When an 85% majority is required for a decision, the US effectively has veto power at the IMF. In addition, the World Bank is 51% funded by the U.S. Treasury.

Journalist John Pilger also provides a political aspect to this: Under a plan devised by President Reagan's Secretary to the Treasury, James Baker, indebted countries were offered World Bank and IMF "servicing" loans in return for the "structural adjustment" of their economies. This meant that the economic direction of each country would be planned, monitored and controlled in Washington. "Liberal containment" was replaced by *laissez-faire* capitalism known as the "free market".

— John Pilger, Hidden Agendas, (The New Press, 1998), p.63

The IMF and World Bank's policies have indeed been heavily criticized for many years and are seen as unhelpful and sometimes, unaccountable, as they have resulted in an increased dependency by the developing countries upon the richer nations, as also mentioned at the top of this page. At the same time, the different cultures are not respected when it comes to prescribing structural adjustment principles, either.

In Africa, the effects of policies such as SAPs have been felt sharply. As an example of how political interests affect these institutions, Africa Action describes the policies of the IMF and World Bank, but also hints at the influences behind them too:

Over the past two decades, the World Bank and International Monetary Fund (IMF) have undermined Africa's health through the policies they have imposed. The dependence of poor and highly indebted African countries on World Bank and IMF loans has given these institutions leverage to control economic policy-making in these countries. The policies mandated by the World Bank and IMF have forced African governments to orient their economies towards greater integration in international markets at the expense of social services and long-term development priorities. They have reduced the role of the state and cut back government expenditure.

The World Bank and IMF were important instruments of Western powers during the Cold War in both economic and political terms. They performed a political function by subordinating development objectives to geostrategic interests. They also promoted an economic agenda that sought to preserve Western dominance in the global economy.

Not surprisingly, the World Bank and IMF are directed by the governments of the world's richest countries. Combined, the "Group of 7" (U.S., Britain, Canada, France, Germany, Italy and Japan) hold more than 40% of the votes on the Boards of Directors of these institutions. The U.S. alone accounts for almost 20%. (The U.S. holds 16.45% of the votes at the World

Bank, and over 17% of the votes at the International Monetary Fund.)

—*Ann-Louise Colgan, Hazardous to Health: The World Bank and IMF in Africa, Africa Action, April 18, 2002*

But it is not just health. Basic food security has also been undermined. An example in 2002 at least made it to mainstream media attention in UK. As Ann Petifor, head of debt campaign organization, *Jubilee Research* noted, the IMF forced the Malawi government to sell its surplus grain in favor of foreign exchange just before a famine struck. This was explicitly so that debts could be repaid. 7 million of the total 11 million population were severely short of food.

"But its worse than that," said Petifor. "Because Malawi is indebted, her economic policies are effectively determined by her creditors—represented in Malawi by the IMF." Malawi spent more than the budget the foreign creditors set. As a result the IMF withheld $47 million in aid. Other western donors, acting on advice from IMF staff, also withheld aid, "*pending IMF approval* of the national budget." (Emphasis added).

"To add to the humiliation of the Malawian government, the IMF has also suspended the debt service relief for which she was only recently deemed eligible—because she is 'off track.'"

That is not the end of the story unfortunately. As Petifor also mentioned, under the economic program imposed by her creditors, Malawi removed all farming and food subsidies allowing the market to determine demand and supply for food. This reduced support for farmers, leading many to go hungry as prices increased. As she also noted, the rich countries, on the other hand, do not follow their own policies; Europe and the US subsidize their agriculture with billions of dollars.

But the US, for example, see this situation as exploitable. Petifor again:

US Secretary for Agriculture, Dan Glickman, illustrates well the US attitude to countries suffering famine and in need of food aid: "Humanitarian and national self interest both can be served by well-designed foreign assistance programs. Food aid has not only met emergency food needs, but has also been a useful market development tool." (OXFAM report: "Rigged Rules and Double Standards: Trade Globalization and the Fight Against Poverty" by Kevin Watkins and Penny Fowler)

— *Ann Petifor, Debt is still the linchpin: the case of Malawi, Jubilee Research, July 4, 2002*

(It is not just the US that uses aid in this way. Most rich countries do this. And it isn't just food aid, but aid in general that is often used inappropriately. The *Guardian* reported (August 29, 2005) how £700,000 (about $400,000) of £3 million in British aid to Malawi was mis-spent on US firms' hotel and meal bills. Even notebooks and pens were flown in from Washington rather than purchased locally. See this site's section on foreign aid for more details about the issue of foreign aid and its misuse.)

IMF and World Bank Reform?

Since the IMF and World Bank protests in Washington, D.C on April 16, 2000, and coinciding with the Meltzer Report criticizing the IMF and World Bank, there has been more talk about IMF reforms. At first thought the reforms sound like the protests and other movements' efforts are paying off. However, as Oxfam notes, some of the reform suggestions may not be the way to go and may do even more harm than good. In their own words:

While some of the reform proposals now being debated are sensible, the thrust of the reform agenda is a source of concern for the following reasons:

- It reflects a growing disenchantment with multilateralism
- It threatens to replace inappropriate IMF conditions with inappropriate conditions dictated by the G7 countries

- It fails to address the real policy issues at the heart of the IMF's failure as a poverty reduction agency
- It does not address the politicization of IMF loans, especially with regard to the US Treasury's influence
- It does not adequately consider the 'democratic deficit' which prevents poor countries from having an effective voice in the IMF

— *Reforming the IMF, Oxfam International Policy Paper, April 2000*

On the one hand it seems appropriate to demand an end to the IMF. However, such an abrupt course of action may itself lead to a gaping hole in international financial policies without an effective alternative. And that is another topic in itself!

IMF and World Bank Hinting That Some of Their Policies Do Not Work

Recently, we have heard members of the World Bank and IMF entertain the possibility that maybe their structural adjustment policies did have some negative effects.

For example, the *Bretton Woods Project* revealed that in 2000, an "internal World Bank report has concluded that the poor are better off without structural adjustment". The report itself is titled The Effect of IMF and World Bank Programs on Poverty. (Requires a PDF reader.)

The report doesn't really look in detail at *why* the poor benefit less from adjustment. Instead it speculates that they "may be ill-placed to take advantage of new opportunities created by structural adjustment reforms" because, as the Bretton Woods Project insinuate, the report implies that the poor "have neither the skills or financial resources to benefit from high-technology jobs and cheaper imports."

Now, it may not have been the intent of the report to do so, but one can't help but notice how it almost seems as though while they may admit that structural adjustment didn't benefit the poor, it is almost as though the Bank tries to subtly absolve itself by sort of blaming the poor for not benefiting from this. When structural adjustments have required cut backs in health, education and so on, then what would one expect?

In March 2003, the IMF itself admitted in a paper that globalization may actually increase the risk of financial crisis in the developing world. "Globalization has heightened these risks since cross-country financial linkages amplify the effects of various shocks and transmit them more quickly across national borders" the IMF notes and adds that, "The evidence presented in this paper suggests that financial integration should be approached cautiously, with good institutions and macroeconomic frameworks viewed as important." In addition, they admit that it is hard to provide a clear road-map on how this should be achieved, and instead it should be done on a case by case basis. This would sound like a move slightly away from a "one size fits all" style of prescription that the IMF has been long criticized for. As mentioned further above, and as many critics have said for a long time, opening up poorer countries in an aggressive manner can leave them vulnerable to large capital volatility and outflows. *Reuters*, reporting on the IMF report also noted that the IMF "sounded more like its critics" when making this admission.

In theory there may indeed be merit to various arguments supporting global integration and cooperation. But politics, corruption, geopolitics, as well as numerous other factors need to be added to economic models, which could prove very difficult. As suggested in various parts of this site, because economics is sometimes separated from politics and other major issues, theory can indeed be far from reality.

Sitglitz, the former World Bank chief economist, is worth quoting a bit more to give an insight into the power that the IMF has, and why accusations of it and its policies being colonial-like are perhaps not too far off:

...The IMF is not particularly interested in hearing the thoughts of its "client countries" on such topics as development strategy or financial austerity. All too often, the Fund's approach to the developing countries has had the feel of a colonial ruler. A picture can be worth a thousand words, and a single picture snapped in 1998, shown throughout the world, has engraved itself in the minds of millions, particularly those in the former colonies. The IMF's managing director, Michel Camdessus (the head of the IMF is referred to as its "Managing Director"), a short, neatly dressed former French Treasury bureaucrat, who once claimed to be a Socialist, is standing with a stern fact and crossed arms over the seated and humiliated president of Indonesia. The hapless president was being forced, in effect, to turn over economic sovereignty of his country to the IMF in return for the aid his country needed. In the end, ironically, much of the money went not to help Indonesia, but to bail out the "colonial power's" private sector creditors. (Officially, the "ceremony" was the signing of a letter of agreement, an agreement effectively dictated by the IMF, though it often still keeps up the pretense that the letter of intent comes from the country's government!)

Defenders of Camdessus claim the photograph was unfair, that he did not realize that it was being taken and that it was viewed out of context. But that is the point—in day-to-day interactions, away from cameras and reporters, this is precisely the stance that the IMF bureaucrats take, from the leader of the organization on down. To those in the developing countries, the picture raised a very disturbing question: Had things really changed since the "official" ending of colonialism a half century ago? When I saw the pictures, images of other signings of "agreements" came to mind. I wondered how similar this scene was to those marking the "opening up of Japan" with Admiral Perry's gunboat diplomacy or the end of the Opium Wars or the surrender of maharajas in India.

— Joseph Stiglitz, Globalization and its Discontents, (Penguin Books, 2002), pp. 40–41

The above from Stiglitz is from his book, *Globalization and its Discontents*. In it, he highlights many, many more issues, criticisms and aspects of IMF/Washington Consensus ideological fanaticism that have hindered development, and in many cases, as he points out, worsened situations. It is surprising and also quite illuminating to get the "insider" image of the workings of some large institutions in this way.

Into mid-2005, and though not as vocal as Stiglitz, others at the IMF are also questioning the institution's strict adherence to the free market doctrine, as *Bretton Woods Project* reveals. One of the authors of a paper from the IMF "concedes the failure of IFI policies for the poorest countries" saying that "Much of sub-Saharan Africa has been under IMF and World Bank programmes during the last three decades, and while a modicum of macroeconomic stability has been achieved, progress has been spotty at best." Another working paper from the IMF suggests that trade liberalization has crippled some governments of poorer countries, and that prospects for further trade liberalization in poor countries may be troubling.

PSRPS REPLACE SAPS BUT STILL SAP THE POOR

The IMF in 1999 replaced Structural Adjustment to Poverty Reduction Growth Facility (PRGP) and their Policy Framework Papers to Poverty Reduction Strategy Papers (PSRP) as the new preconditions for loan and debt relief. However, the effect is still the same, as the preceding disastrous structural adjustment policies, as the World Development Movement reported. Many civil society organizations are increasing their critique of the PSRPs.

> [T]he PRSP process is simply delivering repackaged structural adjustment programmes (SAPs). It is not delivering poverty-focused development plans and it has failed to involve civil society and parliamentarians in economic policy discussions.
>
> *— PRSPs just PR say civil society groups, Bretton Woods Project Update #23, June/July 2001*

As Jubilee Research (formerly Jubilee 2000, the debt relief campaign organization) adds:

Joint World Bank/IMF papers (39) on the PRSP stress "poverty reduction" and that the paper must be "country-driven with the broad participation of civil society". But the IMF in its own papers stresses that this is in addition to everything that was required in the past; none of the old "Washington consensus" policies have been removed. In a paper for a meeting of African finance ministers, 18-19 January 2000, to explain the new PRGF, (40) the IMF stresses that it will demand of all countries "a more rapid privatisation process" and "a faster pace of trade liberalization"—the conditions criticized by Joseph Stiglitz when he was chief economist of the World Bank.

... James Wolfensohn, president of the World Bank, commented that "it is also clear to all of us that ownership is essential. Countries must be in the driver's seat". The theory is fine, but the practice distorts the meaning of these words. Countries are in the driving seat only as the chauffeur of the Washington Consensus limousine. And as Angela Woods and Matthew Lockwood comment, all too often "ownership relates to persuading the public that reforms are necessary and good in order to minimize political opposition to them".

... The implication is that governments wishing to take an alternative economic approach must expect to forgo aid and debt relief. But Wood and Lockwood note that "not only does the Bank define a 'good' policy environment very narrowly, the consensus on what defines 'good' policies is subject to change. What may have been regarded as a good policy yesterday may not be today."

... It is impossible to ignore the sweeping critique, by the second most important man in the World Bank [Joseph Stiglitz], of policies still being imposed on poor countries as a condition of debt cancellation and aid. And it must be remembered that these are being imposed in the names of "good governance", "sound policies" and "poverty reduction".

Stiglitz notes that had the US followed IMF policy it would have not achieved its remarkable expansion.

— *Joseph Hanlon and Ann Pettifor, Kicking the Habit; Finding a lasting solution to addictive lending and borrowing—and its corrupting side-effects, Jubilee Research, March 2000*

Additionally, as this book reports (see pages 37-38 of the PDF online version), "[A] senior [World] Bank official described the PRSP-PRGF as a 'compulsory programme, so that those with the money can tell those without the money what they need in order to get the money.'" It would be worth additionally noting the cruel irony that nations that are "those with the money" today have largely accumulated it through plunder via imperialism and colonialism upon those very nations who today are "without the money." Prescribing how to get "the money," in that context then, is dubious indeed.

For additional information and critique, you can see the following links as well:

- Reports from the World Development Movement:
  - Still Sapping the Poor: A critique of IMF poverty reduction strategies, by Charles Abugre, June 2000
  - Polices to Roll-back the State and Privatize? from the World Development Movement, April 2001 provides additional studies and examples
- From the Bretton Woods Project, an IMF and World Bank monitoring organization:
  - Structural Adjustment/PRSP section of their web site
  - The ABC of the PRSP, an introduction to the new Bank and Fund Poverty Reduction Strategy Papers, by Angela Wood, April 2000
- From the Focus on the Global South:
  - The World Bank and the PRSP: Flawed Thinking and Failing Experiences

THE ASIAN DEVELOPMENT BANK

Like the IMF and World Bank, the Asian Development Bank (ADB) has also fallen under much criticism for its policies, which also require structural adjustments for loans. Through its policies it encourages export-driven, capital and resource-intensive development, just like the other international financial institutions. The largest financing and influence of the bank comes from Japan and the United States. As summarized from chapter 2 of The Transfer of Wealth; Debt and the making of a Global South: The escalating dependence of developing countries in the [Asia] region on debt-financed development has a number of negative consequences. These include:

a. the neglect of domestic savings as a source of development finance;
b. cuts in government expenditure for basic social services and basic infrastructure in order to meet debt servicing requirements;
c. an escalation of export-oriented resource extraction to generate hard currency receipts for debt servicing;
d. a reorientation of agricultural production from meeting local needs to production for export in highly skewed regional and global markets;
e. increased dependence on imported, capital intensive technologies as a consequence of tied procurement and project design processes led by foreign consulting companies;
f. increased dependence on and influence of international financial institutions such as the ADB and the World Bank, particularly through the imposition of debt-induced structural adjustment programs and policy based lending.

Also, as with the IMF and World bank, and mentioned in the above link, "governments are using the rubric of poverty reduction to channel taxpayer funds to their private sector companies via the ADB. This is occurring with little or no pubic scrutiny although government representatives will, if necessary, appeal to commercial self-interest to justify continued contributions to the ADB and other multilateral development banks." As with the IMF for example, loans by the IMF are guaranteed by the creditor country. In essence then, tax payers from the lending countries will bail out the IMF and ADB if there are problems in their policies. (For more details and statistics etc, the above link is a good starting place.) The ADB has mentioned its desires to promote "good governance." However, Aziz Choudry is highly critical in terms of whom this governance would actually be good for: It has nothing to do with democratization, humanitarianism or support for peoples' rights. It is a euphemism for a limited state designed to service the market and undermine popular mandates. The term is explicitly linked to the kinds of structural adjustment measures promoted by the ADB—measures for which there is little popular support and which are rapidly increasing economic inequalities.

— *Aziz Choudry, The Asian Development Bank—"Governing" the Pacific?, June 6, 2002*

Structural adjustment policies have therefore had far-reaching consequences around the world. Yet, this is just one of the mechanisms whereby inequality and poverty has been structured into laws and institutions on a global scale.

TODAY, OVER 26,500 CHILDREN DIED AROUND THE WORLD

Around the world, some 26,500 children die every day.

That is equivalent to:

- 1 child dying every 3 seconds
- 18 children dying every minute
- A 2004 Asian Tsunami occurring every week
- An Iraq-scale death toll every 15–36 days
- Almost 10 million children dying every year
- Some 60 million children dying between 2000 and 2006

The silent killers are poverty, hunger, easily preventable diseases and illnesses, and other related causes. In spite of the scale of this daily/ongoing catastrophe, it rarely manages to achieve, much less sustain, prime-time, headline coverage.

WHY IS THIS TRAGEDY NOT IN THE HEADLINES?

UNICEF's 2000 Progress of Nations report tried to put these numbers into some perspective: The continuation of this suffering and loss of life contravenes the natural human instinct to help in times of disaster. Imagine the horror of the world if a major earthquake were to occur and people stood by and watched without assisting the survivors! Yet every day, the equivalent of a major earthquake killing over 30,000 young children occurs to a disturbingly muted response. They die quietly in some of the poorest villages on earth, far removed from the scrutiny and the conscience of the world. Being meek and weak in life makes these dying multitudes even more invisible in death.

—*A spotty scorecard, UNICEF, Progress of Nations 2000*

Unfortunately, it seems that the world still does not notice. It might be reasonable to expect that death and tragedy on this scale should be prime time headlines news. Yet, these issues only surface when there are global meetings or concerts (such as the various G8 summits, the Make Poverty History campaign in 2005, etc). Furthermore, year after year, we witness that when those campaigns end and the meetings conclude, so does the mainstream media coverage. It feels as though even when there is some media attention, the ones who suffer are not the ones that compel the mainstream to report, but instead it is the movement of the celebrities and leaders of the wealthy countries that makes this issue newsworthy.

Even rarer in the mainstream media is any thought that wealthy countries may be part of the problem too. The effects of international policies, the current form of globalization, and the influence the wealthy countries have on these processes is rarely looked at. Instead, promises and pledges from the wealthy, powerful countries, and the corruption of the poorer ones—who receive apparently abundant goodwill—make the headlines; the repeated *broken* promises, the low quality and quantity of aid, and conditions with unfair strings attached do not.

Accountability of the recipient countries is often mentioned when these issues touch the mainstream. Accountability of the roles that international institutions such as the World Bank and IMF, and their funders (the wealthy/powerful countries), rarely does. The risk is that citizens of these countries get a false sense of hope creating the misleading impression that *appropriate* action is taken in their names. It may be harsh to say the mainstream media is one of the many causes of poverty, as such, but the point here is that their influence is enormous. Silence, as well as noise, can both have an effect.

RECENT HEADLINES IN CONTEXT

When initially writing this, the BBC's top story on prime time television was about a British child kidnapped in Portugal. This is definitely a tragic story that needs reporting, but why, for the BBC and other British media outlets that pride themselves in outstanding international media coverage, is the plight of millions of children not daily headlines?

Another recent tragedy that sustained days of headline and prime time media coverage was the Virginia Tech massacre's in the US. When media critics at *Media Lens* asked for the BBC's rationale for such sustained coverage compared to more people dying each day in Iraq and receiving just a few minutes in comparison, the BBC responded that it happens every day in Iraq. See Putting Virginia Tech in Perspective for the follow up from *Media Lens*. Some people fear there will be fatigue at hearing those depressing stories all the time, or the advertisers will pressure the media companies to put a bit more entertainment or good news on so that buying moods are not affected. However, news of tragedies in Iraq are also depressing, but nevertheless do received regular headline coverage.

Also there is worry that the lack of sensationalism attached to reporting the same news story each day will result in lower television viewing ratings and this may have various consequences—especially where advertising is concerned.

Finally there is the question of whether people want to hear about such depressing news stories. After all the media feels it is delivering what its viewers would like. However, it is difficult for people to know what they do or do not want to see, if they are never given the options of the alternatives. If the magnitude of this suffering is hardly reported in a *sustained* manner, how can viewers judge whether they wish to watch it or not?

About Child Deaths

NICEF also notes that the global child mortality rate declined by almost a quarter between 1990 and 2006:

Global Mortality Rate; Comparing 1990 and 2006		
Region	**Under-5 deaths per 1,000 live births**	
Notes: Percentages are rounded; Each mortality figure shown as follows: • 1990 • 2006		
	1990	2006
Sub-Saharan Africa	187	160
Eastern and Southern Africa	165	131
West and Central Africa	208	186
Middle East and North Africa	79	46
South Asia	123	83
East Asia and Pacific	55	29
Latin America and Caribbean	55	27
CEE/CIS	53	27
Industrialized	10	6
Developing	103	79
Least Developed	180	142
World	93	72

Progress has certainly been made as each year the number of children under 5 dying is slowly coming down. However, as UNICEF cautioned in their State of the World's Children, 2008 report, "progress has been unevenly distributed" (p.25). For example, good progress was made by a few nations with large populations, but many countries made "no progress or insufficient progress" (p.iii)

Why is child mortality important to understand? UNICEF summarizes: The under-five mortality rate, often known by its acronym U5MR or simply as the child mortality rate ... has several advantages as a barometer of child well-being in general and child health in particular.

First, it measures an 'outcome' of the development process rather than an 'input', such as per capita calorie availability or the number of doctors per 1,000 population—all of which are means to an end.

Second, the U5MR is known to be the result of a wide variety of inputs: the nutritional status and the health knowledge of mothers; the level of immunization and oral rehydration therapy; the availability of maternal and child health services (including prenatal care); income and food availability in the family; the availability of safe drinking water and basic sanitation; and the overall safety of the child's environment, among other factors.

Third, the U5MR is less susceptible to the fallacy of the average than, for example, per capita gross national income (GNI per capita). This is because the natural scale does not allow the children of the rich to be 1,000 times as likely to survive, even if the human-made scale does permit them to have 1,000 times as much income. In other words, it is much more difficult for a wealthy minority to affect a nation's U5MR, and it therefore presents a more accurate, if far from perfect, picture of the health status of the majority of children (and of society as a whole).

— *State of the World's Children, 2008 , UNICEF, January 2008, p.2 (see also p.149 for more details)*

NOTES AND SOURCES

Sources for child deaths

These mortality figures are from UNICEF. 60 million covers deaths between 2000 and 2006, the latest figures from UNICEF at time of writing.

The term "Children" in this context means infants under the age of 5. The tragedy is therefore even worse if older children, adults, and the elderly are to be considered.

The approximate number of deaths in those five years is calculated by averaging the deaths per year of known figures and multiplying by 6 years, which gives a total of 62.16 million deaths.

Given the population is increasing, the reducing actual numbers shows a percentage decline in these deaths over those six years, by 0.03%.

In a way, this feels like a very small reduction given that many of the illnesses and conditions that children suffer are easily preventable, technically.

Taking a longer term view, since 1960 (when child mortality numbers were first being recorded) the annual number of child deaths has halved, from 20 million in 1960 to just under 10 million in 2006.

In addition, given the population in 1960 was 3 billion whereas 2006 was about 6.5 billion this means that there has been a four-fold improvement in saving lives of children from a percentage basis. That is, although population has increased (a lot), the number of child deaths has reduced even more.

Explanation for four-fold saving»

- 20 million divided by 3 billion is 0.00667.
- 10 million divided by 6.5 billion is 0.0015.
- 0.00667 divided by 0.0015 is approximately 4.33

The sources are typically the UNICEF web site and their progress of nations reports. They have a statistical database, which (at the time of writing) uses 2005 as the latest available data. In addition, their recently release State of the World's Children 2008 report provides 2006 data.

Child deaths at different intervals							
Year	Per year (millions)	Per day	Per hour	Per minute	Per second	Population (approx)	%
Some values have been rounded for display.							
2000	11	30,137.99	1,255.71	20.93	0.35	6.1 billion	0.18
2003	10.6	29,041.10	1,210.05	20.17	0.34	6.3 billion	0.17
2005	10.14	27,786.30	1,157.76	19.30	0.32	6.45 billion	0.16
2006	9.7	26,575.34	1,107.31	18.46	0.31	6.5 billion	0.15

See also the following:

- Progress of Nations 2000, *UNICEF*, 2000;
- Robert E. Black, Saul S Morris, Jennifer Bryce, Where and why are 10 million children dying every year?, *The Lancet*, Volume 361, Number 9376, 28 June 2003. (Note, while the article title says 10 million, their paper says 10.8 million.)
- State of the World's Children, 2005, UNICEF (this cites the number as 10.6 million in 2003)
- State of the World's Children, 2008 , UNICEF, provides approximate figures for 2006.

Sources for Asia Tsunami comparison

See the article about the Asian Tsunami in December 2004 for comparative numbers.

In summary, approximately 230,000 people died in that disaster. At 26,500 deaths per day, that would be about 8.6 days.

Sources for Iraq Comparison

For the Iraq estimate, the John Hopkins study (reported in the Lancet) found 400,000 to 950,000 deaths since the 2003 Iraq invasion (average of some 655,000). Dividing 400,000 by 26,500 gives 15, and 950,000 by 27,000 gives 36.

As an aside, George Bush and many others dismissed this study in the Lancet as lacking credibility, using discredited methodologies, and instead used the Iraq Body Count statistics (of 30,000 at the time, though it is now reported at about 66,000).

If Iraq Body Count statistics are to be used, then the number of days in which child deaths match the post 2003 Iraq death toll is just two or three days. The Iraq Body Count statistics are often criticized because they rely on mainstream media reporting, which is heavily censored and managed by the US in Iraq. Nonetheless they provided criticism of the John Hopkins study (often referred to as the Lancet study as that is where it was published).

The authors of the study defended it noting that they used the very methodology that the US government is teaching others (and thus dismissed Bush's claim of using discredited methodologies). The full report in the Lancet also notes that casualty reporting in war time tends to be grossly underestimated, so their numbers may not be as hard to accept as it initially sounds.

ECONOMIC DEMOCRACY: THE POLITICAL STRUGGLE OF THE 21ST CENTURY

Capital accumulation advantage increases or decreases exponentially with the differential in pay for equally productive labor: An equally productive worker in the poorly-paid Third World produces a unique model car, is paid $1 an hour, and produces one model car an hour.

An equally productive worker in the developed world produces another unique model car, is paid $10 an hour, and also produces one model car per hour. Each equally productive worker likes, and purchases, the other's model cars. (All true costs are labor costs [capital is stored labor] so we ignore monopoly capital costs, which go to the developed world anyway and calculate the cost of those model cars at the labor cost of production.) The $1 an hour worker must work 10 hours to buy one of the model cars of the $10 an hour worker but, with the money earned in the same 10 hours, the $10 an hour worker can buy 100 of the model cars of the $1 an hour worker. While in a homogenized market of many producers there is a 10 times differential in buying power, in direct trades between each other there is an exponential 100 times differential in retained wealth.

If the pay differential is 5 ($10 to $2), the wealth accumulation advantage is 25 to 1. If the pay differential is 2 ($10 to $5), the wealth accumulation advantage is 4 to 1. When all have access to technology and markets and pay is equal for equally-productive work, the wealth retained (and available for accumulation or consumption) by each nation is equal.

All wealth comes from resources and resources are in the countryside. Thus for 800 years the cities of the Middle Ages raided the countryside to destroy their primitive industrial capital, forcing the countryside to sell their natural resources to the city. City states fought city states over those same resources.

The imperial city states evolved into imperial nations which continued to fight control of resources and trade, the source of their wealth. The imperial nations of Europe colonized the entire world and continued to battle over who would control the wealth producing process.

Military forces of the wealthy world spread all over the world are there for the same purpose as those raiding parties from the imperial cities of Europe, control resources, monopolize industrial technology and control markets-in short, controlling the rules of unequal trade.

Where are Japan's resources? Where are South Korea's resources? Where are Singapore's resources? Where are Hong Kong's resources? Where are Taiwan's resources?

Where are the resources of the old imperial nations of Europe who consume roughly 14 times the resources as lie within their borders? America, with 5 percent of the world's people, consumes 28 percent of the world's resources. The resources from which all wealth comes are primarily in the undeveloped world, the "countryside"q of the developed world.

After World War II, the entire world was breaking free. Africa's new leaders were planning to build a regional economy and emulating the United States. This is why potentially wealthy countries of Africa and Latin America were destabilized. If they had been permitted to develop, the wealth of the world would be in those countries, not in Europe.

Virtually every nation which developed did so under the opposite development philosophies being forced upon the developing world. This creates dependent nations trapped in debt and are the legal structures which-through the formula described above-lay claim to the natural wealth and labors of the impoverished world.

Any nation which attempts to break out will be immediately ostracized, embargoed, quickly impoverished, and forced back within the fold. Like the raiding parties of the Middle ages, the IMF/World Bank/GATT/ NAFTA/WTO/MAI structural adjustments are enforcing arms of imperial capital maintaining the impoverished world in dependency.

Where would America be if a powerful nation undersold their farmers? American farmers would go broke, farm equipment dealers would go broke, and businesses dependent upon the wages of those workers would go broke, simply because they imported their food instead of raising their own.

The same principle works for all industry. If a country is unable to protect their internal markets and imports their needs, there is no buying power within the country to support local industries and they will stay impoverished.

Through organizing into trading regions and receiving full value for their resources and labor, the impoverished world can quickly break out of poverty.

If only 14% of the industry producing arms for the suppression of the world's break for freedom were turned to producing industry for the impoverished world, the entire world could be developed to a sustainable level and poverty largely eliminated in only 45 years. And Capital destroying Capital in trade wars wastes even more capital than that wasted on wars.

The wealthy world gained the support of their citizens for the violence they imposed upon the world through propagandizing them that these people were dangerous enemies. Only by educating impoverished populations on every aspect of why and how they were kept in dependency for centuries can governments gain the support of their citizens for reorganizing into efficient production and trading regions.

Intellectuals in the wealthy world are moral, honest, and want to alleviate poverty. But they have never been taught how the impoverished world was kept dependent and thus they cannot honestly address those causes. Only by this full understanding of economic history can the impoverished world gain their freedom. Wealthy world intellectuals would not push their nonsense when they know that their audience knows a lot better.

Through abandoning control of the world through covert and overt violence and sharing both the world's resources and the wealth those resources produce, world poverty can be quickly eliminated.

This author and others on the staff of The Institute for Economic Democracy are available to lecture at your university and at other conferences. We also have available resource staff with expertise in permaculture and affordable housing.

Reviews: "I feel that this scholarly work will be viewed in the future as a milestone of the new Millennium. It is a work that turns the corner from the mode of thinking of one era to the mode of thinking in the next." — WM. H. Kotke, author of The Final Empire

"This book constitutes an incisive review and analysis of the post-war political economy. J.W. Smith carefully integrates geopolitical, strategic, institutional and human rights issues into the understanding of post-war economic change and transformation." — Michel Chossudovsky, University of Ottawa, Professor.

"With an unusual flair for historical prototypes, Smith strips the Washington Consensus to its underclothes and beyond. A dazzling performance." — William Krehm Editor, Economic Reform

"Smith's exposure of how conscientious professors and reporters are the unwitting carriers of disinformation, and thus unwittingly misinform their students and audience, provides researchers with an invaluable tool for unearthing truth." — Ralph McGehee, originator of the database, CIABASE, and author of Deadly Deceits: My 25 Years in the CIA.

4

World Hunger and Poverty

We often hear about people's desire to solve world hunger, or to be able to feed the world and help alleviate the suffering associated with it. However, meaningful long-term alleviation to hunger is rooted in the alleviation of poverty, as poverty leads to hunger. World hunger is a terrible symptom of world poverty. If efforts are only directed at providing food, or improving food production or distribution, then the structural root causes that create hunger, poverty and dependency would still remain. And so while continuous effort, resources and energies are deployed to relieve hunger through these technical measures, the political causes require political solutions as well. (There are many other issues that also affect poverty and hunger, which this site attempts to start to discuss here in the following sections. Given the number of related issues involved here, over time, expect this section to grow, so do keep coming back to check for updated information!)

Causes of Hunger are related to Poverty

There are many inter-related issues causing hunger, which are related to economics and other factors that cause poverty. They include land rights and ownership, diversion of land use to non-productive use, increasing emphasis on export-oriented agriculture, inefficient agricultural practices, war, famine, drought, over-fishing, poor crop yields, etc. This section introduces some of these issues. Last updated Thursday, February 15, 2007.

Solving World Hunger Means Solving World Poverty

Solving world hunger in the conventional sense (of providing/growing more food etc) will not tackle poverty that leads to hunger in the first place. Further, there is a risk of continuing the poverty and dependency without realizing it, because the act of attempting to provide more food etc can appear so altruistic in motive. To solve world hunger in the long run, poverty alleviation is required. Last updated Saturday, June 15, 2002.

Consider the following:

- Over 9 million people die worldwide each year because of hunger and malnutrition. 5 million are children.
- Approximately 1.2 billion people suffer from hunger (deficiency of calories and protein);
- Some 2 to 3.5 billion people have micronutrient deficiency (deficiency of vitamins and minerals);
- Yet, some 1.2 billion suffer from obesity (excess of fats and salt, often accompanied by deficiency of vitamins and minerals);
- Food wastage is also high:
    - o In the United Kingdom, "a shocking 30-40% of all food is never eaten;"
        - * In the last decade the amount of food British people threw into the bin went up by 15%;
        - * Overall, £20 billion (approximately $38 billion US dollars) worth of food is thrown away, every year.
    - o In the US 40-50% of all food ready for harvest never gets eaten;
    - o The impacts of this waste is not just financial. Environmentally this leads to:
        - * Wasteful use of chemicals such as fertilizers and pesticides;
        - * More fuel used for transportation;

* More rotting food, creating more methane — one of the most harmful greenhouse gases that contributes to climate change.

- The direct medical cost of hunger and malnutrition is estimated at $30 billion each year.
- Sources»

The first three stats come from a report by UK-based Centre for Food Policy, Thames Valley University and UK Public Health Association, titled Why health is the key for the future of farming and food, January 24, 2002. See page 10, Table 1 for the data.

The stats on food wastage come from The best meal you'll never have!, *Costing the Earth*, BBC Radio 4, April 14, 2005.

See also, for example, this site's section on consumption effects for more issues.

Stats on annual deaths and medical costs from from the United Nations Food and Agriculture Organization's State of Food Insecurity in the World 2004 report.

Notes from SellingPower.com points out that:

o "Numerous studies suggest that every dollar invested in well-targeted interventions to reduce undernourishment and micronutrient deficiencies can yield $5 to $20 in benefits."

o The number of children that die every day due to hunger is the "technical equivalent of 45 jumbo jets crashing every single day"

In a world of plenty, a huge number go hungry. Hunger is more than just the result of food production and meeting demands. The causes of hunger are related to the causes of poverty. One of the major causes of hunger is poverty itself. The various issues discussed throughout this site about poverty lead to people being unable to afford food and hence people go hungry. There are other related causes (also often related to the causes of poverty in various ways), including the following:

- Land rights and ownership
- Diversion of land use to non-productive use
- Increasing emphasis on export-oriented agriculture
- Inefficient agricultural practices
- War
- Famine
- Drought
- Over-fishing
- Poor crop yield
- Lack of democracy and rights
- etc.

Some of the above are introduced here. (Over time, this will grow, and more will be added so do check back for updates.)

LAND RIGHTS AND OWNERSHIP

Two inter-related factors which influence hunger that are often ignored are land ownership and who controls land.

The following passage summarizes it very well, asking "Is It Overpopulation or Who Controls the Land?"

The often heard comment (one I once accepted as fact) that "there are too many people in the world, and overpopulation is the cause of hunger", can be compared to the same myth that expounded sixteenth-century England and revived continuously since.

Through repeated acts of enclosure the peasants were pushed off the land so that the gentry could make money raising wool for the new and highly productive power looms. They could not do this if the peasants were to retain their historic *entitlement* [emphasis is original] to a share of production from the land. Massive starvation was the inevitable result of this expropriation.

There were serious discussions in learned circles about overpopulation as the cause of this poverty. This was the accepted reason because a social and intellectual elite were doing the rationalizing. It was they who controlled the educational institutions which studied the problem. Naturally the final conclusions (at least those published) absolved the wealthy of any responsibility for the plight of the poor. The absurdity of suggesting that England was then overpopulated is clear when we realize that "the total population of England in the sixteenth century was less than in any one of several present-day English cities."

The hunger in underdeveloped countries today is equally tragic and absurd. Their European colonizers understood well that ownership of land gave the owner control over what society produced. The most powerful simply redistributed the valuable land titles to themselves, eradicating millennia-old traditions of common use. Since custom is a form of ownership, the shared use of land could not be permitted. If ever reestablished, this ancient practice would reduce the rights of these new owners. For this reason, much of the land went unused or underused until the owners could do so profitably. This is the pattern of land use that characterizes most Third World countries today, and it is this that generates hunger in the world.

These conquered people are kept in a state of relative impoverishment. Permitting them any substantial share of the wealth would negate the historic reason for conquest — namely plunder. The ongoing role of Third World countries is to be the supplier of cheap and plentiful raw materials and agricultural products to the developed world. Nature's wealth was, and is, being controlled to fulfill the needs of the world's affluent people. The U.S. is one of the prime beneficiaries of this well-established system. Our great universities search diligently for "the answer" to the problem of poverty and hunger. They invariably find it in "lack of motivation, inadequate or no education," or some other self-serving excuse. They look at everything except the cause — the powerful own the world's social wealth. As a major beneficiary, we have much to gain by perpetuating the myths of overpopulations, cultural and racial inferiority, and so forth. The real causes must be kept from ourselves, as how else can this systematic damaging of others be squared with what we are taught about democracy, rights, freedom, and justice?

— J.W. Smith, The World's Wasted Wealth: the political economy of waste, (New World's Press, 1989), pp. 44, 45.

Some have pointed out over the years that even the US Founding Fathers understood this very well, to the effect that some elites were able to affect the Constitution in this manner:

Despite the egalitarian rhetoric of the American Revolution and an attempt to place a proclamation in the Constitution for a "common right of the whole nation to the whole of the land," the powerful looked out for their own interests by changing Locke's insightful phrase: "all men are entitled to life, liberty and land." This powerful statement that all could understand coming from a well-read and respected philosopher was a threat to the monopolizers of land, so they restructured those words to "life, liberty and [the meaningless phrase] pursuit of happiness." Knowledge of the substitution for phrases in America's Constitution which would protect every person's rights with phrases that protect only the rights of a few should alert one to check the meaning and purpose of all laws of all societies carefully.

— J.W. Smith, Regaining Rights to a Modern Commons through Eliminating the Subtle-Monopolization of Land, Chapter 24, Economic Democracy; The Political Struggle for the 21st Century, (1st Books, 2002, Second Edition) [Bracketed text is original]

Diversion of land use to non-productive use: When precious arable land use is diverted to non-productive, or even destructive use, the overall costs to society can be considerable. Examples of such land use include, but is not limited to the following:

- The tobacco industry
- Tea and Coffee plantations the world over to be sold to the wealthier countries, primarily

- Floriculture to sell flowers in the wealthier countries comes at a high cost to the growers
- Certain dam projects
- Sugar cane growing for sugar exports
- Beef and fast food industries using other people's resources

THE TOBACCO INDUSTRY

Smoking kills, reduces economic productivity and exacerbates poverty, charges the world's premier health body, the World Health Organization (WHO).

Smoking also contributes to world hunger, as the tobacco industry diverts huge amounts of land from producing food to producing tobacco:

Dr Judith MacKay, Director of the Asian Consultancy on Tobacco Control in Hong Kong, claims that tobacco's "minor" use of land denies 10 to 20 million people of food. "Where food has to be imported because rich farmland is being diverted to tobacco production, the government will have to bear the cost of food imports," she points out.

... The bottom line for governments of developing countries is that the net economic costs of tobacco are profoundly negative— the cost of treatment, disability and death exceeds the economic benefits to producers by at least US$200 billion annually "with one third of this loss being incurred by developing countries".

— John Madeley, Big Business Poor Peoples; The Impact of Transnational Corporations on the World's Poor, (Zed Books, 1999) pp. 53, 57

Madeley also describes in detail other impacts on land from tobacco use:

- The land that has been destroyed or degraded to grow tobacco has affects on nearby farms. As forests, for example, are cleared to make way for tobacco plantations, then the soil protection it provides is lost and is more likely to be washed away in heavy rains. This can lead to soil degradation and failing yields.

- A lot of wood is also needed to cure tobacco leaves.
- Tobacco uses up more water, and has more pesticides applied to it, further affecting water supplies. These water supplies are further depleted by the tobacco industry recommending the planting of quick growing, but water-thirsty eucalyptus trees.
- Child labor is often needed in tobacco farms.
- For more detail, refer to *Big Business Poor Peoples; The Impact of Transnational Corporations on the World's Poor*, by John Madeley, (Zed Books, 1999) ch. 4.

Madeley continues on to point out that heavy advertising of tobacco by TNCs can "convince the poor to smoke more, and to use money they might have spent on food or health care, to buy cigarettes instead."

A report by the Campaign for Tobacco-Free Kids says that from a socioeconomic and environmental perspective, there is little benefit in tobacco growing, and that "While a few large-scale tobacco growers have prospered, the vast majority of tobacco growers in the Global South barely eke out a living toiling for the companies." Furthermore, "the cigarette companies continue to downplay or ignore the many serious economic and environmental costs associated with tobacco cultivation, such as chronic indebtedness among tobacco farmers (usually to the companies themselves), serious environmental destruction caused by tobacco farming, and pesticide-related health problems for farmers and their families."

In fact, it is interesting to note that the tobacco industry has gone to extraordinary level to discredit the World Health Organisation (WHO) and others that are fighting tobacco issues, as a report from the WHO describes. A Committee of Experts had been set up in October 1999 to "enquire into the nature and extent of undue influence which the tobacco industry had exercised over UN organisations." This Committee produced the report that "found that the tobacco industry regarded the World Health Organization as one of their leading enemies, and that the industry had a planned strategy to 'contain, neutralise, reorient' WHO's tobacco control initiatives." They added that the tobacco industry documents show that they carried out their plan by:

- staging events to divert attention from the public health issues raised by tobacco use;
- attempting to reduce budgets for the scientific and policy activities carried out by WHO;
- pitting other UN agencies against WHO;
- seeking to convince developing countries that WHO's tobacco control program was a "First World" agenda carried out at the expense of the developing world;
- distorting the results of important scientific studies on tobacco;
- discrediting WHO as an institution.

While some countries, such as the US have had the resources and political will to tackle the large tobacco corporations, these multinationals have intensified their efforts in other regions of world such as Asia, to continue growing and selling cigarettes, as well as expanding advertising (to *create* demand, not meet).

Reports from the WHO show that there is a lot of political manouvering by large tobacco companies to lower prices, to increase sales, etc. In addition, the poor and small farmers are the ones most affected by the impacts of tobacco companies. The hard cash earned from this "foreign investment" is offset by the costs in social and public health. In effect, profits are privatized; costs are socialized.

If one doesn't wish to give up smoking because it is considered their free choice, how about giving up smoking so others may have a choice?

More issues around tobacco and its impacts, the actions of the tobacco industry, attempts at global regulation, and more are provided on this site's tobacco section.

ENVIRONMENTAL AND ECONOMIC DAMAGE FROM COFFEE PRODUCTION

"Coffee drinkers will be astonished to learn that they hold in their hands the fate of farm families, farming communities, and entire ecosystems in coffee-growing regions like Costa Rica," as *Old Dog Documentaries* notes. Furthermore:

> 25 million coffee growers worldwide are paid a mere pittance in the corporate marketplace while bearing the full brunt of global price fluctuations. When prices crash, farmers go hungry and their children are forced to drop out of school. Families are separated, communities disintegrate, and the land is cleared for other crops or other means of livelihood. That clearing of the land disrupts the ecosystem in ways that have deadly consequences for migratory birds in particular and for global ecological balance in general.
>
> — *Birdsong & Coffee: A Wake Up Call, Old Dog Documentaries, Inc., March 2006*

The ID21 research organization summarizes some the impacts of coffee production: "Coffee production provides a livelihood for 25 million people in developing countries and globally, 10.6 million hectares of land are used for growing coffee beans." Coffee is therefore "one of the most legally-traded agricultural commodities in the world and one of the most important income crops for small farmers in developing countries." Despite its importance, Growing coffee is not always a reliable source of income, however. While coffee production increased by 61 percent between 1960 and 2000, prices fell by 57 percent during the same period.

> ...Growing coffee has significant environmental impacts:
>
> - Establishing coffee plantations results in the clearance of natural forest areas. This trend is made worse by the

increasing demand for high-grade speciality coffee, which requires more land.

- Chemical use contributes to soil degradation. A shift to new production methods (such as full-sun production) has increased pesticide use enormously, resulting in lower insect populations and reduced nutrient recycling by soil.
- As coffee processing has moved away from the farms and fields, waste pulp is dumped in rivers, thus reducing levels of oxygen in the water and degrading freshwater ecosystems. It could instead be used as a soil amendment for coffee crops.

— *Counting the cost of a cup of coffee, ID21, 28 February 2005*

Fair Trade Coffee is often highlighted as a better option than normally produced coffee, for it at least pays the producer a fairer wage. Yet, in a wider context, is such mass coffee consumption healthy for the producing country?

Coffee consumption, in the amounts typically done today, may also be unnecessary. Many consume it in vast quanitites believing the caffeine intake will help them get through the day, especially if working long, stressful hours. A recent program by the *BBC* called the *Truth about Food* compared coffee with a decafenated substitute and concluded the following:

Does caffeine give us the edge over decaf users? No. Once we've recovered from caffeine we can do just as well without it.

— *Caffeine and the Brain, BBC, accessed February 15, 2007*

Some may choose to consume coffee for its taste, but if so many are consuming it to get through work, then it may not be necessary. This may implied "wasted labour" and resources (the details and implications of which are discussed further on this site's section on Behind Consumption and Consumerism).

GROWING FLOWERS CAN HAVE A HIGH COST TO GROWERS

Floriculture too is a growing field in some developing countries. However, as Madeley explains, it too has some negative effects, such as:

- Divert land use away from growing needed food. (In Colombia for example, floriculture was seen as a way to avoid cocaine growing. Food growth could have been more directly positive for the growers and local communities.)
- Very low wages
- Child labor
- Pesticide poisoning and other severe health problems. (Some of these pesticides are banned in the West.)
- Women suffer high miscarriage rates
- For more detail, refer to *Big Business Poor Peoples; The Impact of Transnational Corporations on the World's Poor*, by John Madeley, (Zed Books, 1999) ch. 4, pp 64 - 70 (Non-traditional export crops).

Anuradha Mittal also describes the effects in some parts of India:

In 1999, a UN Population Fund report predicted that India would soon become one of the world's largest recipients of food aid. The report went on to blame the increasing population for the problem. What it did not mention is that the state of Punjab, also known as "the granary of India," grows abundant food even today, but most of it is being converted into dog and cat food for Europe. Nor did the report mention that the neighboring state of Haryana, also traditionally a fertile agricultural state, is today one of the world leaders in growing tulips for export. Increasingly, countries like India are polluting their air, earth, and water to grow products for the Western market instead of growing food to feed their own people. Prime agricultural lands are being poisoned to meet the needs of the consumers in the West, and the money the consumers spend does not reach the majority of the working poor in the Third World.

— *Anuradha Mittal, True Cause of World Hunger, February 2002*

And in Ecuador, *Mother Jones* magazine adds that,

Insecticides, herbicides, fungicides, and soil fumigants used in the greenhouses are causing serious health problems for Ecuador's 60,000 rose workers — especially the women and children who sort and package the flowers prior to shipping. In recent years, studies by the International Labor Organization and Ecuador's Catholic University have found that as many as 60 percent of postharvest workers complain of pesticide-poisoning symptoms, including headaches, blurred vision, and muscular twitching. Women in the industry, who represent 70 percent of all rose workers, experience significantly elevated rates of miscarriages. Children under 18, who make up more than a fifth of the workforce, display signs of neurological damage at 22 percent above average.

— *Ross Wehner, Deflowering Ecuador, Mother Jones, January/February 2003 Issue*

THE EFFECTS OF DAM PROJECTS ON THE POOR

While not necessarily a non-productive use as such, dam projects have long been criticized for displacing millions of people and not providing them the benefits promised, while also degrading the environment and even flooding arable land.

Every year, from the mid-1980s to the mid-1990s, around four million people were displaced from their homes because of hydro-electric dam schemes. These schemes usually created huge resevoirs which flooded homes, forests and fertile land.... Since the electricity generated by the dams was intended to power factories and houses in urban areas, few of the rural poor benefitted from such schemes.

... These [multinational construction] corporations are a vital link in the "big dam" chain. Their experience of such projects means they can provide an expertise that national companies usually lack. Without the TNCs, the big aid-funded dam schemes of the last 40 years could not have gone ahead with such confidence. The schemes give the TNCs security of payment, as the money is coming mostly from foreign aid, and the opportunity to make good profits at low risk — if costs soar they can usually be passed on. Dams often cost more than the original estimates, leaving governments of developing countries to pick up an extra bill.

... The construction of the [Sri Lankan] Mahaweli River scheme effectively witnessed an enormous transfer of wealth from people in one of the poorest developing countries to some of the world's largest TNCs. "We are a poor country", said a critic of the scheme, "we cannot afford this kind of aid".

... The UK had agreed to give aid for Pergau in 1989 as a sweetener for securing a £1.3 billion arms deal with Malaysia. In 1991, Sir Timothy Lankester, a former permanent secretary at the Overseas Development Administration, the British government department which then administered the aid budget, opposed aid for the dam, saying he believed it was neither economic or efficient. He was over-ruled.

— John Madeley, Big Business Poor Peoples; The Impact of Transnational Corporations on the World's Poor, (Zed Books, 1999) pp. 115 - 117

After reactions to a pertinent report by the World Bank, a World Commission on Dams (WCD) was established in 1998 with a mandate to review the development effectiveness of large dams and develop internationally acceptable criteria, guidelines and standards for large dams.

The World Commission on Dams (WCD), released a report at the end of 2000 criticizing dam projects for failing to deliver promised benefits while affecting millions of poor people's lives in developing countries and degrading the environment.

They also pointed out that "dams have made an important and significant contribution to human development, and the benefits derived from them have been considerable." However, "in too many cases an unacceptable and often unnecessary price has been paid to secure those benefits, especially in social and environmental terms, by people displaced, by communities downstream, by taxpayers and by the natural environment. Lack of equity in the distribution of benefits has called into question the value of many dams in meeting water and energy development needs when compared with the alternatives."

The full report from the World Commission on Dams is on their web site.

The World Bank, involved in many dam projects, received criticism for choosing to only reference the WCD report rather than adopt them as rules governing its operations.

BEEF AND FAST FOOD INDUSTRIES USING OTHER PEOPLE'S RESOURCES

Consider the following cited from this web site's section on consumption and beef:

- More than one third of the world's grain harvest is used to feed livestock.
- Breaking that down a little bit
  - o Almost all rice is consumed by people
  - o While corn is a staple food in many Latin American and Sub-Saharan countries, "worldwide, it is used largely as feed."
  - o Wheat is more evenly divided between food and feed and is a staple food in many regions such as the West, China and India.
- The total cattle population for the world is approximately 1.3 billion occupying some 24% of the land of the planet
- Some 70 to 80% of grain produced in the United States is fed to livestock
- Half the water consumed in the U.S. is used to grow grain for cattle feed

- A gallon of gasoline is required to produce a pound of grain-fed beef

— *Anup Shah, Beef*

The beef industry consumes a considerable number of resources, and for a product that is not a "need" as such, but more of a "luxury". Excessive promotion of its consumption has led to many health issues as well as environmental problems. Furthermore, the resources used could be put to more productive uses. In addition, as an example of the vast first world subsidies which the third world often complains about as hypocritical, consider the following: If water used by the meat industry [in the United States] were not subsidized by taxpayers, common hamburger meat would cost $35 a pound. You need 25 gallons of water to produce a pound of wheat — 2,500 gallons to generate a pound of meat.

— *Simone Spearman, Eating More Veggies Can Help Save Energy, San Francisco Chronicle, June 29, 2001. (Emphasis Added) [Previous link is to a reposted version at Commondreams.org]*

The issue of beef and fast food industry is discussed further on this site's section on beef.

Sugar Cane Growing for Sugar Exports

Like beef, sugar too contributes to problems. From the obvious things like health, there are also other concerns such as the environment, and using vast resources to produce an unhealthy product for export when similar resources could be spent in other, more productive ways. This too is further discussed on this site's section on sugar. Like beef, sugar exemplifies issues related to some of the negative aspects of liberalized, industrial agriculture.

Increasing Emphasis on Liberalized, Export-oriented and Industrial Agriculture

In Less Developed Countries the problem of land use is even more acute. Whilst the majority of food produce tends to be grown on small, subsistence farms, the bulk of the best agricultural land is used for the growing of cash crops. Partly a legacy of colonial policies, partly a result of the debt problem and IMF and World Bank solutions to this problem, we find that people in the LDCs, particularly the rural poor, are going hungry whilst the bulk of these countries' agricultural output is exported to Europe and the USA.

— Ross Copeland, The Politics of Hunger, University of Kassel, September 2000

In many cases where food is grown, it is often for exports. In some cases, while local people may be going hungry, they are growing food to export for the hard cash that would be earned. The increasingly export-oriented economies are being promoted by the wealthier Northern countries and the international institutions that they have strong influence over, the IMF and World Bank, as detailed in the Structural Adjustment section on this site. The result of this is that the wealthier nations tend to benefit while poorer countries generally lose out.

[Farmers] producing [fruit and vegetables] for export markets has recently become more common. TNCs are increasingly involved in the production of crops that have traditionally not been exported. But export crops are replacing staple foods in some areas, resulting in food scarcities and rising food prices that hit hard at the poorest.

... Yet [the market success seen by this exporting policy] "has frequently come at a cost in workers' health, inequitable distribution of economic benefits, and environmental degradation in many of the exporting countries."

... Small-scale farmers and consumers in Latin America are paying the price of this drastic shift to export agriculture. In towns and cities across the continent, beans are now frequently scarce as land which once grew beans now grows vegetables for export. Beans contribute around 30 per cent of the protein consumption by the continent's 200 million low-income families. Most bean farmers are now trying to grow vegetables for export and devoting less of their land (often already small) to beans for their own use.

— *John Madeley, Big Business Poor Peoples; The Impact of Transnational Corporations on the World's Poor, (Zed Books, 1999) pp. 64 - 66*

Sometimes, the cost of the food produced can be more than what the local people can afford and has to be exported to earn cash. Land and labor is therefore diverted away from immediate needs. Additionally, the local food growers are then subject to the fashions and preferences of external communities and market demands. If they no longer like the range of products as much, the entire local economy could be affected. The banana trade in the Caribbean is an example of this.

Free trade and other economic agreements that reduce subsidies on local farms etc, has a worse impact on developing countries with few resources. We hear of these subsidies being "barriers" for foreign investment.

Yet, the nature of the foreign investment isn't to help promote self-sufficiency etc. It is to follow on from what the SAPs opened up — that is, SAPs opened up these economies, and foreign multinational companies can now go in and help "export" base foods and commodities. As J. W. Smith has described, this results in the Third World producing for the First World (which was the pattern during imperial and colonial times):

World hunger exists because: (1) colonialism, and later subtle monopoly capitalism, dispossessed hundreds of millions of people from their land; the current owners are the new plantation managers producing for the mother countries; (2) the low-paid undeveloped countries sell to the highly paid developed countries because there is no local market [because the low-paid people do not have enough to pay] ... and (3) the current Third World land owners, producing for the First World, are appendages to the industrialized world, stripping all natural wealth from the land to produce food, lumber, and other products for wealthy nations.

This system is largely kept in place by underpaying the defeated colonial societies for the real value of their labor and resources, leaving them no choice but to continue to sell their natural wealth to the over-paid industrial societies that overwhelmed them. To eliminate hunger: (1) the dispossessed, weak, individualized people must be protected from the organized and legally protected multinational corporations; (2) there must be managed trade to protect both the Third World and the developed world, so the dispossessed can reclaim use of their land; (3) the currently defeated people can then produce the more labor-intensive, high-protein/high-calorie crops that contain all eight (or nine) essential amino acids; and (4) those societies must adapt dietary patterns so that vegetables, grains, and fruits are consumed in the proper amino acid combinations, with small amounts of meat or fish for flavor.

With similar dietary adjustments among the wealthy, there would be enough food for everyone.

— *J.W. Smith, The World's Wasted Wealth 2, Institute for Economic Democracy, 1994), pp. 63, 64.*

Yet, the wealthier nations realize the importance of food security and heavily subsidize their own farming infrastructures:

While subsidies are viewed as barriers by companies outside the region, they are critical incentives for the smallholder farmers especially those in southern Africa, most of whom are still using traditional methods and are only just beginning to acquire vital modern technology.

Large-scale commercial farmers in Europe and the US have been modernized for decades and have benefited from similar subsidies from their own governments for many years.

Paradoxically, the European Union, one of the leading proponents of trade liberalization has one of the most protected agricultural sectors in the world through its Common Agricultural Policy. Such is the double standard of the EU that it forces developing countries, through the western-dominated World Trade Organization (WTO), to open up their economies when Europe's agriculture sector is the most highly subsidized in the world.

—Munetsi Madakufamba, Unequal 'freetrade' threatens food security, The Mail & Guardian (a South African national newspaper), August 13, 2001

Additionally, some of the political dynamics that result in the poverty that most food growers are in, also leads to continued misery:

- Historically, the poor have often been marginalized by forcing them off their lands on to land less suitable for agriculture. This has been achieved through (sometimes violent) change and control of legal land ownership and related laws, especially during the colonial times.
- When much of the colonialized countries broke free from their imperial rulers, this pattern didn't go away.
  - o There was a continued concentration by the newer elites of poor countries (who, as discussed in some of the geopolitics sections of this site, were often placed in power by former colonial and imperial rulers).
  - o In some cases the new elites were dictators and despots. In other cases, the economic relations of the society had been transformed so much, that systems like mass plantation systems continued as those in charge were in favor with former colonial masters, and now had more power.
  - o Combined with the expansion in global trading today, and the promotion of export-oriented economies as a solution to poverty, this has led to local and national elites in poor countries exporting to wealthier nations where the only real "market" for their food and other products can be effectively sold.
- A continuing circle like this produces a downward spiral of deeper poverty and further marginalization.

- The less suitable land also leads to further environmental degradation of those and other areas as well such as forests.

Peter Rosset describes the above very clearly as part of a look at some of the causes of poverty and hunger in his essay "Genetic Engineering of Food Crops for the Third World: An Appropriate Response to Poverty, Hunger and Lagging Productivity?" He goes on to show how this has led to the current downward spiral, quoted in summarized form below:

- The marginalization of the majority leads to narrow and shallow domestic markets
- So landowning elites orient their production to export markets where consumers do have purchasing power
- By doing so, elites have ever less interest in the well-being or purchasing power of the poor at home, as the poor are not a market for them, but rather a cost in terms of wages to be kept as low as possible.
- By keeping wages and living standards low, elites guarantee that healthy domestic markets will never emerge, reinforcing export orientation.
- The result is a downward spiral into deeper poverty and marginalization, even as national exports become more "competitive" in the global economy.
- One irony of our world, then, is that food and other farm products flow *from* areas of hunger and need to areas were money is concentrated, in Northern countries. (Bold emphasis added; italics emphasis is original)

Food as a Commodity

And when food is treated as a commodity, those who can get food are the ones who can afford to pay for it. To illustrate this further, the following is worth quoting at length (bulleting and spacing formatting is mine, text is original):

To understand why people go hungry you must stop thinking about food as something farmers grow for others to eat, and begin thinking about it as something companies produce for other people to buy.

- Food is a commodity....
- Much of the best agricultural land in the world is used to grow commodities such as cotton, sisal, tea, tobacco, sugar cane, and cocoa, items which are non-food products or are marginally nutritious, but for which there is a large market.
- Millions of acres of potentially productive farmland is used to pasture cattle, an extremely inefficient use of land, water and energy, but one for which there is a market in wealthy countries.
- More than half the grain grown in the United States (requiring half the water used in the U.S.) is fed to livestock, grain that would feed far more people than would the livestock to which it is fed....

The problem, of course, is that people who don't have enough money to buy food (and more than one billion people earn less than $1.00 a day), simply don't count in the food equation.

- In other words, if you don't have the money to buy food, no one is going to grow it for you.
- Put yet another way, you would not expect The Gap to manufacture clothes, Adidas to manufacture sneakers, or IBM to provide computers for those people earning $1.00 a day or less; likewise, you would not expect ADM ("Supermarket to the World") to produce food for them.

What this means is that ending hunger requires doing away with poverty, or, at the very least, ensuring that people have enough money or the means to acquire it, to buy, and hence create a market demand for food.

— *Richard H. Robbins, Readings on Poverty, Hunger, and Economic Development*

5

Solving World Hunger Means Solving World Poverty

HUNGER AND POVERTY ARE RELATED ISSUES

A common, often altruistic, theme amongst many is to be able to solve world hunger via some method that may produce more food. However, often missed is the relationship between poverty and hunger. Hunger is an effect of poverty and poverty is largely a political issue. (While manifesting itself as an economic issue, conditions causing poverty are political and end up being economic.)

As shown in the Genetically Engineered Food and Human Population sections on this web site, people are hungry not due to lack of availability of food, but because people do not have the ability to purchase food and because distribution of food is not equitable. In addition, there is also a lot of politics influencing how food is produced, who it is produced by (and who benefits), and for what purposes the food is produced (such as exporting rather than for the hungry, feedstuff, etc.)

[A]ccess to food and other resources is not a matter of availability, but rather of ability to pay. Put bluntly, those with the most money command the most resources, whilst those with little or no money go hungry. This inevitably leads to a situation whereby some sections of humanity arguably have too much and other sections little or nothing. Indeed, globally the richest 20 per cent of humanity controls around 85 per cent of all wealth, whilst the poorest 20 per cent control only 1.5 per cent.

— Ross Copeland, The Politics of Hunger, September 2000

Peter Rosset, co-director of the Institute for Food and Development Policy, quoted at the top of this page, highlights some of the wider issues around hunger. He argues that it is not just a challenge of producing more and more food, but there are many political and economic issues underscoring the problems:

Research carried out by our Institute reveals that since 1996, governments have presided over a set of policies that have conspired to undercut peasant, small and family farmers, and farm cooperatives in nations both North and South. These policies have included runaway trade liberalization, pitting family farmers in the Third World against the subsidized corporate farms in the North (witness the recent U.S. Farm Bill), forcing Third World countries to eliminate price supports and subsidies for food producers, the privatization of credit, the excessive promotion of exports to the detriment of food crops, the patenting of crop genetic resources by corporations who charge farmers for their use, and a bias in agricultural research toward expensive and questionable technologies like genetic engineering while virtually ignoring pro-poor alternatives like organic farming and agroecology.

— Peter Rosset, The World Food Summit: What Went Wrong?, June 4, 2002

Food as a Human Right

Reporting from the World Food Summit 2002, and highlighting some shocking obstacles to getting a declaration on tackling these issues, Peter Rosset reported on day one:

ROME—At 3:00 AM on Monday morning the United States stood alone among all nations of the world in blocking further discussion of the draft text of the declaration that governments will sign at the World Food Summit. What was leading the U.S.

to stop the all night negotiating session? First, the U.S. wanted all references to "food as a human right" to be deleted, and second, the U.S. wanted strong language saying that genetically modified (GM) crops are a key way to end hunger. The Third World nations organized in the Group of 77 wanted mandatory language on the Right to Food, while Europe and Canada held out for the compromise of a voluntary Code of Conduct. No other nation felt strongly that GM crops should receive prominence.

— *Peter Rosset, United States Behavior at World Food Summit: "Reprehensible", Report from the 2002 World Food Summit: Day 1, June 10, 2002 [Emphasis Added]*

And at the end of the summit:

The only positive thing in the official declaration was the proposal for a "voluntary" code of conduct on the Right to Food to be developed over the next two years. The United States, which had vehemently opposed the right to food in any form, finally accepted this version which is a) not mandatory and b) not immediate. Apart from that, the declaration is a disaster as far as ending hunger goes. It repeats the flaws of the 1996 Summit declaration which led to the failure to meet hunger reduction goals over the past five years, including an endorsement of free trade, a recommendation of more structural adjustment for the poorest countries, and a call for greater private investment. It also adds the golden goose that the U.S. wants — biotechnology — and drops a key victory from the 1996 declaration, land reform. All in all, a bad performance by governments.

— *Peter Rosset, Report from the 2002 World Food Summit: Day 4, June 13, 2002*

The U.S.'s position on opposing the right to food comes at odds with most others in the world. The world's premier organization on food issues, the United Nations Food and Agriculture Organization (FAO), is one example. As reported by Europaworld, an international development organization, Jacques Diouf, the FAO's Director-General reiterated the link between hunger, poverty and basic rights, saying, "Failure to address the silent under-nourishment of millions of children and adults in peacetime should also be regarded as a violation of the right to food."

Furthermore, because of the immediate urgency to address hunger, the issue of promoting food itself as a human right, and its denial as an abuse of rights, has been seen by many as paramount. This has been the cry for many years by the Institute for Food and Development Policy (or Food First for short), for example.

Solving Hunger Effectively Requires Addressing Causes of Poverty

While providing solutions to hunger via more efficient food production seems to be a noble endeavor, problems lie in distribution, land ownership, inefficient use of land, politics and powerplay. Currently, food production rates are higher than population growth (although that is no reason to be complacent). Tackling hunger directly by providing more charitable contributions of food, or even finding ways to increase production, is attacking the symptoms of poverty only, not root causes.

That is not to say that research to increasing food production should not be done, just that it should be recognized that the deeper problem of fighting the roots of poverty that causes hunger would allow better use of resources in the long term. Not fighting root causes of poverty and only fighting hunger will be costly in the long run as people will continue to be hungry and resources will be continually diverted to remedy hunger in a superficial manner without addressing its cause.

"Solving" world hunger by only increasing food production and not addressing root causes of hunger (i.e. poverty), would not alleviate the conditions that create poverty in the first place. If the poorer nations aren't given the sufficient means to produce their own food, if they are not allowed to produce and create industry for themselves, then poverty and dependency will continue.

World hunger exists because: (1) colonialism, and later subtle monopoly capitalism, dispossessed hundreds of millions of people from their land; the current owners are the new plantation managers producing for the mother countries; (2) the low-paid undeveloped countries sell to the highly paid developed countries because there is no local market [because the low-paid people do not have enough to pay] ... and (3) the current Third World land owners, producing for the First World, are appendages to the industrialized world, stripping all natural wealth from the land to produce food, lumber, and other products for wealthy nations.

This system is largely kept in place by underpaying the defeated colonial societies for the real value of their labor and resources, leaving them no choice but to continue to sell their natural wealth to the over-paid industrial societies that overwhelmed them. To eliminate hunger: (1) the dispossessed, weak, individualized people must be protected from the organized and legally protected multinational corporations; (2) there must be managed trade to protect both the Third World and the developed world, so the dispossessed can reclaim use of their land; (3) the currently defeated people can then produce the more labor-intensive, high-protein/high-calorie crops that contain all eight (or nine) essential amino acids; and (4) those societies must adapt dietary patterns so that vegetables, grains, and fruits are consumed in the proper amino acid combinations, with small amounts of meat or fish for flavor. With similar dietary adjustments among the wealthy, there would be enough food for everyone.

— J.W. Smith, The World's Wasted Wealth 2, (Institute for Economic Democracy, 1994), pp. 63, 64.

It is worth repeating here the quote from the end of the previous page, about food as a commodity:

To understand why people go hungry you must stop thinking about food as something farmers grow for others to eat, and begin thinking about it as something companies produce for other people to buy.

- Food is a commodity. ...
- Much of the best agricultural land in the world is used to grow commodities such as cotton, sisal, tea, tobacco, sugar cane, and cocoa, items which are non-food products or are marginally nutritious, but for which there is a large market.
- Millions of acres of potentially productive farmland is used to pasture cattle, an extremely inefficient use of land, water and energy, but one for which there is a market in wealthy countries.
- More than half the grain grown in the United States (requiring half the water used in the U.S.) is fed to livestock, grain that would feed far more people than would the livestock to which it is fed. ...

The problem, of course, is that people who don't have enough money to buy food (and more than one billion people earn less than $1.00 a day), simply don't count in the food equation.

- In other words, if you don't have the money to buy food, no one is going to grow it for you.
- Put yet another way, you would not expect The Gap to manufacture clothes, Adidas to manufacture sneakers, or IBM to provide computers for those people earning $1.00 a day or less; likewise, you would not expect ADM ("Supermarket to the World") to produce food for them.

What this means is that ending hunger requires doing away with poverty, or, at the very least, ensuring that people have enough money or the means to acquire it, to buy, and hence create a market demand for food.

— *Richard H. Robbins, Readings on Poverty, Hunger, and Economic Development*

To address the causes of poverty then, is where more effort needs to be. However, that is no easy task.

Just giving/donating food as aid or charity in non-emergency situations is also not always the long term answer, either. The section on food dumping, next, reveals additional details on how food aid has been used as a foreign policy tool by some wealthy nations to their advantage and interests. Rather than benefiting recipients, such "food aid" has amounted to economic dumping, helping destroy local farmers and their production, while supporting and bolstering large agribusiness. Hunger and poverty has increased as an effect.

FOOD DUMPING [AID] MAINTAINS POVERTY

In the industrialized northern countries, we instinctively believe that food aid is a very worthy cause and many do their utmost to genuinely help in this field. Web sites like the hungersite.com allow you to simply click a link and thereby donate food to someone in need in a developing country. However, there is more to it that selecting on a link.

In fact, if priority is not placed on the political root causes of hunger, sites like this may unwittingly contribute to the harm that has already been inflicted on the poor in developing countries because the poor countries will remain dependent. (Providing free food in emergency situations of course is usually welcome, but we are concerned with systemic root causes of hunger in non-emergency situations here as some one sixth of humanity goes hungry each day in non-emergency situations.)

This subsection of the poverty section on the globalissues.org web site provides additional details on this important issue in the following articles:

FOOD AID AS DUMPING

The *way* the food aid programs of various rich countries is structured may be of concern. In fact, food "aid" (when not for *emergency* relief) can actually be very destructive on the economy of the recipient nation. Dumping food on to poorer nations (i.e. free, subsidized, or cheap food, below market prices) undercuts local farmers, who cannot compete and are driven out of jobs and into poverty, further slanting the market share of the larger producers such as those from the US and Europe. Last updated Monday, October 31, 2005.

MYTH: MORE US AID WILL HELP THE HUNGRY

With kind permission from Peter Rosset of the Institute for Food and Development Policy (or FoodFirst.org as it is also known), chapter 10 of *World Hunger: 12 Myths*, 2nd Edition, by Frances Moore Lappé, Joseph Collins and Peter Rosset, with Luis Esparza (fully revised and updated, Grove/Atlantic and Food First Books, Oct. 1998) has been posted here. It describes in details the issue of food aid and the United States of America's aid policies, the problems it causes and who it really benefits. Posted Saturday, November 25, 2000.

FOOD AID AS DUMPING

Some years back, a keynote speaker at the International Famine Centre at Cork, Ireland, detailed how maize was loaded on ships bound for Britain at the height of the great Irish potato famine that killed some 1.5 million people more than 150 years ago. He paused and then lamented: "I wonder what kind of people lived at that time who were not even remotely offended at the sight of millions dying of hunger in the same village where the ships were being loaded."

A hundred years later, the same class of people were largely responsible for the great Bengal Famine in 1943, in which an estimated 1.5 million to 3 million people perished. As Nobel laureate Amartya Sen explains in his now well-known theory of entitlements, the Bengal famine was not the result of a drastic slump in food production but because the colonial masters had diverted food for other commercial purposes. And if you are wondering whether the same evil class of the elite decision-makers has perished with the collapse of the erstwhile colonies, hold your breadth.

In the last 60 years or so, following the great human tragedy of the Bengal famine, food aid was conveniently used as a political weapon... Food was then a political weapon. Food aid has now in addition become a commercial enterprise. Famine or no famine, the Shylocks of the grain trade must have their "pound of flesh".

— *Devinder Sharma, Africa's Tragedy; Famine as Commerce, November 10, 2002*

Certain types of food "aid" (when not for *emergency* relief) can actually be destructive. Dumping food on to poorer nations (i.e. free, subsidized, or cheap food, below market prices) undercuts local farmers, who cannot compete and are driven out of jobs and into poverty, further slanting the market share of the larger producers such as those from the US and Europe.

DESTROYING LOCAL MARKETS; INCREASING HUNGER IN THE NAME OF AID

J. W. Smith, of the Institute for Economic Democracy, in his 1994 book titled the *World's Wasted Wealth II*, has detailed research and summarizes the issue very well and is worth quoting at length:

Highly mechanized farms on large acreages can produce units of food cheaper than even the poorest paid farmers of the Third World. When this cheap food is sold, or given, to the Third World, the local farm economy is destroyed. If the poor and unemployed of the Third World were given access to land, access to industrial tools, and protection from cheap imports, they could plant high-protein/high calorie crops and become self-sufficient in food. Reclaiming their land and utilizing the unemployed would cost these societies almost nothing, feed them well, and save far more money than they now pay for the so-called "cheap" imported foods.

World hunger exists because: (1) colonialism, and later subtle monopoly capitalism, dispossessed hundreds of millions of people from their land; the current owners are the new plantation managers producing for the mother countries; (2) the low-paid undeveloped countries sell to the highly paid developed countries because there is no local market [because the low-paid people do not have enough to pay] ... and (3) the current Third World land owners, producing for the First World, are appendages to the industrialized world, stripping all natural wealth from the land to produce food, lumber, and other products for wealthy nations.

This system is largely kept in place by underpaying the defeated colonial societies for the real value of their labor and resources, leaving them no choice but to continue to sell their natural wealth to the over-paid industrial societies that overwhelmed them. To eliminate hunger: (1) the dispossessed, weak, individualized people must be protected from the organized and legally protected multinational corporations; (2) there must be managed trade to protect both the Third World and the developed world, so the dispossessed can reclaim use of their land; (3) the currently defeated people can then produce the more labor-intensive, high-protein/high-calorie crops that contain all eight (or nine) essential amino acids; and (4) those societies must adapt dietary patterns so that vegetables, grains, and fruits are consumed in the proper amino acid combinations, with small amounts of meat or fish for flavor. With similar dietary adjustments among the wealthy, there would be enough food for everyone.

— J.W. Smith, The World's Wasted Wealth 2, (Institute for Economic Democracy, 1994), pp. 63, 64.

He goes on to show the effects of imports and exports with regards to food production:

The United States lent governments money to buy this food, and then enforced upon them the extraction and export of their natural resources to pay back the debt...

Not only is much U.S. food exported unnecessary, but it results in great harm to the very people they profess to be helping. The United States exported over sixty million tons of grain in 1974. Only 3.3 million tons were for aid, and most of that did not reach the starving. For example, during the mid-1980s, 84 percent of U.S. agricultural exports to Latin America were given to the local governments to sell to the people. This undersold local producers, destroyed their markets, and reduced their production.

Exporting food may be profitable for the exporting country, but when their land is capable of producing adequate food, it is a disaster to the importing countries. [Note that many of the poor nations today are rich in natural resources and arable land.] American farmers would certainly riot if 60 percent of their markets were taken over by another country. Not only would the farmers suffer, but the entire economy would be severely affected.

Imported food is not as cheap as it appears. If the money expended on imports had been spent within the local economy, it would have multiplied several times as it moved through the economy contracting local labor (the multiplier effect) ...

This moving of money through an economy is why there is so much wealth in a high-wage manufacturing and exporting country and so little within a low-wage country that is "dependent" on imports. With centuries of mercantilist experience, developed societies understand this well.

... [S]ubsidies, tariffs and other trade policies eliminate the comparative advantage of other regions to maintain healthy economies in the developed world. ... The result of these First World subsidies [for export] are shattered Third World economies.

*— J.W. Smith, The World's Wasted Wealth 2, (Institute for Economic Democracy, **1994**), pp. **66-67**.*

(One of the U.S. food "aid" programs that J.W. Smith is referring to above is the Food for Peace, or Public Law 480 (PL 480).)

In that final paragraph above, Smith also points out that subsidies to protect industries in the developed world allows products to be produced, which can then lead to dumping on developing countries, whose tariffs etc have been removed due to "free trade" policies and Structural Adjustment, as described earlier.

Anuradha Mittal, of the Institute for Food and Development Policy describes some of the harsh realities of this and is worth quoting at length:

The victims of free market dogma can be found all over the developing world. An estimated 43 per- cent of the rural population of Thailand now lives below the poverty line, even though agricultural exports grew an astounding 65 percent between 1985 and 1995. In Bolivia, following half a decade of the most spectacular agricultural export growth in its history, by 1990, 95 percent of the rural population earned less than a dollar a day. In the Philippines, as acreage under rice and corn declines and the area under "cut flowers" increases, 350,000 rural livelihoods are set to be destroyed.

Similarly, in Brazil during the 1970s, agricultural exports, particularly soybeans (almost all of which went to feed Japanese and European livestock), were boosted phenomenally. At the same time, however, the hunger of Brazilians spread from one-third of the population in the 1960s to two-thirds by the early 1980s. Even in the 1990s, as Brazil became the world's third largest agricultural exporter — the area planted to soybeans having grown 37 percent from 1980 to 1995, displacing forests and small farmers in the process — per capita production of rice, a basic staple of the Brazilian diet, fell by 18 percent.

The Mexican government, meanwhile, has put over 2 million corn farmers out of business over the past few years by allowing imports of heavily subsidized corn from the United States. A flood of cheap imported grain has also driven local farmers out of business in Costa Rica. From 1984 to 1989, the number growing corn, beans, and rice, the staples of the local diet, fell from 70,000 to 27,000. That is the loss of 42,300 livelihoods. The same has taken place in Haiti, which the IMF forced open to imports of highly subsidized U.S. rice at the same time as it banned Haiti from subsidizing its own farmers. Between 1980 and 1997, rice imports grew from virtually zero to 200,000 tons a year, at the expense of domestically produced staples. As a result, Haitian farmers have been forced off their land to seek work in sweatshops, and people are worse off than ever: according to the IMF's own figures, 50 percent of Haitian children younger than 5 suffer from malnutrition and per capita income has dropped from around $600 in 1980 to $369 today.

Kenya, which had been self-sufficient until the 1980s, now imports 80 percent of its food, while 80 percent of its exports are accounted for by agriculture. In 1992, European Union (EU) wheat was sold in Kenya for 39 percent cheaper than the price paid to European farmers by the EU. In 1993, it was 50 percent cheaper. Consequently, imports of EU grain rose and, in 1995, Kenyan wheat prices collapsed through oversupply, undermining local production and creating poverty.

Far from ending hunger and promoting the economic interests of small farmers, agricultural liberalization has created a global food system that is structured to suit the interests of the powerful, to the detriment of poor farmers around the world.

— *Anuradha Mittal, Land Loss, Poverty and Hunger, Alternet.org, December 3, 2001*

Mittal, quoted above, is also worth quoting again, in an interview:

Of the 830 million hungry people worldwide, a third of them live in India. Yet in 1999, the Indian government had 10 million tons of surplus food grains: rice, wheat, and so on. In the year 2000, that surplus increased to almost 60 million tons — most of it left in the granaries to rot. Instead of giving the surplus food to the hungry, the Indian government was hoping to export the grain to make money. It also stopped buying grain from its own farmers, leaving them destitute. The farmers, who had gone into debt to purchase expensive chemical fertilizers and pesticides on the advice of the government, were now forced to burn their crops in their fields.

At the same time, the government of India was buying grain from Cargill and other American corporations, because the aid India receives from the World Bank stipulates that the government must do so. This means that today India is the largest importer of the same grain it exports. It doesn't make sense — economic or otherwise.

This situation is not unique to India. In 1985, Indonesia received the gold medal from the UN Food and Agriculture Organization for achieving food self-sufficiency. Yet by 1998, it had become the largest recipient of food aid in the world. I participated in a fact-finding mission to investigate Indonesia's reversal of fortune. Had the rains stopped? Were there no more crops in Indonesia? No, the cause of the food insecurity in Indonesia was the Asian financial crisis. Banks and industries were closing down. In the capital of Jakarta alone, fifteen thousand people lost their jobs in just one day. Then, as I traveled to rural areas, I saw rice plants dancing in field after field, and I saw cassava and all kinds of fruits. There was no shortage of food, but the people were too poor to buy it. So what did the U.S. and other countries, like Australia, do? Smelling an opportunity to unload their own surplus wheat in the name of "food aid," they gave loans to Indonesia upon the condition that it buy wheat from them. And Indonesians don't even eat wheat.

Remember the much-publicized famine in Ethiopia during the 1980s? Many of us don't realize that, during that famine, Ethiopia was exporting green beans to Europe. [Emphasis Added]

But the deeper issue here has to do with the fact that food aid is not usually free. It is often loaned, albeit at a low interest rate. When the U.S. sent wheat to Indonesia during the 1999 crisis, it was a loan to be paid back over a twenty-five-year period. In this manner, food aid has helped the U.S. take over grain markets in India, Nigeria, Korea, and elsewhere.

— Anuradha Mittal, True Cause of World Hunger, Institute for Food and Development Policy, February 2002

More generally, international policies relating to agriculture have been politically weighted towards the more powerful nations who are more influential. While the European Union (EU) and U.S. for example are strong and vocal in demanding that poor countries remove tariffs and other barriers to trade and that it will give them prosperity, they do the opposite. Devinder Sharma, a food and trade policy analyst comments:

a new Farm Bill pending before the U.S. Congress provides for support of a staggering $170 billion to American agriculture in the next ten years. On the other hand, the EU, paradoxically one of the leading proponents of trade liberalization, has one of the most protected agricultural sectors in the world through its Common Agricultural Policy. Such is the double standard of the EU that it forces developing countries, through the Western-dominated World Trade Organization (WTO), to open up their economies when Europe s agriculture sector is the most subsidized in the world.

"Dollar for dollar, America exports more meat than steel, more corn than cosmetics, more wheat than coal, more bakery products than motorboats, and more fruits and vegetables than household appliances," Mattie Sharpless, Acting Administrator, Foreign Agriculture Service of the U.S. Department of Agriculture recently told the Senate Agriculture Committee. She also added that agriculture is one of the few sectors of the U.S. economy that consistently contributes a surplus to its trade balance. In fact, the U.S. projections for the current year are that 53% of its wheat crop, 47% of cotton, 42% of rice, 35% of soybeans, and 21% of corn will be exported. This has only been made possible by the heavy subsidies and the removal of trade barriers or QRs in the developing countries.

— *Devinder Sharma, Food Supremacy, Foreign Policy In Focus, 13 February, 2002*

This mercantile process above shows how "aid" can be used as a foreign policy tool.

Farm subsidies have also contributed to surpluses which have been dumped on poorer nations, as discussed in further detail on this site's section that looks at foreign aid from rich nations. For example, Europe subsidizes its agriculture to the tune of some $35-40 billion per year, even while it demands other nations to liberalize their markets to foreign competition. The U.S. also introduced a $190 billion dollar subsidy to its farms through the U.S. Farm Bill, also criticized as a protectionist measure.

Oxfam illustrates how this can then translate into dumping and other effects:

Europe's sugar-production costs are among the world's highest but, paradoxically, the EU is the world's second biggest sugar exporter. This is made possible by setting the domestic sugar price at three times international prices, and subsidizing exports of excess production onto the world market. EU consumers and taxpayers are forced to pay the hefty bill of (Euro)1.6bn, but the impact falls hardest on developing countries. This is because the EU sugar regime has the following effects:

- It blocks developing-country exporters, including some of the world's poorest countries like Mozambique, from European markets,
- It undercuts developing countries in valuable third markets, such as the Middle East, by subsidizing exports to prices below international costs of production,
- It depresses world prices by dumping subsidized and surplus production, so damaging foreign-exchange earnings for low-cost exporters such as Brazil, Thailand, and southern Africa.

... the real winners are a few European sugar processors, and large farmers, who together form a powerful lobby which has blocked change for decades.

...In Jamaica, some 3,000 poor dairy farmers are being put out of business because of unfair competition from heavily subsidized European milk dumped on their market. The subsidies on the 5,500 tons shipped annually cost the European taxpayer $3m. Many of the farmers are women running their own small businesses. They are literally throwing away thousands of liters of milk from overflowing coolers. Many are leaving the industry that has supported their families for decades.

> -- *Europe's Double Standards. How the EU should reform its trade policies with the developing world, Oxfam Policy Paper, April 2002, p.11 (Link is to the press release, which includes a link to the actual PDF document from which the above is cited.)*

In addition, Oxfam also continues (p.12) that "Before the Bill passed, White House officials admitted that it would greatly encourage overproduction, fail to help US farmers most in need, and jeopardize markets abroad. According to the European Commission, 'there is no doubt that the vast bulk of payments under the Farm Bill will go to the largest agri-businesses'. Third World producers will find it harder to sell to the US market and, since the USA exports 25 per cent of its farm production, they will find it harder to sell in other international markets or to resist competition from US products in their home markets. The disposal of increased US surpluses as 'food aid' is likely to compound the loss of livelihoods."

Poverty and hunger are not just simple economic issues then; they are results of complex factors and decisions and aspects of a political economy; an ideological construct. President Aristide of Haiti faced this food dumping in Haiti as well:

What happens to poor countries when they embrace free trade? In Haiti in 1986 we imported just 7000 tons of rice, the main staple food of the country. The vast majority was grown in Haiti. In the late 1980s Haiti complied with free trade policies advocated by the international lending agencies and lifted tariffs on rice imports. Cheaper rice immediately flooded in from the United States where the rice industry is subsidized. In fact the liberalization of Haiti's market coincided with the 1985 Farm Bill in the United States which increased subsidies to the rice industry so that 40% of U.S. rice growers' profits came from the government by 1987. Haiti's peasant farmers could not possibly compete. By 1996 Haiti was importing 196,000 tons of foreign rice at the cost of $100 million a year. Haitian rice production became negligible. Once the dependence on foreign rice was complete, import prices began to rise, leaving Haiti's population, particularly the urban poor, completely at the whim of rising world grain prices. And the prices continue to rise.

What lessons do we learn? For poor countries free trade is not so free, or so fair. Haiti, under intense pressure from the international lending institutions, stopped protecting its domestic agriculture while subsidies to the U.S. rice industry increased. A hungry nation became hungrier.

— Jean-Bertrand Aristide, Eyes of the Heart; Seeking a Path for the Poor in the Age of Globalization, (Common Courage Press, 2000), pp. 11-12

Note in the above quote, the effect this created dependency has. Free trade and globalization and its effects are discussed on this web site as well.

As a further example, Aristide continues by describing how the eradication of the Creole pigs in Haiti in the 1980s and replacing them with "healthier" pigs resulted in further poverty and hunger:

Haiti's small, black, Creole pigs were at the heart of the peasant economy. An extremely hearty breed, well adapted to Haiti's climate and conditions, they ate readily-available waste products, and could survive for three days without food. Eighty to 85% of rural households raised pigs; they played a key role in maintaining the fertility of the soil and constituted the primary savings bank of the peasant population. Traditionally a pig was sold to pay for emergencies and special occasions (funerals, marriages, baptisms, illnesses and, critically, to pay school fees and buy books for the children when school opened ...)

In 1982 international agencies assured Haiti's peasants their pigs were sick and had to be killed (so that the illness would not spread to countries to the North). Promises were made that better pigs would replace sick pigs. With an efficiency not since seen among development projects, all of the Creole pigs were killed over a period of thirteen months.

Two years later the new, better pigs came from Iowa. They were so much better that they required clean drinking water (unavailable to 80% of the Haitian population), imported feed (costing $90 a year when the per capita income was about $130), and special roofed pigpens.... Adding insult to injury, the meat did not taste as good. Needless to say, the repopulation program was a complete failure. One observer of the process estimated that in monetary terms peasants lost $600 million dollars. There was a 30% drop in enrollment in rural schools, there was a dramatic decline in protein consumption in rural Haiti, a devastating decapitalization of the peasant economy and an incalculable negative impact on Haiti's soil and agricultural productivity. The Haitian peasantry has not recovered to this day.

— *Jean-Bertrand Aristide, Eyes of the Heart; Seeking a Path for the Poor in the Age of Globalization, (Common Courage Press, 2000), pp. 13-15*

THE IMPACT ON BIODIVERSITY AND THE ENVIRONMENT

The way trade agreements and so called aid and economic policies such as the structural adjustment policies have been formulated with respect to agriculture is such that the diversity of crops and species is to be sacrificed for monocultures for their hard cash that exporting would earn. As seen in the biodiversity section of this web site, diversity is important because of the free services offered by nature, that allow species to survive, resist disease and provide resources for everyone. Reducing genetic diversity is therefore extremely costly.

Climate change will have a greater impact on the environment where biodiversity has been reduced.

The *Guardian* summarizes a United Nations warning that, "One in six countries in the world face food shortages this year because of severe droughts that could become semi-permanent under climate change."

Drought and desertification are starting to spread and intensify in some parts of the world already.

Some of UK's top environment and development groups have formed a coalition known as the *Working Group on Climate Change and Development*. In a report the coalition released, they say that efforts to alleviate poverty in Africa will ultimately fail unless urgent action is taken to halt dangerous climate change. "If not addressed, climate change is estimated to place an additional 80–120 million people at risk of hunger; 70 to 80 per cent of these will be in Africa." (p. 6).

In addition, not only are smaller farms more productive, but they are less costly:

> Highly diverse systems, as opposed to commercial monocultures, have been shown time and again to be more resilient — and more productive. Farming based on expensive and energy intensive artificial inputs will be both vulnerable to fuel price rises and further add to the problem of climate change.
>
> *— Africa — Up in Smoke?, Second report from Working Group on Climate Change and Development, June 20, 2005, p. 3*

The report also notes that:

- A lack of financial resources has meant there has been little investment in much-needed drought-resistent farming
- Rainy seasons are become less predictable and frequent due to climate changes, yet some important types of farming in Africa relies on rain a lot
- Farmers therefore need access to seeds that are adapted to drought or reduced rainfall at crucial stages in the growing season. However, "A variety of forces have led to a reduced availability of local seeds, and increased

dependence on hybrid seeds and crops like maize that are not well adapted to these conditions."

- "Another pressure comes from the concentration of ownership in the seed industry into a handful of large corporations. Ten companies now control one-third of the global seed industry, further threatening agricultural biodiversity."
- Diverse cropping systems, rather than monocropping, "is also much more suited to the harsh conditions in which most farmers in Sub-Saharan Africa operate."

(See also pages 6-18 of the above report for more details on climate change impacts, the environment, and agriculture.) The report hints at the fact that there are many, many things that can be done to improve agriculture in such a way that it does not require extensive — and expensive — inputs, while increasing yield and the integrity of the environment. Food security can increase, thus reducing dependency on others, and therefore minimizing the chances of food dumping, and the politicization and commercialization of food aid.

Indian scientist and activist, Vandana Shiva, for example, has done extensive research for many years on this aspect and is quoted here at length: Industrial agriculture has not produced more food. It has destroyed diverse sources of food, and it has stolen food from other species to bring larger quantities of specific commodities to the market, using huge quantities of fossil fuels and water and toxic chemicals in the process.... Since cattle and earthworms are our partners in food production, stealing food from them makes it impossible to maintain food production over time, and means that the partial yield increases [during the Green Revolution] were not sustainable.

... More grain from two or three commodities arrived on national and international markets, but less food was eaten by farm families in the Third World.

The gain in "yields" of industrially produced crops is based on a theft of food from other species and the rural poor in the

Third World. That is why, as more grain is produced and traded globally, more people go hungry in the Third World. Global markets have more commodities for trading because food has been robbed from nature and the poor.

... [I]ndustrial breeding [and growing of crops] actually increases pressure on the land, since each acre of a monoculture provides a single output, and the displaced outputs have to be grown on additional acres, or "shadow" acres.

... Wasting resources creates hunger. By wasting resources through one-dimensional monocultures maintained with intensive external inputs, the new biotechnologies create food insecurity and starvation.

— *Vandana Shiva, Stolen Harvest, (South End Press, 2000), pp. 12-13*

In fact, Shiva goes on to discuss other aspects that show economic factors overriding common sense, such as:

- Dumping BSE-infected beef onto the Third World, after the people of the First World rejected it (*Ibid, pp. 65-66*)
- Promoting beef, soy and other non-traditional diets into various developing countries that do not consume these foods normally, so that the first world can again benefit from these larger markets of consumers (*Ibid, pp. 21-37, 66-70*)
- In 1991, then chief economist for the World Bank Larry Summers, (and currently US Treasury Secretary, until the elected Bush and the Republican party come into power), wrote in an internal memo:

Just between you and me, shouldn't the World Bank be encouraging more migration of dirty industries to the LDCs [less developed countries]?... The economic logic behind dumping a load of toxic waste in the lowest wage country is impeccable, and we should face up to that... Under-populated countries in Africa are vastly under-polluted; their air quality is probably vastly inefficiently low compared to Los Angeles or Mexico

City... The concern over an agent that causes a one in a million change in the odds of prostate cancer is obviously going to be much higher in a country where people survive to get prostate cancer than in a country where under-five mortality is 200 per thousand.

— Lawrence Summers, Let them eat pollution, The Economist, February 8, 1992. Quoted from Vandana Shiva, Stolen Harvest, (South End Press, 2000) p.65; See also Richard Robbins, Global Problems and the Culture of Capitalism (Allyn and Bacon, 1999), pp. 233-236 for a detailed look at this.

- Dumping genetically engineered food to cyclone suffers in Orissa, India. (See bottom of this interview with Vandana Shiva.)

SIMILAR PROCESSES GO ON TODAY, ESPECIALLY WITH GENETICALLY ENGINEERED FOODS

And while the next section will describe how food dumping in the recent past has created hunger and poverty that doesn't suggest it has stopped today. In fact, protests by farmers in Brazil and around the world in April 2001 marked an "International Day of Farmers' Struggle" highlighting and protesting various issues such as police massacres of rural workers, genetically modified seeds, and agricultural trade that jeopardizes food security.

The Institute for Food and Development Policy (also known as Food First) also reveals that "US taxpayer dollars are being used through foreign assistance programs to subsidize the export of genetically engineered (GE) foods to the Third World and to finance GE research" thus raising "very serious ethical questions about [U.S. tax payers'] foreign aid dollars."

They additionally point out that this is a form of corporate welfare, at the expense of U.S. tax payers, because the U.S. government ends up "subsidizing agribusiness by buying surplus GMO crops and distributing them through foreign aid programs. This helps large corporations to penetrate new markets abroad.

Funds intended to assist the poor instead wind up in corporate coffers."

The science journal, *Nature*, also comments on the issue of GM food aid to African nations during the 2002 famine, adding that,

> In the case of US food aid, including some of the emergency aid currently flowing into southern Africa, grants or loans are normally made available only for the procurement of grain from US farmers. That makes the decision to grant the aid more politically palatable, because it is, in effect, just a few dollars more on top of the billions already being lavished on domestic farm support....
>
> It is certainly to be hoped that the United States is not using the current famine threat to get its GM crops into Africa through the back door to expand the restricted export market for them.
>
> The United States donates almost 60% of the world's food aid and, as long as much of that aid is tied to the procurement of food from US farmers, the region facing famine will probably have to accept GM food.
>
> — *Poverty and transgenic crops, Nature 418, 569, August 8 2002 (registration may be required to view content)*

Friends of the Earth for example, have also started a campaign about GM food in food aid. Amongst other concerns, they have found that GM foods not approved for human consumption have been part of the food aid.

Furthermore, such foods, which are still controversial, as described in the Genetically Engineered Food section on this web site, for example, are often not labeled as such.

FOOD AID AND FAMINES EXPLOITED AS COMMERCIAL OPPORTUNITY

When hunger's roots are to be found in the inability to purchase available food, and in the lack of access to available food, then such food "aid" doesn't do much for addressing such issues. Although, it does help corporations get funding for research and testing on unsuspecting people as pointed out by the following:

> The US food aid system appears to disregard the rights and concerns of recipient citizens in order to assure profits for US agribusiness giants. It is a system that allows for the misspending of public funds in ways that benefit the private sector; a system that takes advantage of the lack of regulation concerning the genetic engineering of food; and a system that undermines democratic decision making about food consumption.
>
> — *Food Aid in the New Millennium — Genetically Engineered Food and Foreign Assistance, Institute for Food and Development Policy, December 2000*

The *International Relations Center* (IRC) also notes the profit motive behind food aid dumping: "Agroexporters such as Cargill and Archer-Daniels Midland, which provide one-third of U.S. food aid, and U.S. charity organizations such as CARE, World Vision, and Catholic Relief Services, which account for four-fifths of food aid delivery, directly collaborate with and benefit from this" food aid policy. US food aid accounts for nearly 60 percent of the world's food aid currently.

Canada, another large provider of food aid, has recently decided to use half its food aid budget to provide buy food locally in developing countries, rather than dump its own. This encourages local economies, rather than destroy them. The *IRC* also summarized a report from the OECD noting that:

- Foreign assistance shipped in the form of food often arrives late, disrupts local markets, and costs up to 50% more to deliver than cash.
- Commodity shipments often arrive too late and are more expensive than local purchases.
- US food aid being shipped to famine-struck Niger will likely coincide with the a bumper harvest in the region, thereby competing directly with area farmers.

Dumping Genetically Modified Food as Aid During Famine

Devinder Sharma, quoted right at the beginning of this article is quite blunt about how the tying the use of famine relief and food aid to genetically modified crops is leading to profiteering from famines:

> What is arguably one of the most blatantly anti-humanitarian act, seen as morally repugnant, is the decision of the United States Agency for International Development (USAID) to offer US $50 million in food aid to famine-stricken Zimbabwe provided that it is used to purchase genetically modified maize. Food aid therefore is no longer an instrument of foreign policy. It has now become a major commercial activity, even if it means exploiting the famine victims and starving millions. That is the official line at the USAID about the corn it has offered to Zambia, Zimbabwe, Lesotho, Mozambique and Malawi, where an estimated 13 million people face severe hunger and possibly live under the spectre of an impending famine after two years of drought and floods.
>
> For the genetically modified food industry, reeling under a growing rejection of its untested and harmful food products, there is money in hunger, starvation and death. Spearheaded by USAID, the industry has made it abundantly clear that it has only genetically modified maize to offer and was not willing to segregate....
>
> ... the biotechnology industry is using all its financial power to break down the African resistance [to GM crops]. Once the GM food is accepted as humanitarian aid, it will be politically difficult for the African governments to oppose the corporate take-over of Africa's agricultural economy. For the industry, Africa provides a huge market.
>
> — *Devinder Sharma, Africa's Tragedy; Famine as Commerce, November 10, 2002*

The previous sections above have shown commercial issues trumping famine and food aid issues. In the summer of 2002, the issue came to the forefront with various Southern African nations being offered aid as long as they purchased GM foods, while they were going through famine. In that context, as well as food aid being a foreign policy tool, famines and food aid is now also seen as a commercial opportunity.

Food Security Undermined by Debt Repayments

Countries ravaged by poverty are susceptible to this type of commercial opportunism. Devastating Structural Adjustment programs from the IMF and World Bank have left poor countries unable to determine their own economic future, as they are forced to export their raw materials and resources to earn foreign exchange with which to pay off debts. Health, education and other important services then get a back seat.

Basic food security has also been undermined. An example in 2002 at least made it to mainstream media attention in UK. As Ann Petifor, head of debt campaign organization, *Jubilee Research* noted, the IMF forced the Malwai government to sell its surplus grain in favor of foreign exchange just before a famine struck. This was explicitly so that debts could be repaid. 7 million of the total 11 million population were severely short of food.

"But its worse than that," said Petifor. "Because Malawi is indebted, her economic policies are effectively determined by her creditors — represented in Malawi by the IMF." Malawi spent more than the budget the foreign creditors set. As a result, the IMF withheld $47 million in aid. Other western donors, acting on advice from IMF staff, also withheld aid, "*pending IMF approval* of the national budget." (Emphasis added).

"To add to the humiliation of the Malawian government, the IMF has also suspended the debt service relief for which she was only recently deemed eligible — because she is 'off track.'"

That is not the end of the story unfortunately. As Petifor also mentioned, under the economic program imposed by her creditors, Malawi removed all farming and food subsidies allowing the market to determine demand and supply for food. This reduced support for farmers, leading many to go hungry as prices increased. As she also noted, the rich countries, on the other hand, do not follow their own policies; Europe and the US subsidize their agriculture with billions of dollars.

But the US, for example, see this situation as exploitable. Petifor again:

> US Secretary for Agriculture, Dan Glickman, illustrates well the US attitude to countries suffering famine and in need of food aid:
>
> "Humanitarian and national self interest both can be served by well-designed foreign assistance programs. Food aid has not only met emergency food needs, but has also been a useful market development tool." (OXFAM report: "Rigged Rules and Double Standards: Trade Globalization and the Fight Against Poverty" by Kevin Watkins and Penny Fowler)
>
> — *Ann Petifor, Debt is still the lynchpin: the case of Malawi, Jubilee Research, July 4, 2002*

It is not just the US that uses aid in this way. Most rich countries do this. And it isn't just food aid, but aid in general that is often used inappropriately. The *Guardian* reported (August 29, 2005) how £700,000 (about $400,000) of £3 million in British aid to Malawi was mis-spent on US firms' hotel and meal bills. Even notebooks and pens were flown in from Washington rather than purchased locally. See this site's section on foreign aid for more details about the issue of foreign aid and its misuse.

Dumping Undesirable Food During Emergency Relief

Another example is British food aid to the United States, in the wake of the devastation caused to some southern states after hurricane Katrina:

> The *Washington Post* (October 14, 2005) reported that most of the food that arrived at a particular facility, worth $5.3

million, "never reached the victims of Hurricane Katrina ... because of fears about mad cow disease and a long-standing ban on British beef, the rations routinely consumed by British soldiers".

On first thoughts, it may not be surprising that the US appears to have received criticism of this, especially as the entire disaster recovery effort after Katrina has been described (by the *Post*) as "slow, inefficient and at times wasteful".

However, in this circumstance, the US government may be justified in their action:

- Since 1997, the United States has banned beef products from Britain and several other European countries that have been affected by bovine spongiform encephalopathy, known as mad cow disease. This is fatal in cattle and can lead to a similar illness in humans.
- As was noted further above, a few years earlier when some countries in Africa were facing famine, some chose to reject food aid that contained genetically modified food, on safety concerns, despite a lot of pressure (ironically, it may seem, from the US) to accept them.
- The US should also be allowed to reject food aid on safety grounds, if they feel that is best for their citizens. In addition, as the *Post* noted, generally people were no longer going hungry in the aftermath of Katrina as they were mostly in shelter of some sort. As a result, the need for food has not been as urgent as it could have been, and in that case, there may have been more consideration about whether or not to accept this particular package of food.

However, there is a twist in this for which the US could be criticized, and that is what they want to do with all that food that's been sitting in a warehouse in the meantime. As the *Post* adds,

State Department officials have considered sending the food to Guatemala, which was devastated by mudslides. But the impoverished country does not have vehicles to transport the enormous pallets. For cultural reasons, the meals would be inappropriate for Pakistani earthquake victims.

"Everyone wants a happy ending," said a senior State Department official who requested anonymity, given the already bruised feelings in Britain. "No one wants them to go to waste. Everyone wants them to be put to good use."

> — *Ceci Connolly, Katrina Food Aid Blocked by U.S. Rules; Meals From Britain Sit in Warehouse, Washington Post, October 14, 2005; Page A01 (Emphasis Added)*

What the *Post* did not seem to question was how it could be "good use" to dump this food onto another country if they themselves find it unfit for consumption by their own citizens. Would that really be a "happy ending?" Does "everyone" include the Guatemalan government and people in this case?

Such types of "aid" are not likely, therefore, to help the hungry, but instead, help those large agribusiness firms, and even risks increasing hunger even more, as the next section details.

Myth 10: More U.S. Aid Will Help the Hungry

MYTH: In helping to end world hunger, our primary responsibility as U.S. citizens is to increase and improve our government's foreign aid.

OUR RESPONSE: Once we learned that hunger results from antidemocratic political and economic structures that trap people in poverty, we realized that we couldn't end hunger for other people. Genuine freedom can only be won by people for themselves.

This realization doesn't lessen our responsibility, but it does profoundly redefine its nature. Our job isn't to intervene in other countries and set things right. Our government is *already* intervening in countries where the majority of people are forced to go hungry. Our primary responsibility as U.S.

citizens is to make certain our government's policies are not making it harder for people to end hunger for themselves.

In light of the demonstrated generosity of many Americans, most of us would probably be chagrined to learn that U.S. foreign aid is only 0.15 percent of our nation's gross national product — that's less than half the percentage of GNP Germany provides, for example, and less than one-fifth of that provided by the Netherlands. Total U.S. bilateral assistance dropped greatly during the first half of the 1990s, as it has for most other wealthy nations. From a high of $20.2 billion in 1985, it fell to $12.3 billion by 1994 and has remained low.

For the world's hungry, however, the problem isn't the stinginess of our aid. When our levels of assistance last boomed, under Ronald Reagan in the mid-1980s, the emphasis was hardly on eliminating hunger. In 1985, Secretary of State George Shultz stated flatly that "our foreign assistance programs are vital to the achievement of our foreign policy goals." But Shultz's statement shouldn't surprise us. Every country's foreign aid is a tool of foreign policy. Whether that aid benefits the hungry is determined by the motives and goals of that policy — by how a government defines the national interest.

During the postwar decades of the Cold War, U.S. foreign assistance was largely defined by a view of the world as divided into two opposing camps. That often meant arming and propping up undemocratic and repressive governments — in Iran, the Philippines, El Salvador, Indonesia, and many other countries — only because they were loyal U.S. allies.

The U.S. government acted as if our vital interests were threatened by any experiment that didn't mimic the U.S. economic model — the free market and unlimited private accumulation of productive assets. Any nation seeking to alter its economic ground rules — Nicaragua, for example — was immediately perceived as having "gone over to the other camp" and thus an enemy. Punishment was swift-usually including the suspension of aid and the arming of opponents of the offending government.

In the rather negative panorama of the Cold War, U.S. foreign assistance did nevertheless have poverty alleviation as a goal, albeit not for the best of motives. Driven by the fear that "communism" would defeat capitalism in the battle for the "hearts and minds" of poor third world populations — by offering them the possibility of greater improvements in material well-being — the United States followed an on-again-off-again policy of funding "basic needs."

In Central America, while propping up corrupt dictatorships with Economic Support Funds (ESF) — basically cash disbursements — and keeping them in power with generous military aid and training, the United States also pressed for and financed basic poverty alleviation policies.

The latter included very limited land reforms, marketing boards to help small farmers sell their grain, basic infrastructure development, etc. These reforms were seen as necessary complements to military aid to mollify the populace and keep our friendly strongmen from being overthrown by the disgruntled masses.

During the entire Cold War it often seemed as though the real goal of foreign aid was making the world safe for U.S.-based corporations. Nevertheless, this goal was often mixed up with Cold War strategic aims, making such a black-and-white analysis difficult. Since the end of the Cold War, however, the more blatant economic aims of foreign assistance have come to the forefront.

From defending freedom in the face of the "communist threat," the goals of foreign aid have more clearly emerged as the promotion of the free market and free trade-of the sort we described in chapters 7 and 8.

A 1997 newsletter of the U.S. Agency for International Development (USAID), the government agency in charge of U.S. foreign assistance, put it this way: "The principal beneficiary of America's foreign assistance has always been the United States. . . . Foreign assistance programs have helped the United

States by creating major markets for agricultural goods, new markets for industrial exports and hundreds of thousands of jobs for Americans." The same report argued forcefully that the amount of money spent on aid be upped significantly in order to maintain U.S. "leadership in the global arena."

Defining our national interest as opening markets for free trade lines up our nation's might — with our tax dollars and our country's good name — against the interests of the hungry. As we have seen, a different kind of change — profound, society-wide change in control over food-producing resources — is a *sine qua non* for ending hunger. It is impossible to be both against this kind of change and for the hungry.

HIGH CONCENTRATION ON A FEW GOVERNMENTS

With kind permission from Peter Rosset of the Institute for Food and Development Policy (or FoodFirst.org as it is also known), chapter 10 of *World Hunger: 12 Myths*, 2nd Edition, by Frances Moore Lappé, Joseph Collins and Peter Rosset, with Luis Esparza (fully revised and updated, Grove/Atlantic and Food First Books, Oct. 1998) has been reproduced and posted here. Due to the length of the chapter, it has been split into sub pages on this site.

First, U.S. economic assistance is highly concentrated on a few governments. Its focus has nothing to do with poverty. Out of the 130-odd governments receiving U.S. bilateral economic assistance in the mid-1990s, just 15 countries got over half of the total (see table).

Israel and Egypt-representing U.S. geopolitical interests-together got almost one-third. The world's 10 poorest countries-most of them in Africa-received less than 5 percent of all U.S. bilateral economic assistance in fiscal year 1994.

Despite widespread poverty in sub-Saharan Africa, for example, only two of the top ten recipients, South Africa and Ethiopia, are in that region, and the former is its most economically developed nation.

Top 15 Recipients of U.S. Economic Assistance* in 1996 ($ millions)

*Economic assistance includes development assistance, Economic Support Fund, Food Aid, Peace Corps, International Narcotics Control*Source:* U.S. Agency for International Development, *Congressional Presentation, Fiscal Year 1996 Request.*

1.	Israel	1,200.0
2.	Egypt	815.0
3.	Russia	263.0
4.	Ukraine	161.4
5.	India	156.3
6.	South Africa	131.9
7.	Peru	123.9
8.	Bolivia	121.0
9.	Haiti	116.0
10.	Ethiopia	108.0
11.	Turkey	105.8
12.	Bosnia-Hercegovina	80.6
13.	Bangladesh	77.8
14.	West Bank/Gaza	76.0
15.	Philippines	74.9

Lured by the opportunities of virgin markets, U.S. foreign policy and assistance have found a new target: Eastern Europe and the former Soviet Union, which now compete for aid with the much poorer third world countries.

AID—A LEVER TO IMPOSE STRUCTURAL ADJUSTMENT ON THIRD WORLD

With kind permission from Peter Rosset of the Institute for Food and Development Policy (or FoodFirst.org as it is also known), chapter 10 of *World Hunger: 12 Myths*, 2nd Edition, by Frances Moore Lappé, Joseph Collins and Peter Rosset, with Luis Esparza (fully revised and updated, Grove/Atlantic and Food First Books, Oct. 1998) has been reproduced and posted here. Due to the length of the chapter, it has been split into sub pages on this site.

Second, aid is used as a lever to impose structural adjustment packages on the third world. Since the 1980s U.S. foreign assistance worldwide has been conditioned on the adoption of structural adjustment packages designed by the World Bank and the International Monetary Fund, policies that we described in chapters 7 and 8.

Making a grant or loan conditional on some action being taken by the recipient is called "conditionality." Conditionality works by "tranching" economic assistance packages-that is, dividing the total sum to be donated or loaned to a recipient country into a series of smaller disbursements to be made over time, called tranches. Before each disbursement is made, the recipient must make policy changes spelled out in the "covenants" of the aid agreement that they must sign with USAID.

Between 1982 and 1990 nine U.S. economic assistance packages provided to the Costa Rican government contained a total of 357 "covenants" that made disbursement conditional on more than twenty structural changes in the domestic economy. These included eliminating a grain marketing board that assisted small farmers; slashing support prices for locally grown corn, beans, and rice; allowing more imports from the United States; easing regulations on foreign investment and capital flows; and complying with specific clauses in similar agreements signed with the World Bank and the IMF.

Such conditionality works in a carrot-and-stick fashion. When the Costa Rican congress balked at approving an outrageous new law demanded by the United States that would allow aid to bypass the government and go directly to the private sector, USAID suspended a $23 million disbursement. Ironically, this came at the very moment at which the Costa Rican Central Bank had exhausted the foreign exchange reserves needed for the daily operation of the economy. An internal USAID memo written several months before the incident occurred-which we obtained access to years later-showed just how cynical the United States can be. A top USAID administrator predicted the month in which the reserves would run dry and recommended timing a key disbursement to take advantage of that moment as leverage to guarantee that the desired law would be passed.

It was precisely the replication of changes like this-and of structural adjustment-throughout the third world that produced rising inequalities in the 1980s and 1990s. For most of the third world the 1980s were a lost decade, during which living standards of impoverished majorities fell to pre-1960s levels. Not surprisingly, this became a period of widespread economic, social, and ecological crisis. Millions of the rural and urban poor were cut out from opportunities for progress. Credit, extension, subsidies, and technical education all fell by the wayside as budgets were slashed, and the lifting of tariffs flooded local economies with imported foodstuffs often placed on the world market at prices below local costs of production. As a consequence, poor farmers were caught in a squeeze between the high price of chemicals and other farm inputs and low crop prices, often losing their lands and moving to cities.

FOOD AID OFTEN DOES NOT TARGET THE HUNGRY

With kind permission from Peter Rosset of the Institute for Food and Development Policy (or FoodFirst.org as it is also known), chapter 10 of *World Hunger: 12 Myths*, 2nd Edition, by Frances Moore Lappé, Joseph Collins and Peter Rosset, with Luis Esparza (fully revised and updated, Grove/Atlantic and Food First Books, Oct. 1998) has been reproduced and posted here. Due to the length of the chapter, it has been split into sub pages on this site.

Third, food aid often does not target the hungry. When they hear about foreign aid, many people automatically think of ships loaded with food, but such aid constitutes only a fraction of total U.S. bilateral foreign aid, hovering around 9 percent during the 1990s. Moreover, only about 5 percent of total aid is for emergency relief. Of the nearly 3 million tons of food aid provided by the United States in 1996, almost one-quarter was in the form of PL 480 Title I sales, in which food is sold to third world governments on easy credit terms for resale to local livestock industries as feed, and to local food-processing companies who make pasta, bread, cooking oil, and other products for urban consumers. While the proceeds from these sales must generally be used for "development" purposes, which are specified by USAID, Title I has long been used as a primary tool to create new markets for U.S. grain exports. In practice, it functions as corporate welfare. According to a study published by the University of Nebraska Press:

> The food-aid program represents a free government service designed to help grain-trading companies expand both their current and future sales. Title I sales generate the same profits for the big U.S. grain companies as does any other commercial export. The only difference is that the U.S. government immediately pays the bill. From the point of view of the grain corporations, then, Title I creates immediate markets by having the U.S. government finance purchases that otherwise might not have been made. The recipient countries, meanwhile, come to depend on these foreign food supplies. . . . By encouraging the growth of poultry farms, wheat mills, and soap and vegetable-oil factories, PL 480 helps create a structural dependence on continued imports. When the food aid stops, these industries, needing the supplies to continue their level of operations, will pressure their governments to keep importing the commodities on commercial terms.

USAID bragged in a 1996 report on food aid that "nine out of ten countries importing U.S. agricultural products are former recipients of food assistance." Far from feeding the hungry, Title I food aid first of all puts money in the pockets of giant grain corporations like Cargill, who provide and ship the products; second, supports factory-style poultry producers and food processors; and finally, helps shift consumer tastes in recipient countries away from locally grown crops toward wheat products like bread and pasta.

Much aid to Africa, for example, has been in the form of wheat, even though wheat grows well in very few parts of the tropics. For many countries, such a shifting of tastes is no small concern-it makes long-term self-reliance even more difficult. South Korea became the largest third world importer of U.S. agricultural goods after years of food aid coupled with intensive marketing of wheat products by AID. This marketing campaign changed the South Korean diet drastically by creating a growing demand for wheat.

Even the funds earned from food sales that are earmarked for "development" frequently end up working against the hungry. These often go for so-called "self-help" measures, like the promotion of further trade with the United States, and market-development activities like trade fairs and port construction.

A second kind of food aid, Title III, works just like Title I but is for poorer countries, allowing the United States to forgive the loans for the purchased food. In 1996 it accounted for about one-eighth of total food shipped.

The Food for Progress program, another type of food aid, was created in 1985 to reward governments who undertake structural adjustment programs. According to the enabling legislation, Food for Progress was "designed to expand free enterprise elements of the economies of developing countries through changes in commodity pricing, marketing, import availability, and increased private-sector involvement." In other words, food is once again being used as a lever to open markets for U.S.-based corporations. While Food for Progress was originally targeted at the third world, the emphasis soon shifted: In 1996, thirty-seven of the thirty-eight donations made under this program went to former socialist countries in Eastern Europe, the newest frontier in market opportunities for U.S. food exporters. Food for Progress shipments accounted for one-seventh of the food donated that year.

The remaining category of food aid, Title II, consists of food that is donated either to support specific development projects or for emergency relief, generally in poor countries, and it accounted for slightly more than half of the food shipped in 1996. These, finally, are the proverbial shiploads that we imagine being sent to the poor in third world countries. Yet even this food often has less than positive impacts.

Title II development food aid is usually distributed through so-called "food-for-work" programs that hire the jobless to provide manual labor for road improvement, irrigation development, and other infrastructure projects, in exchange for food. In theory, society as a whole benefits from this sort of program-the jobless get to eat, while the rest of society gains from the public works projects. Yet a careful examination shows that food-for-work benefits the well-off disproportionally, while the poor receive no long-term gains.

An example from Haiti, where so many people are deprived of enough to eat, makes this clear. In a particular village, one family controlled the local government and community offices. When a U.S. relief agency came to the village with a food-for-work program, this same family was chosen to administer it. Jobless villagers built roads and tended the gardens of a well-to-do village leader, which took them away from their lands five days a week. The wealthy family gained benefits through the improvement of their lands, better access to markets for their produce, and increased patronage power. The workers gained temporary work, which provided food during the slack agricultural season, at the cost of not attending to their own plots, but they did not gain long-term, fundamental changes or a sustainable lessening of their poverty and hunger. Similar stories dot the landscape of food-for-work programs.

FOOD AID FORESTALLS DEVELOPMENT

With kind permission from Peter Rosset of the Institute for Food and Development Policy (or FoodFirst.org as it is also known), chapter 10 of *World Hunger: 12 Myths*, 2nd Edition, by Frances Moore Lappé, Joseph Collins and Peter Rosset, with Luis Esparza (fully revised and updated, Grove/Atlantic and Food First Books, Oct. 1998) has been reproduced and posted here. Due to the length of the chapter, it has been split into sub pages on this site.

Fourth, food aid can actually forestall agricultural development that could otherwise alleviate hunger. The inflow of food aid-even in many emergency cases-has proved time and again to be detrimental to local farm economies. Cheap, subsidized, or free U.S. grains undercut the prices of locally produced food, driving local farmers out of business and into cities.

Somalia is only one case in point. When a civil war began in 1991, domestic transportation was interrupted, precipitating a food crisis in large regions of the country. The UN estimated that almost 4.5 million people-over half of the estimated total population of the country-were threatened by severe undernutrition and malnutrition-related diseases at that time.

Yet in December of 1992, when U.S. troops landed under the UN banner to distribute food and achieve a cease-fire among hostile factions, the worst of the famine was already over. The death rate had dropped from three hundred per day to seventy, and good crops of rice, sorghum, and corn from the agricultural regions of Afgoye and the Shebell River valley had already been harvested. Nonetheless, food aid poured in, driving down the prices received by local farmers for their harvest by a whopping 75 percent. Sometimes they couldn't sell their crops even at the lower prices. Mrs. Faaduma Abdi Arush, a Somali farmer, tried to sell her corn to six relief agencies. None would buy it, as the U.S. government only provided them with funds to buy American food from U.S. companies. Many Somali farmers, unable to make a living by selling their produce, were forced to abandon their farms and join the lines for handouts of imported food.

Nonemergency Title II food aid is sometimes used to support activities such as mother and child health, nutrition, and education programs. The cash for the programs is raised by selling food aid in the recipient country. Or the food is used for lunch programs as an incentive for children to stay in school, or mothers at health centers receive food when they bring their babies to be treated.

While many of these activities seem at first glance to be laudable, we need to look deeper. First and foremost, this kind of food aid is still about the injection of food into the economy of recipient countries, which results in the distortion of food markets. Just as it does with other forms of food aid, this distortion weakens the local food system, drives farmers off the land, and ultimately creates long-term dependency on imported U.S. agricultural commodities. These effects remain whether we are talking about food-for-work, health, or school programs.38 That is not to say that all programs supported by food aid are misguided. Rather, other ways are needed to carry them out.

For example, mother and child health and nutrition programs can offer substantial benefits to recipients. The alternative to using imported food for these programs should be to purchase food from surrounding areas. This system would strengthen farmers, local merchants, and the economy of the country, as local expertise, knowledge, and resources are utilized to produce the food. As income is generated internally, communities become self-sufficient and sustainable.

However, food aid-based development projects continue to depend on foreign expertise, knowledge, and outside resources to generate income. These projects are not self-sufficient, nor are they sustainable when the aid ends. Not surprisingly, food aid-based development projects have historically been failures. Says former food-aid manager Michael Maren, "Africa is littered with the ruins of such projects."

U.S. CONTRIBUTES DIRECTLY TO ARMED CONFLICTS AROUND THE WORLD

With kind permission from Peter Rosset of the Institute for Food and Development Policy (or FoodFirst.org as it is also known), chapter 10 of *World Hunger: 12 Myths*, 2nd Edition, by Frances Moore Lappé, Joseph Collins and Peter Rosset, with Luis Esparza (fully revised and updated, Grove/Atlantic and

Food First Books, Oct. 1998) has been reproduced and posted here. Due to the length of the chapter, it has been split into sub pages on this site.

Fifth, through military aid, the United States contributes directly to armed conflicts around the world-which are a major cause of hunger and famine. Since the end of the Cold War, U.S. military aid has declined, yet in 1998 it still totaled $6 billion, outweighing development assistance by a six-to-one ratio. Arms sales add significantly to the impact of our military aid. Needing to cope with an overproduction problem in the post-Cold War era, American defense contractors have aggressively sought overseas markets, usually with government subsidies to do so. U.S. arms sales in the early 1990s exceeded those of all other nations combined. Global military expenditure by governments is estimated at $1 trillion annually, and that doesn't take into account illicit arms trafficking to nongovernmental belligerents. For every four weapons involved in such trafficking, three are estimated to come from the United States, many of them originally via aid or credits.

Between 1985 and 1995, the belligerent parties in forty-five conflicts around the globe obtained $42 billion worth of weapons from the United States. In 90 percent of the fifty most significant conflicts in 1993-94, one or more parties received U.S. weapons or military technology. Through trafficking, arms sales, and military aid, the United States helps keep dozens of civil wars and other armed conflicts around the world alive and kicking. This is particularly alarming in light of our conclusion in chapter 3 that contemporary episodes of famine are often the product of armed conflicts like that which took place in Somalia. U.S. arm sales and military aid make that possible.

"GOOD" AID PROJECTS OBSCURES AN UGLIER REALITY

Sixth, "good" aid projects serve a public relations, "window dressing" or "fig leaf" function that obscures an uglier reality. Focusing on the best projects funded by USAID can be misleading as to the overall impact of foreign aid. There are no doubt some projects that when viewed outside of the larger context appear unambiguously positive-but in the final analysis they really facilitate the far more common programs that have net negative impacts, simply because the "best projects" make the very idea of aid more palatable.

In the 1990s "humanitarian relief" missions, festooned with journalists and slick publicity, have been key to building a positive image of USAID-even though such activities represent a tiny proportion of the agency's budget and have ample problems of their own as described above. Environmental projects can also play a public relations role.

One of us had the opportunity to work with such an environmental effort during the 1980s and early 1990s, the Integrated Pest Management Project for Central America. Initially funded with $5 million from USAID, the project's laudable goal was to reduce pesticide use among small farmers in Central America. Who could argue with that? Nevertheless, our experience makes us think twice whenever we see something from USAID that seems too good to be true.

The project suffered from a typical design flaw, namely, a top-down conception of technological change. Project scientists-mostly Ph.D.-trained expatriates-were to research alternatives to pesticides and then train national "experts" in each country, who were to train local extension agents, who would then transmit the new information to farmers. Of course, this rarely happened-because of kinks in the long chain of collaborating institutions and individuals and because the alternatives finally presented to farmers rarely fit their reality.

The initial funding was approved at the tail end of the "basic needs" period of U.S. foreign assistance, so the project was said to be targeted at small farmers growing food crops, but project implementation coincided with the new emphasis in the 1980s on structural adjustment and related export promotion. Thus, USAID functionaries continually pressed project staff and the host institution to switch our focus to export crops and larger farmers. The host institution and staff held out against these changes, eventually leading USAID to discontinue its support for the project and redirect its funds to more pliable host organizations.

Before the project's funding was terminated, an incident occurred that would be comical if it were not so sad. Congress passed a new requirement that USAID projects incorporate both "women and men" as beneficiaries, in response to criticisms that assistance favored men and left women out. This regulation was imposed when the project came up for renewal. A memo went out from USAID headquarters instructing all field staff to be sure to incorporate the new requirement in future funding requests. In response, the project leader had a secretary do a universal "search and replace" in her word processor. Each time the words "people," "persons," "farmers," "students," "beneficiaries," etc., were used in the renewal request they were replaced with, or preceded by, "women and men." Thus, one section read that "24 women and men farmers will be invited to the field day." No other changes were made to the proposal, which was approved without comment. In subsequent congressional hearings, USAID staff were able to argue that gender was now an integral component of development aid.

But these details about the project actually miss the real reason its overall impacts have been negative. The project was frequently used by USAID to show policy makers, journalists, Central American government functionaries, and others the friendly face of U.S. policy in the region. Even though it accounted for a tiny fraction of USAID money spent during the 1980s, it had a high profile.

Thus, it served as a fig leaf hiding the true thrust of aid spending in the region: the overthrow of the revolutionary Sandinista government in Nicaragua and the structural adjustment of the region's other economies. In the end, its real function in the larger scheme of things was to make the overall U.S. presence in Central America more palatable, thus indirectly facilitating less beneficent ends.

EVEN MOST DEVELOPMENT ASSISTANCE FAILS THE POOR AND HUNGRY

Finally, even most "development assistance" fails to help the poor and hungry. Only 18 percent of U.S. bilateral aid is even called development assistance. How is this development aid spent? During the 1960s and early 1970s, much of it went to install infrastructure (power plants, transportation and communication facilities, and the like) benefiting mainly businessmen, landlords, and others in an economic position to take advantage of such facilities. In the late 1970s and early 1980s, the trend was more toward smaller-scale projects, including agricultural credit programs and the development of small and medium-size businesses. But even these smaller-scale projects failed to reach the poorest, concluded a major study by the World Bank and the International Monetary Fund.

This general finding was borne out by USAID's own program evaluations. One report reviewing twelve years of small-farm credit programs noted that benefits were "highly skewed against the small farmer and the landless poor." The reasons for this failure were clear enough-very few of the poor had titles to farms large enough to satisfy the requirements of a credit application. Since the majority of rural poor in most third world countries are landless, even the best farm credit program could never help them.

In the 1980s and 1990s a major trend has been to promote nontraditional exports. In Central America, for example, USAID has been pushing farmers into hopelessly competing for volatile niche markets by promoting new export crops. These Non-Traditional Agricultural Exports (NTAEs) range from passion fruit and broccoli to macadamia nuts and melons and have been vigorously advanced through massive foreign aid subsidies and fierce pressure on local governments. Central American farmers and governments now find themselves saddled with risky agricultural ventures that have destabilized traditional production of food crops for local consumption. The net result is deepening poverty and economic insecurity in agricultural communities throughout Central America. In stark contrast to USAID's stated aim of stabilizing Central America's economies, NTAE programs have intensified the inequities between small farmers and wealthy landowners.

A 1983 USAID project in the Guácimo district of Costa Rica offers a poignant yet not atypical case in point. Investing money, credit, technical assistance, and marketing expertise, USAID encouraged poor farmers at the El Indio land settlement to switch from traditional yellow corn production to cocoa, tuber crops, and ayote squash for export to the growing Latino market in the United States. In the project's first season, farmers were provided with imported, disease-free seed, a full-time extension agent, and an advance purchase contract. The incomes of the farmers who participated soared in the first year, up to forty times more per acre than their neighbors who continued growing corn.

But just one year later, the El Indio venture began to unravel. The NTAE project no longer provided seeds, there was no marketing contract, and the extension agent was employed only part-time. Still, enticed by the previous year's success, more farmers took the plunge. The results were disastrous. Crop prices dropped as global competition heightened. Due to the low-grade seeds used the second year, much of the harvest was hit by disease-discouraging buyers from all but a small portion of the crops. Half of the farmers defaulted on their credit, and the forty who persisted defaulted in the following year.

The El Indio experience and many others like it provide a cautionary tale of the pitfalls of pushing exports at all costs. Promoting capital-intensive crops for unproven markets, NTAE projects are a high-stakes gamble for peasants. Small farmers face hurdles at every step along the way.

In Guatemala, for example, the initial investment to plant nontraditional export crops ranges from five to fifteen times higher than that for traditional corn and beans. Crossing this barrier means taking out risky credit and loans that frequently have interest rates biased against poor farmers and can easily lead to losing the farm after a bad harvest. The fate of small farmers in the nontraditionals industry has been similar to their fate with traditional exports and in the Green Revolution. Nontraditionals are expensive to produce-requiring enormous quantities of pesticide, fertilizer, and technical expertise, favoring larger, better capitalized producers. Because these are perishable products, small farmers are often unable to place their produce in Northern markets with quality standards, giving the edge to the giant fruit companies.

Unable to compete with better-financed growers, and heavily in debt because of high production costs, many small farmers have been driven out of business by trying to produce nontraditional exports. At the same time, chemical pesticides and fertilizers have seriously degraded the productive capacity of the soil in many regions and contaminated the environment.

Growing corn and other basic staples is no longer profitable either, due to the flooding of local markets with cheap grain via free trade, and to cutbacks in price supports and marketing imposed by structural adjustment programs. As a result, small farmers have migrated to cities and to developed countries in huge numbers, fleeing the policy-driven collapse of rural livelihoods. The winners under current policies have been, first and foremost, international companies able to compete in the emerging global food system, and the net losers have clearly been the rural poor and the environment.

While the poor may not be the chief beneficiaries of development assistance projects, one group that does benefit handsomely includes the U.S. corporations, consulting companies, and universities that get USAID contracts. An independent study found that 29 percent of U.S. development assistance was 100 percent tied to purchases from companies in the United States-an amount greater than the total of U.S. assistance to sub-Saharan Africa.

Funds for aid pass though many hands before reaching the supposed beneficiaries. So the question we must ask is, How likely is it that resources channeled through the *powerful* will help the *powerless*?

The already better off are positioned to capture a disproportionate share of any economic gains offered by development aid. And with their new resources, they can often further tighten their grip over land and other productive resources, thereby worsening the plight of the poor. Thanks to a bribe to a technician, an irrigation pump earmarked for a cooperative of poor farmers in Bangladesh winds up belonging to the village's richest landowner; he graciously allows his neighbors water from the new well in exchange for a third of their harvests. The pump and the added revenue give the "waterlord" the incentive to take over more land by foreclosing on the small farmers in debt to him. Thanks to his heightened prosperity, the landowner can now buy an imported tractor, eliminating desperately needed jobs for the village's landless families.

This and similar scenarios, endlessly repeated, entrench the already well off and add to their incentive to fight demands for democratic control over productive resources. In many countries, rich landowners are known to hire thugs to intimidate and even murder villagers who dare to protest or organize self-help cooperatives.

Only projects that reinforce the poor's initiatives to tackle the extreme inequalities in power within the village have a chance of improving the lives of the majority. However, most governments are unlikely to look kindly on such activities, for fear of antagonizing powerful elites.

But we hesitate even to use this space to question the possibility of government-sponsored development projects helping the poor within elite-dominated societies. To do so may mislead, for it is so easy to lose sight of the big picture.

No matter how sensitively designed the aid project, prospects for the poor majority-whether they will have land, jobs, food, and economic security-hinge largely on forces *outside* their villages. To whom is their government accountable? To whom are international bankers who make loans to their government accountable? And what about the corporations dominating trade in their country's exports? Such questions point us to what we call the iceberg. Foreign aid is only the tip.

The Iceberg

Focusing only on official aid can blind us to many other ways we citizens of the United States are linked to the lives-and hopes-of the hungry. We need to take responsibility not just for what our government does in the name of "aid" and otherwise-but also for what corporations and other institutions based in our country do (often supported directly or indirectly by our "aid" and other subsidies).

The iceberg is the action of the private sector-transnational corporations, investors, and currency speculators-and the less visible actions of the United States and other Northern governments to support their free rein in the third world. Some forty thousand corporations control two-thirds of global trade in goods and services, and most of that is in the hands of only a few hundred corporate giants. In 1995, for example, General Motors' sales were greater than the gross national product of 169 countries, including Saudi Arabia, South Africa, Malaysia, and Norway.

In the last few years, there has been a tremendous increase in private foreign investment, concentrated in the wealthier developing countries. The World Bank reports that the overall volume of private-capital flows to developing countries quadrupled in the first half of the 1990s, accounting for three-quarters of all long-term flows to developing countries. While governments are backing out, private investors are taking their place. Private investment has become the main source of external financing for many middle-income countries, though the majority of low-income countries still rely primarily on official sources of financing. That may yet change as corporations seek virgin territory for new investments.

In 1996 the Clinton administration announced plans to boost the 8 percent U.S. share of the sub-Saharan Africa market, meager in comparison to Europe's 40 percent share. The United States is using free-trade language to argue that Africa, the "last frontier of American business," should open up to greater U.S. trade and investment. Key, high-profit sectors of African economies, such as infrastructure (roads, telecommunications) and mining are targeted. In June of 1997, at the G-8 Africa Summit in Denver, reminiscent of the famous 1883 Berlin Conference scramble for Africa, the future of African trade was discussed by the Northern countries, in the conspicuous absence of African delegates.

Over and above its foreign aid program, through numerous other public channels (not to mention covert ones like the CIA), the U.S. government supports policies that promote business interests, often in ways diametrically opposed to the interests of the hungry.

U.S. government agencies like the Export-Import Bank (EXIMBANK) and the Overseas Private Investment Corporation (OPIC) can have a greater impact on the economy and policies of a third world country than official U.S. foreign aid, although few Americans have ever heard of them. Both offer financing and loan guarantees-backed by U.S. taxpayers-to finance exports of goods and services. In accordance with the turn toward greater private capital flows relative to official aid, EXIMBANK loans, guarantees, and insurance rose from $12 billion in 1980 to $53 billion in 1995, more than five times greater than total U.S. foreign assistance. In more than one case of corporate welfare, EXIMBANK largely backs the efforts of transnational corporations like Boeing, General Electric, and Westinghouse to penetrate overseas markets and outcompete local companies. Small U.S.-based businesses receive only 12-15 percent of EXIMBANK financing. In the mid-1990s OPIC supported $84 billion of investments by U.S. corporations in 140 countries and played a key role in the corporate takeover of the former Soviet bloc countries in Eastern Europe.

HOW AID COULD BENEFIT THE HUNGRY

Whether U.S. foreign aid can benefit the hungry depends on how our government defines our national interest. Thus, a first step in putting ourselves on the side of the hungry is to work to *change our government's definition of our national interest.* Less control-less striving to make the world conform to the U.S. model and respond to U.S. fears-would actually mean more security for all.

After years of studying our foreign aid program, we have learned that foreign aid is only as good as the recipient government. *Foreign aid only reinforces the status quo.* It cannot transform an antidemocratic process working against the majority into a participatory government shaped in its interests. Where the recipient government answers only to a narrow economic elite or foreign corporations, our aid not only fails to reach the hungry, it girds the very forces working against them.

We do not suggest that we simply abolish foreign aid. The accumulated debt "owed" to the third world by Northern countries for centuries of unbridled profit taking through conquest, colonialism, mineral and other natural resource extraction, unequal trade, labor exploitation, and other forms of corporate pillage is too great to say nothing should be sent back.

The problem is *how* to give something back, since as we've seen in this chapter, even the best-intentioned humanitarian aid can have negative consequences if the recipient government is based on elite local and foreign interests.

An immediate step that we as citizens can take is to tell our representatives that the best use for our money is not supporting the status quo but alleviating the largest economic barrier to true development in the third world-its foreign debt.

The combined debt of third world countries reached almost $2 trillion in 1996. The bulk was accumulated largely as a result of Northern banks-flush with the "petrodollars" deposited with them by oil-producing countries in the 1970s-needing to place an unprecedented volume of loans. Once developed countries were"borrowed out," the banks turned to the third world, like snake-oil salesmen, selling huge loans for megaprojects that many knew would never pan out. The structural adjustment programs of the 1980s and 1990s have been designed in part to induce the third world to pay off that debt; the IMF and World Bank acting out the role of debt collectors for private banks. In various refinancing agreements, the debt owed to private banks has been assumed by agencies like the IMF, who are ultimately funded by taxpayers, and to whom much of the debt is now owed.

That debt-for which the lenders bear as much or more responsibility than the borrowers, is now stifling economic development and social services throughout the third world. Repayments from Zambia to the IMF between 1991 and 1993 were $335 million, compared to $37 million spent on primary education. In Honduras, annual debt payments exceed the amount spent on health and education combined.

In fact, annual interest payments alone by all third world countries amounted to $81 and $85 billion in 1994 and 1995, respectively, roughly equal to the $80 and $90 billion they received in total direct foreign investment and easily outstripping the $48 and $64 billion they received in total development assistance from Northern countries. Total debt payments (principal plus interest) were $190 and $213 billion in the same years, greater than the sum of investment plus assistance.

Our institute and two hundred other organizations have joined together in the 50 Years is Enough Campaign against the IMF and the World Bank. These two institutions, which celebrated their fiftieth anniversaries in 1994, play key roles in policing the third world's debt. The campaign calls for debt relief for third world countries. Aid dollars could be made into something positive and noninterventionist if they were spent on debt relief-as long as they were not tied to structural adjustment-like conditions, which are so onerous for the poorer majorities.

One could argue that such unconditional debt relief might not end up benefiting the hungry, either-because most third world governments do not truly represent their poor majorities. This is a legitimate concern-yet, in the end, if we have learned anything, it is that real change starts with people themselves. Our job is to not block that change through conditional aid, or equally conditioned debt relief, that mandates the strengthening of a status quo in which the rich get more powerful and the poor more marginalized. If we allow our government and major lending institutions to "get a foot in the door" by agreeing that debt relief be conditioned-with our conditions, of course-we will most likely see the conditions distorted to meet ends other than those we support, just as has happened with originally well-intentioned foreign aid.

Rather, we must make our government and corporations stop blocking change-that is perhaps the most important step in making real change possible in third world countries. As individuals, and through the organizations we belong to, we can also support the movements of local people to bring about change on their own terms. We should not think or act as though we know better than they-or that we can or should tell them what to do or how to do it.

Understanding the nature of U.S. foreign aid-that it does not, and in most countries, cannot, help the hungry-does not lead necessarily to a there's-nothing-I-can-do dead end. It is actually the first step in perceiving the many and varied actions open to all who are determined to end world hunger. In our concluding essay, and in the other publications of our institute, we offer suggestions as to how to seize the opportunities all around us.

Corruption

Corruption is both a major cause and result of poverty around the world. It occurs at all levels of society, from governments, civil society, judiciary functions, military and other services and so on. The impact of corruption in poor countries on the poorer members of those societies is even more tragic.

The issue of corruption is very much inter-related with other issues. At a global level, the "international" (Washington Consensus-influenced) economic system that has shaped the current form of globalization in the past decades requires further scrutiny for it has also created conditions whereby corruption can flourish and exacerbate the conditions of people around the world who already have little say about their own destiny.

A difficult thing to measure or compare, however, is the impact of corruption on poverty versus the effects of inequalities that are *structured into law*, such as unequal trade agreements, structural adjustment policies, so-called "free" trade agreements and so on. It is easier to see corruption. It is harder to see these other more formal, even legal forms of "corruption." It is easy to assume that these are not even issues because they are part of the laws and institutions that govern national and international societies and many of us will be accustomed to it—that is how it works, so to speak. Those deeper aspects are discussed in other parts of this web site's section on trade-related issues.

RICH COUNTRIES INVOLVED IN CORRUPTION ABROAD

When asking why poor countries are poor, it is quite common to hear, especially in wealthier countries that are perceived to have minimal corruption (at least domestically) that other countries are poor because of corruption. Yet, corruption is not something limited to third world despots. Rich countries too have been involved in corrupt practices around the world.

As Professor Robert Neild from Trinity College, Cambridge University writes in *Public Corruption; The Dark Side of Social Evolution* (London: Anthem Press, 2002), "Rich countries and their agencies ... commonly have been and are accomplices in corruption abroad, encouraging it by their actions rather than impeding it...." (p.209). Specific problems he highlights include:

- The impact of Cold War corruption (supporting dictatorships, destabilizing democracies, funding opposition, etc);
- Firms from rich countries bribing rulers and officials from developing countries to gain export contracts, particularly in the arms trade and in construction (even justifying it by suggesting bribery is "customary" in those countries, so they need to do it to, in order to compete);
- The "corruption-inducing effects of the purchase, by the rich countries and their international corporations, of concessions in Third World countries to exploit natural deposits of oil, copper, gold, diamonds and the like." Payments made to rulers often violate local (and Western) rules, keeping corrupt rulers in power, who also embezzle a lot of money away.
- The drug trade. Neild suggests that international law and national laws in rich countries that prohibit drugs may serve to "produce a scarcity value irresistible to producers, smugglers and dealers." Governments and civil society in the third world are often "undermined, sometimes destroyed" by the violence and corruption that goes with the drug trade. "This is probably the most important way in which the policies of rich countries foster corruption and violence. Yet the effect on the Third World seems scarcely to enter discussion of alternative drug policies in the rich countries." Legalizing drugs, a system of taxation and regulation, comparable to that applied to tobacco and alcohol might do more to reduce corruption in the world than any other measure rich countries could take, he suggests.

Rich countries have been used to it, too:

Bribery may be pervasive, but it is difficult to detect. Many Western companies do not dirty their own hands, but instead pay local agents, who get a 10 per cent or so "success fee" if a contract goes through and who have access to the necessary "slush funds" to ensure that it does. Bribery is also increasingly subtle.... Until recently, bribery was seen as a normal business practice. Many countries including France, Germany and the UK treated bribes as legitimate business expenses which could be claimed for tax deduction purposes.

— *Dr Susan Hawley, Exporting Corruption; Privatisation, Multinationals and Bribery, The Corner House, June 2000*

A COLD WAR LEGACY: THE CURSE OF NATURAL RESOURCES; INVITING CORRUPTION

Professor Neild is worth quoting at extensive length on the impacts the Cold War had in terms of encouraging or exacerbating corruption in the developing countries:

Many Western covert and overt military operation were motivated, in part at least, by the view, which may have been fearfully exaggerated, that the West's supplies of raw materials and oil were threatened by communist intrusion into Third World countries. A feeling of vulnerability was understandable. The Soviet Union ... was largely self-sufficient ...; the West, in need of increasing supplies for its growing industrial production, depended heavily on imports from Third World countries.... Western governments used diplomacy plus overt and covert military operations to counter the Communists. Meanwhile western firms paid rulers to obtain concessions to extract oil and minerals.

The business of obtaining oil and mineral concessions has aways been conducive to the use of bribes, omissions, gifts, and favors, and remains so since there are huge "rents" (i.e. windfall profits) to be shared by the parties to a deal.... Third World governments rarely use auctions [for concession, which, when done honestly, removes the opportunity for buyers to bribe sellers]. They commonly sell concessions by negotiation. For which there are some good reasons. It is often necessary for the foreign company that buys a concession to build infrastructure, such as ports, pipelines, roads and dormitory towns for their staff; to make this worthwhile, a whole oil field or major mineral deposit has to be given to one foreign company, rather than split between many competitors; and that one company, which will become the source of a significant, perhaps dominant, part of the nation's revenue, will acquire substantial economic power *vis-à-vis* the government. Hence strategic and diplomatic consideration enter the calculation: the government will want to give the concession to a company backed by a government which it believes will be helpful to it in its international relations—and in supplying it with arms and mercenaries. But .... there is [also] the prospect of bribes. Those who run a government that has a concession to sell will know that negotiation creates a strong incentive to the potential buyers to offer them bribes: they will know this from the point of view of the buyers, a sum that will only add a small percentage to, say, a billion dollar deal, will be worth paying in order to win the concession. Once negotiation is adopted as the means of allocating concessions, the dominant incentive is for bidders to engage competitively in the bribery of local rulers and fixers.

— Robert Neild, Public Corruption; The Dark Side of Social Evolution, (London: Anthem Press, 2002), pp. 136-137 [Emphasis added]

But Neild feels that this same attitude has affected rich countries' domestic political behavior, too. Of particular concern to Neild in this is the apparent tendency for bribery, which is intense in the business of seeking resource concession and selling arms, to become a secret habit of western firms and politicians that infects their domestic political behavior. Of this there has been considerable evidence in scandals that have occurred recently in Britain, France and Germany.... *Le Monde* published an outspoken editorial commenting on the [French company, Elf Aquitaine, corruption] affair: For too long French policy in Africa has been neither moral nor effective.

... It would be wrong to deny that corruption is indispensable in the obtaining of drilling concession, though that does not mean that one should not try to stop it. M. Tarallo [a senior Elf Manager] is unfortunately right when he says that all petrol companies use it... But the sins of others do not absolve Elf. Added to which ... Elf has used its money to keep in power dictators whose principle aim has been not the development of their country but their personal enrichment. In exchange, Paris could count on their support in its diplomatic battles and could offer captive markets to French firms...

This "neo-colonialism" was put in place during the presidency of General de Gaulle and has been maintained by subsequent governments regardless of party...

Looked at today the picture is not glorious. A former colonial power has taught corruption to its African clients—who were willing pupils—and there is nothing to persuade us that they have not rewarded their friends in Paris...

... In one case at least, lack of natural resources has apparently been an incentive to anticorruption policies: the tough ruler of Singapore, Lee Kuan Yew, is reported to have said that he came down hard on the corrupt because his tiny country with no natural resources has to rely on its good name to remain a center of banking and technology.

— Robert Neild, Public Corruption; The Dark Side of Social Evolution, (London: Anthem Press, 2002), p. 138 [Emphasis added]

GLOBALIZATION, MULTINATIONAL CORPORATIONS, AND CORRUPTION

Corruption scandals that sometimes make headline news in Western media can often be worse in developing countries. This is especially the case (as the previous link argues) when it is multinational companies going into poorer countries to do business. The international business environment, encouraged by a form of globalization that is heavily influenced by the wealthier and more powerful countries in the world makes it easier for multinationals to make profit and even for a few countries to benefit. However, some policies behind globalization appear to encourage and exacerbate corruption as accountability of governments and companies have been reduced along the way. For example, For multinationals, bribery enables companies to gain contracts (particularly for public works and military equipment) or concessions which they would not otherwise have won, or to do so on more favorable terms. Every year, Western businesses pay huge amounts of money in bribes to win friends, influence and contracts. These bribes are conservatively estimated to run to US$80 billion a year—roughly the amount that the UN believes is needed to eradicate global poverty.

— *Dr Susan Hawley, Exporting Corruption; Privatization, Multinationals and Bribery, The Corner House, June 2000*

Dr Hawley also lists a number of impacts that multinationals' corrupt practices have on the "South" (another term for Third World, or developing countries), including:

- They undermine development and exacerbate inequality and poverty.
- They disadvantage smaller domestic firms.
- They transfer money that could be put towards poverty eradication into the hands of the rich.
- They distort decision-making in favor of projects that benefit the few rather than the many.
- They also
    - o Increase debt;
    - o Benefit the company, not the country;
    - o Bypass local democratic processes;
    - o Damage the environment;
    - o Circumvent legislation; and
    - o Promote weapons sales.

IMF and World Bank Policies that Encourage Corruption

At a deeper level are the policies that form the backbone to globalization. These policies are often prescribed by international institutions such as the World Bank and IMF. For years, they have received sharp criticism for exacerbating poverty through policies such as Structural Adjustment, rapid deregulation and opening barriers to trade before poorer countries are economic ready to do so. This has also created situations ripe for corruption to flourish:

> As Western governments and the World Bank and IMF shout ever more loudly about corruption, their own policies are making it worse in both North and South. Particularly at fault are deregulation, privatization, and structural adjustment policies requiring civil service reform and economic liberalization. In 1997, the World Bank asserted that: any reform that increases the competitiveness of the economy will reduce incentives for corrupt behavior. Thus policies that lower controls on foreign trade, remove entry barriers to private industry, and privatize state firms in a way that ensure competition will all support the fight.
>
> The Bank has so far shown no signs of taking back this view. It continues to claim that corruption can be battled through deregulation of the economy; public sector reform in areas such as customs, tax administration and civil-service; strengthening of anti-corruption and audit bodies; and decentralization.
>
> Yet the empirical evidence, much of it from the World Bank itself, suggests that, far from reducing corruption, such policies, and the manner in which they have been implemented, have in some circumstances increased it.
>
> *— Dr Susan Hawley, Exporting Corruption; Privatization, Multinationals and Bribery, The Corner House, June 2000*

Jubilee Research (formerly the prominent Jubilee 2000 debt relief campaign organization) has similar criticisms, and is also worth quoting at length: Rich country politicians and bank officials argue that because dictators like Marcos, Suharto, and Mobutu were kept in power with western arms and were given loans to squander on ill-judged and repressive schemes, that the people of those countries—who often fought valiantly against those dictators—cannot be trusted not to waste the money released by debt cancellation. This may seem confusing to people not familiar with the logic of the IMF and World Bank. In summary:

- Creditors colluded with, and gave loans to dictators they knew were corrupt and who would squander the money.
- Creditors gave military and political aid to those dictators—knowing arms might be used to suppress popular opposition
- Therefore, successor democratic governments and their supporters, who may have been victims of corruption and oppression, cannot be trusted.

To many people in the South, this seems irrational and illogical—the logic of blaming the victim. It is the logic of power rather than of integrity, and is used to benefit the rich rather than the poor in developing countries.

A similar logic argues that if the World Bank and government export credit agencies promoted inappropriate and unprofitable projects, then southern governments proved their inability to control money because they accepted the ill-advised projects in the first place. Thus, if money is released by debt cancellation, it must be controlled by agencies which promoted those failed projects.

This is the logic that says if people were stupid enough to believe cigarette advertising, then they are too stupid to take care of themselves and the "reformed" cigarette companies should be put in charge of their health care.

The same institutions who made the corrupt loans to Zaire and lent for projects in Africa that failed repeatedly are still in charge, but their role has been enhanced because of their success in pushing loans. Can we trust these institutions to suddenly only lend wisely; to not give loans when the money might be wasted?

Preventing new wasted loans and new debt crises, and ensuring that there is not another debt crisis, means that the people who pushed the loans and caused this crisis cannot be left in charge.

The creditors or loan pushers cannot be left in charge, no matter how heartfelt their protestations that they have changed. Pushers and addicts need to work together, to bring to an end the entire reckless and corrupt lending and borrowing habit.

— *Joseph Hanlon and Ann Pettifor, Kicking the Habit; Finding a lasting solution to addictive lending and borrowing—and its corrupting side-effects, Jubilee Research, March 2000*

And in terms of how lack of transparency by the international institutions contributes to so much corruption structured into the system, Hanlon and Pettifor continue in the same report as cited above:

Structural adjustment programs cover most of a country's economic governance.

... The most striking aspect of IMF/World Bank conditionality [for aid, debt relief, etc] is that the civil servants of these institutions, the staff members, have virtual dictatorial powers to impose their whims on recipient countries. This comes about because poor countries must have IMF and World Bank programs, but staff can decline to submit programs to the boards of those institutions until the poor country accepts conditions demanded by IMF civil servants.

There is much talk of transparency and participation, but the crunch comes in final negotiations between ministers and World Bank and IMF civil servants The country manager can say to the Prime Minister, "unless you accept condition X, I will not submit this program to the board". No agreed program means a sudden halt to essential aid and no debt relief, so few ministers are prepared to hold out. Instead Prime Ministers and presidents bow to the diktat of foreign civil servants. Joseph Stiglitz also notes that "reforms often bring advantages to some groups while disadvantaging others," and one of the problems with policies agreed in secret is that a governing elite may accept an imposed policy which does not harm the elite but harms others. An example is the elimination of food subsidies.

— *Joseph Hanlon and Ann Pettifor, Kicking the Habit; Finding a lasting solution to addictive lending and borrowing—and its corrupting side-effects, Jubilee Research, March 2000*

As further detailed by Hanlon and Pettifor, Christian Aid partners (a coalition of development organizations), argued that top-down "conditionality has undermined democracy by making elected governments accountable to Washington-based institutions instead of to their own people." The potential for unaccountability and corruption therefore increases as well.

CORRUPTION EVERYWHERE; RICH AND POOR COUNTRIES, INTERNATIONAL INSTITUTIONS

It goes without saying, almost, that corruption is everywhere. Corruption in poor countries is well commented on (sometimes used dismissively to explain away problems caused by other issues, too). It would be futile to provide examples here (see also the sources of information at the end of this document for more on this).

Rich countries, also suffer from corruption. Examples are also numerous and beyond the scope of this page to list them here. However, a few recent examples are worth mentioning because they are varied on the type of corruption involved, and are very recent, implying this is a massive problem in rich countries as well as poor.

The first example is the US government, accused of outsourcing many contracts without an open bid process. Jim Hightower notes that "An analysis by the Times found that more than half of their outsourcing contracts are not open to competition. In essence, the Bushites choose the company and award the money without getting other bids. Prior to Bush, only 21% of federal contracts were awarded on a no-bid basis."

Another example is Italy, where former Italian Prime Minister Silvio Berlusconi and some of his close associates were held on trial for various crimes and corruption cases (though Berlusconi himself has not, to date, been found guilty of any charges). Many key teams in the massive Italian soccer league, Serie A were also found to be involved in a massive corruption ring.

In the United Kingdom, the arms manufacturer, BAE was being investigated for bribing Saudi officials to buy fighter planes, but the government intervened in the investigation citing national interests. The *Guardian* also reported that BAE gave a Saudi prince a £75 airliner ($150m approx) as part of a British arms deal, with the arms firm paying the expenses of flying it. This seemingly large figure is small compared to the overall deal, but very enticing for the deal makers, and it is easy to see how corruption is so possible when large sums are involved.

International institutions, such as the United Nations and World Bank have also recently come under criticism for corruption, ironically while presenting themselves in the forefront fighting against corruption.

The recent example with the UN has been the oil for food scandal, where the headlines were about the corruption in the UN. In reality, the figures of $21 billion or so of illicit funds blamed on the UN were exaggerations; it was $2 billion; it was the UN Security Council (primarily US and UK) responsible for much of the monitoring; US kickbacks for corrupt oil sales were higher, for example. (This is discussed in more detail on this site's Iraq sanctions, oil for food scandal section.)

At the World Bank, headlines were made when its recent president, Paul Wolfowitz, was forced to resign after it was revealed he had moved his girlfriend to a new government post with an extremely high salary without review by its ethics committee.

Paul Wolfowitz's appointment was also controversial, due to his influential role in architecting the US invasion of Iraq. A former member of staff at the World Bank also noted concerns of cronyism related to Wolfowitz's appointment way before the scandal that forced him to resign.

The US nominee for the next president is the former US Trade Representative and currently an executive at Goldman Sachs, Robert Zoellick. His nomination is also coming under criticism. Bush supports it, saying Zoellick "is the right man to succeed Paul in this vital work." Former World Bank chief economist, and Nobel Prize winner for economics, Joseph Stiglitz feels that instead of a political appointee, it would be better to get an economist who understands development.

As also reported by the BBC, Paul Zeitz, executive director of the Global AIDS Alliance, said that he thought Mr Zoellick was a terrible choice because "Zoellick has no significant experience in economic development in poor countries," and that "he has been a close friend to the brand-name pharmaceutical industry, and the bilateral trade agreements he has negotiated [for the US] effectively block access to generic medication for millions of people."

While the US typically gets its preferred nomination to head the World Bank, Europe has typically got its preferred person to head the IMF. Critics have long argued that this lacks transparency and is not democratic. While not illegal as such, it does feel like a form of corruption.

TACKLING CORRUPTION

What can be Done to Tackle this Problem?

The above-cited report by Hanlon and Pettifor also highlights a broader way to try and tackle corruption by attempting to provide a more just, democratic and transparent process in terms of relations between donor nations and their creditors:

Campaigners from around the world, but particularly the South, have called for a more just, independent, accountable and transparent process for managing relations between sovereign debtors and their public and private creditors.

An independent process would have five goals:

- to restore some justice to a system in which international creditors play the role of plaintiff, judge and jury, in their own court of international finance.
- to introduce discipline into sovereign lending and borrowing arrangements—and thereby prevent future crises.
- to counter corruption in borrowing and lending, by introducing accountability through a free press and greater transparency to civil society in both the creditor and debtor nations.
- to strengthen local democratic institutions, by empowering them to challenge and influence elites.
- to encourage greater understanding and economic literacy among citizens, and thereby empower them to question, challenge and hold their elites to account.

— Joseph Hanlon and Ann Pettifor, Kicking the Habit; Finding a lasting solution to addictive lending and borrowing—and its corrupting side-effects, Jubilee Research, March 2000

The *Bretton Woods Project* organization notes that the World Bank, under pressure of late, has suspended a number of loans due to concerns of corruption. These include loans to Chad, Kenya, Congo, India, Bangladesh, Uzbekistan, Yemen, and Argentina. The Bank has also started internal investigations of Bank corruption. However, "despite high-profile moves by president Paul Wolfowitz, the root causes of corruption—underpaid civil servants, an acceptance of bribery by big business, and dirty money—remain largely unaddressed."

The *Bretton Woods Project* adds that the "normalization of petty corruption in developing countries has in part been driven by"

- IFI conditions;
- The aid industry for "overpaying consultants" and turning a blind eye to corruption in some regimes; and

- The "World Bank's 'pressure to lend' culture where staff are rewarded for the volume of the portfolio they manage;"
- The World Bank's slow pace in investigating and disbarring companies found guilty of corrupt practices such as bribery, fraud or malpractice;
- Failing to increase transparency of some of its own procedures;
- The IFI's "central part of an international financial system which has both actively and tacitly supported the global proliferation of dirty money flows" including, for example, the financing of various despotic rulers that have siphoned off a lot of money to personal offshore accounts.

To help address these problems, the *Bretton Woods Project* suggests a few steps:

- Greater transparency of World Bank processes, allowing greater visibility for elected officials and civil society in recipient countries;
- Strengthening internal mechanisms within the Bank itself, to monitor integrity of Bank functions, and allow truly independent audits of Bank operations;
- Minimum standards in governance, transparency and human rights that must be fulfilled before approving oil, gas and mining projects in institutionally weak countries.
- Not always tying loans with economic policy conditions in such a way that some governments surrender their policy-making space.

During the 2002 World Summit on Sustainable Development, the *BBC* broadcast a mini debate on globalization, poverty, and related issues, and had a panel of around 30 experts, from both the developing and rich countries. One person on that panel was Vandana Shiva, a vocal critic of the current form of globalization and its impact on the environment and people in the third world. She was asked why people should listen to concerns from the third world when they cannot sort out the rampant corruption first. Her answer was simple: rich countries need to stop dictating policies that encourage corruption in the first place.

Like Shiva, Professor Neild feels that the solution is philosophically simple. However, as Neild acknowledges, in reality it is far harder to do, due to the power interests involved:

> It is hard to see how the international economic agencies and their member governments can introduce incentives that would cause corrupt rulers to [attack corruption]... Not only are the rich countries and their agencies in this respect impotent, they commonly have been and are accomplices in corruption abroad, encouraging it by their action rather than impeding it.
>
> ... It is hard to see any solution other than transparency and criticism. It would take an unprecedented degree of united dedication to the checking of corruption for the international community to agree that the oil and mining companies of the world should boycott corrupt regimes, somehow defined, let alone manage to enforce an agreement.
>
> *— Robert Neild, Public Corruption; The Dark Side of Social Evolution, (London: Anthem Press, 2002), pp. 208-210, [Emphasis added]*

Purpose of Summit: Review Progress on Millennium Declaration

The main purpose for this World Summit was to review progress since the Millennium Declaration, adopted by all Member States in 2000. This Declaration contained what became known as the Millennium Development Goals. These goals, which all 191 member states have pledged to meet, all for 2015, include:

- A halving of hunger and poverty;
- Attaining universal primary education;
- Drastic reductions in child and maternal mortality;

- Promoting gender equality;
- Improved environmental sustainability;
- A fairer global trading system; and
- Reversing the spread of HIV/AIDS and other deadly diseases.

The above would form a major part of the Summit dubbed "Freedom from want." Other issues that the Summit were to be addressed included:

- Security (Freedom from fear)
- Human rights (Freedom to live in dignity)
- UN reform (Strengthening the United Nations)

CONCERNS LEADING UP TO THE MEETING

There were a number of serious concerns leading up to the meeting.

Fears that Primary Purpose of UN Summit May take Back Seat

In the wake of the Iraq war, the Security Council issues that it highlighted and a scandal about corruption in the United Nations Oil For Food Program, UN reform has been back on the agenda in a major way.

Under pressure after the beginning of 2005, in the wake of these Iraq-related issues and scandals, UN General Secretary Kofi Annan, released a report titled *In Larger Freedom* calling attention to the need for UN reform.

In particular he wanted Security Council reform issues to be resolved before the 2005 World Summit. Unfortunately, that has not happened.

Inter Press Service (IPS) reported (August 16, 2005) that many developing country diplomats were worried that development issues would take a backseat, in favor of UN reform as that would be of more interest to richer and powerful nations.

Draft Outcome Document Leads to Concerns of Weak Text

Leading up to the Summit, a number of drafts of the outcome document for the Summit were released. However, various countries and blocs have concerns for different reasons. For example, the 117 members of the Non-Aligned Movement sought to weaken the text on issues such as the proposed new Human Rights Council and the increasing powers for the UN Security Council to intervene militarily in conflicts around the world.

Reasons that these countries have typically been weary of such issues include that

- They often have poor human rights records themselves;
- They see the richer countries being more influential in these areas, especially the UN Security Council, where they have little say and thus could feel quite powerless, and sometimes even threatened.

Equally of concern was that the drafts failed to take into account legitimate concerns raised by developing countries on various development issues, and instead had adhered to an approach favoring richer countries.

US Wants to Do Away With Most Text, even the Millennium Development Goals

It is perhaps the US stance that had concerned most countries, though, including allies.

As the *Washington Post* reported (August 24, 2005), "the Bush administration has thrown the proceedings in turmoil with a call for drastic renegotiation" of the draft agreement that all the attending world leaders would sign.

The proposed changes, submitted by controversial US Ambassador to the UN, John Bolton, touched on "virtually every aspect of UN affairs and provide a detailed look at US concerns about the world body's future." For example:

- As the *Post* continued, the United States introduced more than 750 amendments that would
  - o Eliminate new pledges of foreign aid to impoverished nations;
  - o Scrap provisions that call for action to halt climate change and urge nuclear powers to make greater progress in dismantling their nuclear arms;
  - o Strengthen language to underscore the importance of taking tougher action against terrorism, promoting human rights and democracy, and halting the spread of the world's deadliest weapons.
  - o Strike any mention of the Millennium Development Goals
  - o Impose greater oversight of U.N. spending
  - o Eliminate any reference to the International Criminal Court
  - o Oppose language that urges the five permanent members of the Security Council not to cast vetoes to block action to halt genocide, war crimes or ethnic cleansing.
- Additional examples noted by *The Guardian* include:
  - o Deleting "respect for nature";
  - o For the right of self-determination of peoples, deleting "which remain under colonial domination and foreign occupation";
  - o Deleting "to provide the [United Nations] organisation with the resources needed to fully implement its mandates";
  - o Deleting "remain concerned, however, by the slow and uneven implementation of the internationally agreed development goals, including the Millennium development goals";
  - o Deleting "corporate responsibility and accountability" when discussing fighting corruption;

- o Deleting "encourage pharmaceutical companies to make anti-retroviral drugs affordable and accessible in Africa" in regards to fighting AIDS;
- The administration publicly complained that the document's section on poverty was too long!
- Instead, the United States sought to highlight the importance of the Monterrey Consensus, a 2002 summit in Mexico that focused on free-market reforms, and required governments to improve accountability in exchange for aid and debt relief.

The *Post* also added that "In meetings with foreign delegates, Bolton has expressed concern about a provision of the agreement that urges wealthy countries, including the United States, to contribute 0.7 percent of their gross national product in assistance to poor countries." This is despite the fact that the Monterrey Consensus reiterates that commitment (which the US was pushing and signed up to) and that countries agreed to this over 30 years ago, and the US, along with many other rich nations, have hardly ever provided close to that amount.

Furthermore, Bolton "has also objected to language that urges nations to observe a moratorium on nuclear testing and to sign the Comprehensive Test Ban Treaty, which the Bush administration opposes."

Why would the US be so hostile to the United Nations goals, considering it is its largest funder? The answer is complex and perhaps too deep to answer quickly here. In short though, a few reasons include:

- The US, as sole superpower, has often found itself going against international opinion, which is often expressed at the United Nations.
- The ability of the US to flex its muscles, so to speak, is often constrained (or attempted to be) at the United Nations, as the recent Iraq War exemplified. This has led to people in the US to call for withholding even more

UN funding than it already withholds until it is reformed (in the ways that best meet US interests), or some to even say that they should pull out of the body all together.

- Some in the US also see a conspiracy in the UN trying to be a sort of world government which would restrict the rights of the US.

Some of the above reasons are quite extreme, but gain popular attention in the right wing of US politics.

Take for example, John Bolton himself. He is a member of the ultra-conservative Project for a New American Century (PNAC) and was Senior Vice President of the ultra-conservative American Enterprise Institute.

PNAC has outlined the ideas behind global dominance and empire in the form of a global Pax Americana and has described peace-keeping missions as "demanding American political leadership rather than that of the United Nations" and hence this is a view that Bolton is associated with.

In addition, in 1994, Bolton said of the United Nations: "There is no such thing as the United Nations. There is only the international community, which can only be led by the only remaining superpower, which is the United States." He also stated that "The Secretariat building in New York has 38 stories. If it lost ten stories, it wouldn't make a bit of difference."

Yet, he has also said that "the United Nations can be a useful instrument in the conduct of American foreign policy." In other words, Bolton sees *using* the UN for America's own agendas as ok. Indeed, he adds that "No one ... should be under any illusions that American support for the United Nations as one of several options for implementing American foreign policy translates into unlimited support for the world organization. That is not true now, and it will not be true for a long time to come, if ever." See also the UN and Development page (warning, that page is quite old, though may provide some context), and various sections through the geopolitics section of this web site for more information.

POWER: USING A BARGAINING POSITION BECAUSE ONE CAN

Recently the developing countries have become more united in a positive sense, to withstand further unfair trade rules that rich countries have tried to push in the past. However, this means they can also try to use their new power to resist changes that most would like to see, such as improved human rights. The US, however, typically has a far more reaching impact as it is far more influential and powerful than the poorer countries.

In short, the US looks to make the outcome of the whole document a weak one without much substance. Given the enormous number of changes the US is proposing, one would not expect them all to happen. However, the US has played a clever tactic here:

- As the biggest donor to the United Nations, and, its biggest critic, as well as being the most powerful nation on the planet, it therefore has a real bargaining position which it has exploited here;
- Other countries will have to typically compromise on US terms in order to get the US in on the outcome agreement.
- The result will therefore be a much weakened document, even if the US does not get most of its 750 changes in there.

This type of "bargaining" occurred with the Kyoto protocol, for example; other countries agreed to a watered down text to get the US in, but the US later pulled out anyway.

And this all comes at a time when a new UN report warns that globalization is driving inequality.

Summit Meeting Outcome

Unfortunately, the above prediction of a weaker final document came true. But, also controversial was the manner in which the final document was drafted right at the end.

UNDEMOCRATIC PROCESS IN GETTING A FINAL DOCUMENT

Also of concern was the way in which the final outcome document was agreed to. Because of the turmoil created mostly by the US leading up to this meeting and with all the reservations and changes they put forward in the document, there resulted a "closed-door consensus-based negotiations (which resulted in the final outcome document) where a few governments were allowed to exercise a veto over the will of the overwhelming majority of member states" as *Inter Press Service* noted (in the same article as linked to above). This was seen as a concern for it was undemocratic.

Furthermore, as the Venezuelan delegation noted, the manner in which the final document was then presented to the rest of the UN General Assembly was illegal. It was presented a few minutes before the meetings started, when one of the rules General Assembly, that "no proposal shall be discussed or put to the vote at any meeting of the General Assembly unless copies of it have been circulated to all delegations not later than the day preceding the meetings."

Another *IPS* report cited Bill Pace, executive director of the *World Federalist Movement*, who said that "the five permanent members of the Security Council, namely the United States, Britain, France, China and Russia, behave in the General Assembly as if they have veto rights and fiercely refuse to allow any consideration of peace and security issues. And a few others, mostly military governments or permanent member wannabes, wreck the negotiations from the other side."

That same article also ended with criticism of the US: On Wednesday, the New York Times squarely blamed the United States — and specifically its "notoriously undiplomatic" Ambassador John Bolton — for the impending failure of the summit.

The Times accused Bolton of insisting on a very long list of unilateral demands. "The predictable effect was to transform what had been a painful and difficult search for workable diplomatic compromises into a competitive exercise in political posturing."

As a result, said the Times editorial, the most tragic loss is a genuine opportunity to help the one billion people around the world who each live on less than a dollar a day.

— *Thalif Deen, UN Summit of World Leaders Under Heavy Fire, Inter Press Service, September 14, 2005*

This meant other countries would not have time to understand any changes, which for such a meeting is crucial. This may seem "efficient" for some, but on such important issues this slight bit of "bureaucracy" is important.

Former British Secretary for Development, Clare Short is quite vocal in her criticism of the United States, and is worth quoting in length:

It is hardly surprising that, in a bitterly divided world where the world's hegemonic power has set aside international law and declared that it will act unilaterally whenever its interests are suited, it has been difficult to agree on a reform package for strengthening the UN.

... The ambition [to review progress on the Millennium Development Goals progress] has widened to try to agree on a major package of UN reform.... But given George Bush's resistance and the sour atmosphere post-Iraq, the reform agenda has been too ambitious and generated strong opposition for reasons that were often self-contradictory.

... n particular, those who advocate a new convention on terrorism fail to understand how deeply unhappy people are about the hypocrisy of those who use state power unlawfully and cause massive loss of civilian life - and then expect all countries to sign up to a definition of terrorism that fails to acknowledge the right to resist occupation.

Despite all of this, the commitment to the Millennium Development Goals has probably been strengthened by the US challenge and then the recognition that even for the US, this was a step too far.

In addition, the focus on monitoring country-by-country progress against the goals has set up a new spirit of competition between states over reductions in poverty, children in school, better health care for the poor and more sustainable use of environmental resources. Progress is being made.

... We are, without doubt, living through a very disappointing period in world history.

— Clare Short, Depression and Mistrust Prevail at the UN, The Independent, September 15, 2005

STRENGTHS AND WEAKNESSES OF THE OUTCOME DOCUMENT

Many non governmental organizations also criticized the final outcome document in this way. *Inter Press Service* quoted Jim Paul, executive director of *Global Policy Forum* as saying the final outcome document was "weak and full of platitudes and generalities."

Some of the positive aspects of the outcome included the following:

- On the human rights front, there was agreement to create a Peace Building Commission, and a Human Rights Council.
- Stopping genocide. Wording on this was more concrete that other issues: nations agreed on a collective responsibility to protect civilians facing genocide and similar atrocities. Governments can no longer use sovereignty and non-intervention norms as excuses to avoid having to act to protect civilians from mass killings.
- Countries reiterated the need to achieve MDG, even though US initially wanted to strike all mention of it.
- Education: supporting elimination of user fees for primary education

- Debt relief: acknowledges the G8 commitments (which were imperfect, though a starting point), and acknowledges that others such as middle-income countries may also need some sort of debt relief.
- HIV/AIDS: endorsed the G8 commitment to universal access to HIV treatment by 2010
- Tax evasion: more mention of this problem
- Reiterated the need for member states to provide the UN with adequate resources as needed (because the UN has a financial crisis of its own whereby some states, the US in particular, has long withheld its dues — and then blamed the UN for being ineffective!)

A number of problems or weaknesses included the following:

- Generally the final document was quite vague in many areas, and often simply reaffirming past commitments, without adding anything new or substantial.
- The urgency of reaching the Millennium Development Goals was lacking, it was felt by many. That most of the world is behind on this right now was not really stressed.
- Trade: risks remaining unequal. There was not much text and what there was was weak and favored rich countries, mostly. There was mention of endorsing trade liberalization but nothing about eliminating the harmful and hypocritical rich country subsidies, or giving more power to smaller/poor countries to have more say in their destiny
- Poor countries are still subject to neoliberal economic policies prescribed and pressured onto poorer countries by the richer countries and institutions such as the IMF and World Bank
- Nuclear non-proliferation and Nuclear disarmament was not mentioned. "This is a real disgrace," Kofi Annan said (recently the US has indicated the desire to use nuclear weapons more offensively than previously

indicated, which is a reverse of the direction the UN wants to go)

- Terrorism: did not get a definition of terrorism, so while condemnation of it was strong by all, more specific issues were not discussed.
- The International Criminal Court was not mentioned either
- Aid: not only was there little commitment to foreign aid, but it was again tied to conditions often deemed as unfair.

6

IMF and World Bank Protests, Washington D.C.

To complement the public protests in Seattle, the week leading up to April 16th/17th 2000 saw the other two global institutions of the so-called "unholy trinity", the International Monetary Fund (IMF) and World Bank, as the focus of renewed protests and criticisms, in Washington, D.C.

As with the WTO protests in Seattle, the purpose of the mass demonstrations was to protest against the *current form* of globalization, which is seen as unaccountable, corporate-led, and non-democratic. It has also been to further the calls for more justice and democracy in the globalization process.

It further shows the links between tremendous odious debt and poverty in the developing countries with the effects of the current forms of globalization that marginalizes a vast majority of people around the world.

While not the only part of the global financial system that has been destructive for most people of the world, the IMF and World Bank policies have been a major instrument to structure the global economy (via structuring the national economies of developing countries) to allow a form of neoliberal globalization to be pursued that has led to the criticisms mentioned above.

Critics also point out that the beneficiaries will be largely the wealthy people in western nations and the transnational corporations, while the majority of people in the world will not benefit. For more about the flawed Structural Adjustment policies of the IMF and World Bank on developing countries, and the race to the bottom effect it has predictably had, go to this web site's Structural Adjustment part of the Poverty Section.

While not as large a turn out as Seattle, estimates vary from ten thousand to twenty thousand or more that turned up during the week long protests.

MAINSTREAM MEDIA REPRESENTATION

As with the poor Seattle coverage, the media have concentrated more on the sensationalism.

- Again the mainstream ignored the in-depth issues around the IMF and World Bank and why they are being criticized by so many around the world.
- As with Seattle, the mainstream media also ignores the protesting of lack of democracy and global justice in the current process to achieve globalization and in the major institutions to realize it.
- According to the IMF's own official statement, they themselves did "not provide press accreditation to public access TV, community radio, nor student or academic publications to attend our meetings." See this alert from Fairness and Accuracy in Reporting for more information. In fact, the Washington, D.C. corporate media, for example, sensationalized the traffic disruptions and policing efforts as the headlines and then occasionally mention the meeting, the protests and the reasons.
    - o A small number of people unfortunately did clash with police, but compared to the thousands of peaceful protestors the media's coverage has so far been disproportionate.
    - o In fact there was little discussion on the police tactics, who
        - * "used illegitimate preemptive arrests

  * set out a huge restricted area around the World Bank and IMF keeping activists from even the vicinity of their focus of dissent
  * invaded and closed the Convergence Center as intimidation
  * used a mixture of arrests, aggression, and sometimes even forbearance in an effective brew to try to channel outcomes
  * and worked hard to goad protesters into acting out, though unsuccessfully" as summarized by Michael Albert in a reflection on the week long protests.
 - o (It is interesting to note how some US Republicans were shocked at the aggressive police raid in Miami to take Elian Gonzalez to return him to his father. They commented that such tactics are typical of somewhere like Cuba, not the United States. However, there wasn't even a slight comment to that effect when there was an equally, if not more brutal, crackdown on more people at Seattle and Washington D.C. protests.)

- With little debate between IMF/World Bank officials/ spokespersons and major protestor representatives in the news and very short sound-bites from each side, the issues were not covered and presented very well.
- However, to be fair to the mainstream media, compared to Seattle, they did at least look into some of the concerns that the protestors were raising a bit more, which is a good indication of the positive effects of the protests.
- Often, the majority of the "experts" interviewed were economists who support the current policies. There had been a few interviews with economists critical of current policies, but hardly any with human rights activists, subject experts from developing countries, or others who could also provide valid insights and perspectives into the issues at hand and the effects on societies of

so many countries that are affected by the decisions and policies made at the IMF and World Bank (and supportive industrialized countries and multinational corporations).

MEDIA REDUCES A COMPLEX MATTER TO JUST TWO "SIDES"

[Interviewer] Thomas Friedman, writing in the New York Times, called the demonstrators at Seattle "a Noah's ark of flat-earth advocates."

From his point of view that's probably correct. From the point of view of slave owners, people opposed to slavery probably looked that way. For the 1 percent of the population that he's thinking about and representing, the people who are opposing this are flat-earthers. Why should anyone oppose the developments that we've been describing?

— An interview with Noam Chomsky, by Nation Magazine, April 24, 2000

A complex subject matter is reduced to "either you are protectionist, or you are pro free trade." Instead, most protesters are pro international trade but with more emphasis on a fairer, accountable and democratic process to get there. It doesn't mean that the current way is the only way. The globalization debate has many perspectives, not just two. For example, the following are some broad categories of perspectives, but by no means exhaustive:

- People who are pro free trade in its current form because it allows them and the corporations to continue and benefit from exploitative practices.
- People who are pro free trade because they genuinely believe that it will be a positive force in the long run.
- People who are pro free trade, but not in its current, largely corporate-led form.
- People who are pro international trade and globalization, but not "free" where free is defined by economic neoliberal

definitions, which is different to political liberalism. An approach with more regulatory measures in the international arena to help protect local industries and people from the possible effects of runnaway, free captial (as seen in the global financial crisis toward the end of the 1990s) would be preferred.
- People who are against free trade because of nationalistic, isolationist or overly protectionist ideals
- and so on.

There are many other perspectives. Some have a mix of the above and so on. The point is that the media often looks to accidentally, or purposely, simplify the picture in order to get their sound bites in and hence the level and range of discourse on the topic is sorely affected. For example, in Seattle, as well as Washington D.C, many protestors were often portrayed as the same people as right wing protectionists, like Pat Buchannan, who also oppose the WTO, IMF, World Bank etc, but for very nationalistic, purposes. As noted in the mainstream media section, most corporate media are pro free trade, hence, this also affects the presented perspectives.

The term "anarchist" has always had a very weird meaning in elite circles. For example, there was a headline in the Boston Globe today on a small article saying something like "Anarchists Plan Protests at IMF Meeting in April." Who are the anarchists who are planning the protest? Ralph Nader's Public Citizen, labor organizations and others. There will be some people around who will call themselves anarchists, whatever that means. But from the elite point of view, you want to focus on something that you can denounce in some fashion as irrational. That's the analogue to Thomas Friedman calling them flat-earthers.

— *An interview with Noam Chomsky, by Nation Magazine, April 24, 2000*

There was some media coverage that tried to look at the issues and criticisms of the IMF and World Bank, and while for a moment it was hopeful that more people in the United States, as well as around the world, would be more aware of the issues the coverage proved not to be too indepth and without sustained analysis. Once the meeting was over, so was the concern it seemed.

The US is influential at the IMF and World Bank. As mentioned in the structural adjustment part of this web site, the IMF and World Bank are largely controlled and "owned" by the developed nations such as USA, Germany, UK, Japan etc. The US, for example, controls 17 to 18% of the voting power at the IMF and when an 85% majority is required for a decision, the US effectively have veto power. The World Bank is also 51% funded by the U.S. Treasury. (See this site's section on Structural Adjustment for more details and sources on this.)

A continued rising awareness within the US would hopefully help stimulate increased debate with a wider range of discourse. American citizens are honest and caring people. However, if the mainstream media, from where a large functioning aspect of democracy proves to not provide all relevant information, the opinions and decisions of the American people are also affected. Hence their ability to hold their leaders properly accountable is also affected.

For more on media portrayal and coverage, you could start with the following:

- The Independent Media Center is a collective of media producers offering non-corporate grassroots coverage. You could start there to find out about the actual coverage.
- The MediaChannel has a good section of articles.
    - TV Can't Tell You How It Is by Robin Andersen, presented on the MediaChannel, is a very good summary of the media coverage of the protests.
- Fairness and Accuracy in Reporting has a section on the IMF & World Bank
    - Media Distortion of World Bank/IMF Protests Starts Early is an example of some of the articles from the above-mentioned FAIR site.

- Protests in Washington Clash with Media Spin by media critic Norman Solomon
- When Corporate Media Cover "Independent Media" also by Norman Solomon, who starts off "During the recent protests in Washington against the World Bank and IMF, the leading cable news network became fascinated with independent media. Journalism free of huge economic interests — what a concept!"
- IMF, World Bank Bar Independent Journalists From Events
- Democracy Now has provided on-going grassroots coverage as well.
    - o The April 2000 archives has the continued coverage of the various issues and aspects
    - o As an example, the April 18 radio broadcast was about some of the issues and concerns around the policing and their tactics.
- Taking A16 Seriously by Jason Vest, points out that "A16 proved that the mainstream media is not averse to reporting a good story, even when the story involves protests against corporate global power. But what it did prove is that the mainstream buck stops well before deep, historical analysis."

More Information

The following sources provide good information about the meeting. It is also a useful set of resources to see the criticisms of current globalization models and current forms of free trade practices.

- Mobilization for Global Justice". This is the main web site about the process. It it brought together by three main organizations who also have a lot of information:
    - o The 50 Years Is Enough campaign is a coalition of 205 organizations dedicated to the profound transformation of the World Bank and the International Monetary Fund (IMF).

  - o Global Exchange, a human rights organization dedicated to promoting environmental, political and social justice around the world.
  - o Direct Action Network, a decentralized, directly democratic organization working to create a movement to overcome corporate globalization and all forms of oppression.
- CorpWatch have a section on globalization and the role of the two Bretton Woods institutions.
- Global Economic Crisis from Z magazine provides a lot of in-depth and background articles on the problems of the current forms of globalization.
- This Web Site's section on Poverty
- The Third World Network takes a look at liberalization
- Some articles from Foreign Policy in Focus:
  - o Structural Adjustment Programs & Poverty Reduction Strategy
  - o The IMF and Good Governance
  - o IMF: Case of a Dead Theory Walking
- UNCTAD: Time to Lead, Time to Challenge the WTO This article suggests that the United Nations Conference on Trade And Development could be a more appropriate and inclusive body for issues of international trade and development. As the article says, "UNCTAD may not have the material resources of these institutions, but it has something that the billions of dollars of the World Bank and IMF could not buy: legitimacy among developing countries."
- Fighting Corporate Sponsored Globalization, by Robin Hanhel
- The DC Cop Crackdown looks at some of the police tactics leading up to the protests, especially given the events in Seattle, earlier.
- The IMF & World Bank Campaign section from OneWorld provides more articles from other organizations as well.

- The Bretton Woods Project, in their own words, "works to monitor and reform the World Bank and IMF. It tracks key policy statements and reports, and provides critiques and early warnings used by non-governmental organisations across the world." They also show that it isn't just Washington D.C. seeing protests of this nature. In other countries around the world, people are protesting. Sometime the number of people who turn out are even larger. For an example, you can see towards the end of section 2 of this update.
- What I learned at the world economic crisis. The Insider by Joseph Stiglitz, former Chief Economist at the World Bank, until the beginning of 2000, when he resigned, harshly criticizing the IMF.
- Time to Rein in Global Finance by William Greider, suggests that while the IMF and World Bank are problematic, a reform, rather than complete closure could be the way foreward (afterall, they were created with a more positive goal in mind initially, before their roles changed to promote Friedman's neoliberalism in the 1970s) and that they are only a part of the global financial system that needs to be addressed.
- Growth May Be Good for the Poor — But are IMF and World Bank Policies Good for Growth? is a detailed critique of the World Bank's report showing that globalization is good for the poor. It claims to show that "growth generally does benefit the poor and that anyone who cares about the poor should favor the growth-enhancing polices of good rule of law, fiscal discipline, and openness to international trade." However, there have been many criticisms about the report for making far too many assumptions and not considering many interrelated issues.

7

Poverty and Economics in South Africa

The following document has been prepared as an input paper for the national hearings on poverty – *Speak Out On Poverty* – organised by the South African NGO Coalition (SANGOCO), the Human Rights Commission, and the Commission on Gender Equality. The focus is on economics, poverty, and socio-economic rights, the topic of the Gauteng poverty hearings.

Examining the linkages between economics, poverty, and socio-economic rights in a comprehensive way is a mammoth undertaking. Therefore, this paper should not be seen as a comprehensive treatment of these issues, but rather as a survey of a number of relevant topics concerning the operation of the economy and the persistence of poverty in South Africa. Although this is meant to be a survey, an outline of what to expect will be useful.

The first section gives a brief introduction to economic aspects and definitions of poverty. This is followed, in the second section, by selected statistical evidence of the extent of poverty and economic inequality in South Africa. "The Economy and Socio-Economic Rights" briefly explores what socio-economic rights mean in relationship to the functioning of an economy.

The forth section focuses on GEAR, current government policies, and their impact on socio-economic rights and poverty. "Economics and Causes of Poverty" looks at different approaches to economics and poverty, arguing that effectively addressing the crisis of poverty demands an alternative approach to economics. Elements of an alternative economic analysis are sketched out in some detail. Finally, the last section suggests shifts in economic policy which arise from an alternative economic framework.

This paper is meant to be a resource and guide for discussion on economics and poverty. Therefore, readers should focus on those parts of the paper which are most useful to them. It is hoped that this paper will stimulate useful debate and discussion around the critical issue of poverty in South Africa.

ECONOMICS AND POVERTY

The 1995 World Summit for Social Development in Copenhagen defines poverty as follows:

"Poverty has various manifestations, including lack of income and productive resources sufficient to ensure sustainable livelihoods; hunger and malnutrition; ill health; limited or lack of access to education and other basic services; increased morbidity and mortality from illness; homelessness and inadequate housing; unsafe environments; and social discrimination and exclusion. It is also characterised by lack of participation in decision-making and in civil, social and cultural life ..."

Economic factors are but just one set of the multiple factors that gives expression to poverty. Nevertheless, how an economy functions can either give rise to, or alternatively begin to eradicate, poverty. The focus of this paper is on the relationship between poverty and economics with an emphasis on the distribution of human and material resources – for example, income, land, finances, jobs, education, and housing. An economy does not operate on the basis of a collection of iron laws which cannot be altered and changed. The type of economy a society embraces, and subsequently the level of poverty it is willing to endure, must claim a central place in any discussion of strategies to eliminate poverty in South Africa. While economics is only one facet of the problem of poverty in society, poverty cannot be eradicated without addressing the dynamics of a modern economy.

Understanding how a modern economy functions must include examining such issues as unemployment, ownership, wages, prices, and government policies. To understand the relationships between poverty and economics, however, the scope of economics must be broadened. For example, gender dynamics play a critical role in allowing a modern economy to operate.

Women are largely responsible for performing a vast amount of unpaid labour – childcare, household work, informal services, and caring for the sick and elderly – without which the economy could not function. In addition, women are frequently denied access to financial resources, they are often limited to low-paying and insecure jobs, they face much higher rates of unemployment, and they carry a disproportionate burden of the costs of sustaining a family. These gender relationships structure modern capitalist economies and, because of their position within the economy, women and female-headed households face a substantially higher risk of poverty.

Part of the definition above equates poverty with a certain level of material deprivation, below which an individual suffers physically, emotionally, and socially. Therefore, poverty is often narrowly defined and measured in terms of a broad threshold of income or resources which separates the poor from the non-poor. But there are two ways of seeing this threshold - as a fixed point of reference or as measured against the ability of others to command resources in the economy. The first approach can be called an *absolute definition of poverty* and the second approach can be called a *relative definition of poverty.*

Absolute Poverty

The absolute approach to poverty can be helpful if poverty is to relate to a basic, fixed level of economic resources which will prevent physical and social suffering due to material deprivation. If incomes or economic resources were to fall below this level (often called the "poverty line"), then that person would be considered to be poor in absolute terms. For example, individuals must have access to enough food to prevent malnutrition, to clean water, to a durable form of shelter, to simple clothing, and to basic educational and health services. The resources necessary to ensure the provision of these basic needs would then form the threshold for determining the absolute level of poverty in an economy.

When poverty is seen in absolute terms, then steadily increasing standards of living across an entire population will be sufficient to eventually eliminate poverty. The rate at which poverty is eradicated would be determined by the rate at which the incomes of those people living in poverty, including social security provisions, increase. Often, general increases in standards of living are linked to the level of economic growth. Therefore, it is often argued that steady levels of economic growth will be sufficient to eventually eliminate poverty.

Relative Poverty

Using a relative understanding of poverty instead of an absolute definition provides a much more textured and complex engagement with the issue of economic deprivation in society. A relative approach would identify poor households as those whose incomes (or more broadly, the economic resources they command) fall significantly below the *average* level of income in the economy. Relative poverty captures a sense of "economic distance" and injustice in society. Relative definitions of poverty begin to take on board issues of social cleavages and economic distinctions between different groups. This definition of poverty will change with economic growth and reflects the shifting norms of society with respect to basic needs as an economy develops. Unlike the case of absolute poverty, rising standards of living will not be sufficient to eliminate relative poverty if the resources available to the wealthy increase at a faster rate than the resources available to the poor. Increases in relative poverty are not necessarily less onerous than increases in absolute poverty - they can lead to social disintegration, growing violence, segmentation, emotional suffering, and ethnic and racial conflict.

In South Africa, high levels of both absolute and relative poverty exist. The disastrously unequal distribution of income inherited from the apartheid years means that deprivation of basic needs is accompanied by a vast economic gulf between the rich and the poor. Although the World Bank classifies South Africa as an "upper-middle income" country because of its *per capita* gross domestic product (GDP), the average income level of South Africa hides more than it reveals. The unequal distribution of income - one of the worst in the world - has created a huge pool of poverty which surrounds a small island of wealth. South Africa is poor, not because it is a "poor country," but because the economic distance between the haves and the have-nots is enormous.

Poverty and Growth

This is not to deny the role of economic growth in raising living standards, but growth is clearly not enough. The existence of staggering income inequalities in South Africa makes the concept of relative poverty as important as absolute poverty in analysing the economics of poverty. An absolute scarcity of resources is not the primary issue, as many mainstream approaches to economics would vehemently argue. Rather a socially constructed scarcity due to a skewed distribution of assets and incomes is at the heart of the problem. In this context, counting on economic growth alone to reverse the legacy of deprivation is not sufficient.

An economic analysis of poverty must explicitly incorporate a theory of economic distribution in order to explain the situation in South Africa and to develop strategies for the eradication of poverty. Before turning to an analysis of the causes of the problem and the manner in which economic resources are distributed in South Africa, it is important to document the evidence as to the extent of absolute and relative poverty in the country.

THE EXTENT OF POVERTY IN SOUTH AFRICA

The following sections describes, from the available data, the extent of both absolute and relative poverty in South Africa. In keeping with the emphasis of this paper, the focus is mainly on the economic indicators of poverty as opposed to other manifestations of compromised human development, for example infant mortality; illiteracy; lack of access to infrastructure, water, education, and health care; and inadequate housing. The following economic measurements of poverty are also largely limited to measurements of income distribution due to the data available. Other economic factors– e.g. the extent of inequality in the ownership of assets or a detailed account of different household economic relationships– are not reflected in these statistics. Nevertheless, they can serve as a general indication of the extent of the problem in South Africa.

Absolute Poverty - South African Statistics

Table 1: Poverty head count and ratio per province

Province	*Number of poor household*	*% household living in poverty*	*Number of poor individuals*	*% individuals living in poverty*
Western Cape	125 208	14.1%	635 557	17.9%
Northern Cape	51 466	38.2%	267 992	48.0%
Eastern Cape	710 257	56.8%	4 115 332	64.0%
KwaZulu Natal	626 889	40.4%	4 216 184	50.0%
Free State	263 112	36.1%	1 331 649	47.1%
Mpumalanga	208 419	33.8%	1 275 517	45.1%
Northern Province	608 528	61.9%	3 565 492	69.3%
North West	232 947	29.7%	1 248 724	41.3%
Gauteng	299 821	15.4%	1 443 204	21.1%
Total	**3 126 647**	**35.2%**	**18 099 651**	**45.7**

(Source: HSRC, 1995: A Profile of poverty, inequality and human development in South Africa). See footnote 7 for an explanation of the poverty line used.

Poverty rates in South Africa - meant to measure the extent of absolute poverty - are extremely high and tend to increasein rural regions, in provinces containing one of the former homelands, and in areas whose economies have been underdeveloped by apartheid-era policies. In most provinces the level of poverty is shockingly high, with poverty rates for individuals near or exceeding 50 percent. Table 1 gives the estimated poverty rates by province in South Africa.

Poverty rates also are much lower for whites than for other historical racial groupings in South Africa. Table 2 illustrates these stark differences. The degree in which poverty is concentrated in South Africa is astounding - of all poor individuals, 95 percent are African.

Table 2: Poverty Rates in South Africa

	Proportion of Households Living in Poverty	*Proportion of Individuals Living in Poverty*
African	47.2%	57.2%
Asian	6.2%	6.8%
Coloured	18.5%	19.8%
White	2.1%	2.1%
Total	35.2%	45.7%

(Source: HSRC, 1995: A Profile of poverty, inequality and human development in South Africa). See footnote 7 for an explanation of the poverty line used.

Relative Poverty and Income Distribution – South African Statistics

Measurements of relative poverty can be more complex that those which try to gauge absolute poverty because relative poverty refers to the extent of economic distance or inequalities in society. One indication of income distribution is the Gini coefficient. The Gini coefficient is simply a number between 0 and 1 which indicates the level of income inequality within a population. A value of 0 indicates perfect equality (everyone has the same income). A value of 1 indicates perfect inequality (one person or household has all the income). As the Gini coefficient becomes larger and closer to 1, the extent of inequality increases. Table 3 below shows the Gini coefficients for different countries whose economies are roughly at the same level of development as South Africa. From the comparison in the table, and even when compared to 64 countries around the world, South Africa has one of the most unequal distributions of income of any country world-wide - only Brazil and Guatemala are worse.

Table 3: Gini Coefficients and Income Inequality

Country	Gini Coefficient
Slovak Republic	0,195
Czech Republic	0,266
Hungary	0,270
Poland	0,272
Estonia	0,395
Peru	0,449
Thailand	0,462
Malaysia	0,484
Russian Federation	0,496
Mexico	0,503
Venezuela	0,538
Chile	0,565
SOUTH AFRICA	0,584
Brazil	0,634

(Source: World Development Report, World Bank, 1996).

Gini coefficients do not have to be calculated for an entire country. They can also be constructed for different populations within a particular country. Table 4 below shows the estimated Gini coefficients for different population groups within South Africa. Within all population groups there is a high degree of inequality. Interestingly, the overall Gini coefficient of 0.59 is greater than the Gini coefficients within each of the historical racial classifications. This means that inequalities are more pronounced across these groupings than within each category. Note that the variation in income across male-headed households is much greater than across female headed households. This most likely reflects a uniform level of poverty among female headed households and high levels of inequality among male headed households.

Table 4. Gini coefficients of different types of South African households

Type of household	Gini coefficient
All households	0,59
Race of head of household:	
African	0,52
Coloured	0,50
Indian	0,44
White	0,49
Gender of head of household:	
Male	0,75
Female	0,55
Type of area:	
Urban	0,57
Non-urban	0,55

Source: CSS(1997). Income and Expenditure Survey 1995.

The unequal distribution of income in South Africa occurs across many dimensions - including geography, gender, and race. Figure 5 below shows the average household income by province and historical racial classification. It is useful to note the following:

- Among African-headed households, the average annual household income is R23 000.
- Among coloured-headed households, it is R32 000.
- Among Indian-headed households, it is R71 000.
- Among white-headed households, it is R103 000, 4.5 times the average for African families.
- Average annual household income varies depending on whether the household is in an urban or a non-urban

area. Households living in urban areas have more than double the average annual income (R55 000) of those living in non-urban areas (R23 000).

- Average annual household income also varies according to type of dwelling, with those living in informal (R15 000) and traditional dwellings (R14 000) having a far lower average annual income than those living in formal houses (R52 000).

Table 5. Average Household Income. Thousands of Rand.

Province	Average annual household income				
	African R 000	Coloured R 000	Indian R 000	White R 000	Total R 000
Eastern Cape	17	24	58	90	24
Free State	14	16	*	72	25
Mpumalanga	20	30	78	82	30
North West	21	25	*	93	30
Northern	26	43	*	140	31
Province	13	18	34	79	31
Northern	24	41	61	98	37
Cape	22	33	54	98	53
KwaZulu-	37	53	111	118	71
Natal					
Western Cape					
Gauteng					

* Number of households in the survey was too small for this analysis.

Source: CSS (1997). *Income and Expenditure Survey 1995*

Another way of looking at income distribution is to examine income quintiles for different segments of the population.What is an income quintile? Suppose all the households in South Africa were put in order according to their incomes - from lowest to highest. Then suppose this list of households were divided into five equal parts. The one-fifth containing the lowest incomes (the lowest 20 percent) would be called the bottom quintile. The next portion (the second quintile) would consist of the next highest 20 percent of incomes. The top one-fifth would contain the highest incomes and is often called the top quintile. Table 6 contains estimated income quintiles for South Africa by gender, historical racial classification, and urban geography by household. Note that, because of the small number of households contained in the sample, data on Asian households are not reported. If incomes were equally distributed across the population, then we would expect each quintile category to contain 20 percent of a particular population segment. 37 percent of African, non-urban, female-headed households, however, fall into the poorest quintile while less than 1 percent of white, urban, male-headed households fall into the same category. Female headed households are much more likely to be low-income households than are male-headed households, and non-urban households are more likely to fall into a lower income quintile than are urban households.

The relationship between gender and income inequalities must be stressed. Gender dynamics cannot be brushed aside when examining issues of relative poverty in society. The following statistics describe the extent of economic gender inequalities in South Africa:

- Irrespective of race, 26% of female-headed households are in the bottom income quintile, as compared to 13% of male-headed households.
- On the other hand, 27% of male-headed households are in the top income quintile, compared with 11% of female-headed households.
- Three in every ten (31%) African, female-headed, and one in every five (19%) African, male-headed households, are in the bottom income category. On the other hand fewer than one in every hundred (less than 0,5%) white, male-headed households, are in the bottom income category.
- At the upper end of the scale, almost three-quarters (73%) of white, male-headed households are in the top income category, as against approximately one in eighteen (6%) African, female-headed households.

Table 6. Income distribution by race and gender in urban and non-urban areas by household

Income quintile (20% each) by race	Non-urban female headed	Non-urban male headed	Urban female headed	Urban male headed	Total
	%*	%*	%*	%*	%*
African:	3	7	11	19	10
Top quintile:	12	15	24	29	19
Quintile 1	18	25	25	27	24
Quintile 2	28	28	21	17	24
Quintile 3	37	26	19	8	23
Quintile 4	**100**	**100**	**100**	**100**	**100**
Bottom quintile:					
Quintile 5					
Total					
Coloured:	6	3	12	24	17
Top quintile:	14	13	26	35	29
Quintile 1	21	25	28	23	25
Quintile 2	28	39	19	13	18
Quintile 3	31	20	15	5	11
Quintile 4	**100**	**100**	**100**	**100**	**100**
Bottom quintile:					
Quintile 5					
Total					
White:	52	75	38	73	65
Top quintile:	31	18	32	19	22
Quintile 1	7	4	17	6	8
Quintile 2	8	2	8	2	4
Quintile 3	2	1	5	0	1
Quintile 4	**100**	**100**	**100**	**100**	**100**
Bottom quintile:					
Quintile 5					
Total					

Due to rounding, figures may not always add up to exactly 100%

Source: CSS (1997) *Income and Expenditure Survey 1995.*

Summary

In summary, it is clear that South Africa suffers from high levels of both absolute and relative poverty. The likelihood of being poor is much greater for women, non-urban households, individuals living in rural provinces, and African families. The high level of poverty is linked to a vastly unequal access to economic resources, making it impossible to speak of eliminating poverty without examining how the economic flows which sustain households are determined. It is to this issue that we now turn.

III. THE ECONOMY AND SOCIO-ECONOMIC RIGHTS

In the Bill of Rights of the South African constitution, a number of socio-economic rights are guaranteed including:

- a right to adequate housing
- a right to health care services
- a right to sufficient food and water
- a right to social security
- a right to basic and on-going education

All of these rights have important economic dimensions. For this reason, the constitution limits the obligation of the state to deliver these rights *within its available resources*. The amount of resources which is available, however, is determined by government's macroeconomic policy, its budget priorities, and the structures of the South African economy. The state is under no obligation in the constitution to ensure that adequate resources will be forth-coming to implement and sustain these socio-economic rights.

Many of the rights put forward in the constitution reflect specific areas of basic needs or delivery of particular goods and services. The right to social security, however, could be interpreted very broadly to include jobs, public support, and access to productive assets. This begs the more general question of what rights a person should have within the functioning of the economy. Determining what should constitute an "economic bill of rights" is a critical area of engagement and potentially extremely threatening to the *status quo*. Furthermore, the links between economics and poverty become much clearer when a list of such rights is suggested. An example of a possible core set of economic rights – interpreted generally as the rights an individual should have with respect to the functioning of an economic system – could be the following. This suggested list would necessarily complement the areas of basic need contained within the Constitution (housing, health care, food, water, and education) in order to ensure that poverty, including its non-income aspects, is broadly addressed.

- a right to a basic income and access to a minimal level of economic resources
- a right to participate in the productive and reproductive work of society
- a right to non-discrimination – on the basis of gender, race, sex, pregnancy, marital status, ethnic or social origin, colour, sexual orientation, age, disability, religion, conscience, belief, culture, language and birth – in the distribution of income, productive output, and economic resources
- a right to non-exploitation in all work – in the labour market, in the household, and in the informal economy
- a right to a just share of the production of the economy
- a right to an equitable distribution of the powers and privileges associated with the ownership of productive assets

The realisation of these rights would require a fundamental transformation of the current South African economy. Nevertheless, the above collection of rights could form the basis for beginning to formulate a vision for economic justice and the eradication of poverty.

ECONOMICS RIGHTS AND CURRENT POLICIES IN SOUTH AFRICA

Having outlined a possible collection of socio-economic rights linked to the functioning of an economy, it would be useful to turn to the current policy situation in South Africa and to evaluate these policies in terms of how and to what extent they make allowance for achieving these rights and address the crisis of poverty in the country. The policy framework of the *Growth, Employment, and Redistribution* strategy, or GEAR, is a relatively compact statement of in which direction the Department of Finance and much of government sees economic policy going. The primary focus of the GEAR document is growth, achieved through greater export-competitiveness, growing foreign investment, and productivity improvements. A number of policy positions make up the GEAR document. Full implementation of this collection of policies, GEAR argues, will grow the South African economy, create jobs, and redistribute incomes.

The GEAR Policies

GEAR stresses the need to adopt economic policies which will encourage investment in the economy and allow South Africa to compete in the global marketplace. Some of the primary components of the GEAR strategy are as follows.

Deficit Reduction – When government spending is greater than government revenues, the shortfall must be borrowed. The amount which must be borrowed is called the budget deficit. GEAR argues that the deficit must be reduced in South Africa in order to improve business confidence and encourage investment. GEAR also argues that taxes should not be increased as a fraction of the total economy. This means that in order to reduce the deficit, government spending, as a percent of the total economy, must decline. Total government spending, therefore, can only increase if the size of the economy grows.

Tight Monetary Policy – Tight monetary policy means that GEAR supports high interest rates to keep inflation low, maintain the value of the rand, and discourage increases in credit availability. GEAR argues that financial stability achieved through restrictive monetary policy will encourage domestic and foreign investment.

Trade Liberalisation – Trade liberalisation, or free trade, refers to the gradual elimination of any restrictions on foreign trade. This means that tariffs, which are taxes on goods coming into South Africa, should be eliminated. GEAR argues that removing tariffs will keep prices low (i.e. reduce inflation) and allow South Africa to integrate into the world economy.

Remove Exchange Controls – Exchange controls are laws which limit the ability of people to take money in and out of South Africa. GEAR states that exchange controls must be gradually eliminated in order to attract foreign investment into the country.

Regulated Flexibility of Labour Markets – According to the macroeconomic strategy, labour markets should have some degree of regulation. In particular, collective bargaining should maintained as a method of negotiating labour market outcomes. Substantial flexibility, however, should be introduced. This could mean downward variations in employment standards, less protection for youth and other groups facing high unemployment, and moderation of wages.

Productivity Improvements – In order to compete internationally, GEAR argues that productivity – that is, the amount produced by each worker – must increase. In order to ensure that productivity improvements mean lower costs of production, the macroeconomic strategy also argues that wages should not increase faster than productivity.

Education and Training – GEAR argues for substantial improvements in the education and training of the workforce. These improvements will help increase productivity and attract investment.

If these policies are put into place, GEAR predicts that economic growth will improve dramatically. Once high levels of growth are achieved, poverty will be addressed through redistributive developments. The most important of these developments is supposed to be job creation, brought about through an acceleration in the growth of the economy. The logic of GEAR is straight-forward: as unemployment drops, poverty will gradually disappear. In addition, economic growth, once it happens, will also generate additional public resources which can then be used to provide public services and poverty relief. The document claims that reducing government spending in order to bring down the deficit will actually pave the way for increased spending in the future, made possible by rapid economic growth.

Evaluating GEAR

GEAR should be evaluate in terms of both its promised effects – job creation and growth – and the ability to provide socio-economic rights to the people living in South Africa.

GEAR's primary aim, to promote higher levels of growth in South Africa, might not be achieved given the policies outlined above. Cutbacks in government spending and high interest rates tend to slow down, not speed up, economic growth. Trade liberalisation could mean that cheap imports would quickly replace domestically produced goods. And the removal of exchange controls could lead to the movement of money out of South Africa in search of higher rates of return abroad.

Furthermore, job creation has not been forthcoming with the adoption of GEAR. In fact, job losses have been the recent phenomenon accompanying slower rates of economic growth. This should not be surprising. Government spending reductions mean that the public sector cannot support the current level of employment. Free trade has meant job losses in sensitive industries such as clothing and textiles. Productivity has improved among workers but the reward has not been economic growth. Rather more efficient employees have made themselves redundant; productivity improvements mean that it takes fewer workers to produce the same output than in the past.

GEAR and Socio-Economic Rights

GEAR can also be evaluated with respect to the provisions made in the Bill of Rights. The deficit reduction plans mean that, without strong economic growth, government resources will be constrained. Fewer available resources, in turn, means that the ability to ensure adequate housing, affordable food, clean water, accessible health care, and quality education will be compromised. In addition, the fiscal austerity measures (i.e. cutbacks in spending) proposed by GEAR has meant that pensions to the elderly have increased at a rate slower than inflation and it has meant that the process of restructuring the family maintenance grants demanded that the size of the grants had to be restricted to a level which provides only marginal poverty relief for children.

One of the reasons for these reductions in spending is to reduce the size of the national debt. A large portion of this debt was built-up during the final years of the apartheid regime and is therefore frequently called the "apartheid debt." The interest payments on this debt account for over one fifth of the combined national and provincial budgets – an amount roughly equal to the combined education budgets. These high interest payments divert public resources away from the socio-economic rights outlined in the Bill of Rights. GEAR has responded, not by restructuring the debt or taxing the beneficiaries of apartheid, but by cutting government spending.

The GEAR policy framework – through its negative impacts on jobs, its cutbacks to government spending, and its curtailing the availability of economic resources – means that social security, broadly defined to include jobs, public support, and access to productive assets, will be reduced. This reduction in the ability to participate in the South African economy and to share in the country's resources will only exacerbate the problems of relative and absolute poverty.

What is Missing

What is most alarming about the current framework is the number of economic issues which the document completely ignores. For example, asset redistribution is hardly mentioned, except for a brief statement calling for land reform. The document's preference for a more restrictive monetary policy means that interest rates would remain high, access to credit and productive capital would be limited, and financing land redistribution and housing development could be prohibitively expensive.

The informal sector is also largely ignored within the policy framework, naturalising the vision of the sector as a residual economy. The failure of the GEAR strategy to create jobs will probably place pressures on the living standards of the informally employed as more people crowd into the informal sector.

Gender and GEAR

In addition, gender issues and household dynamics are almost completely invisible within the current macroeconomic strategy, contributing to the on-going marginalisation of women. While GEAR might be called "gender blind," it is certainly not "gender neutral." For example, GEAR calls for greater labour market flexibility in order to attract foreign investment and to improve competitiveness. The implications of this are that the most vulnerable workers (that is, women) will remain unprotected and discriminated against, and that where jobs are created they will perpetuate the poor working conditions experienced by many women workers. With greater labour market flexibility the position of women will actually worsen, since this implies decreased benefits (such as maternity benefits) and less flexibility with regard to working time and parental responsibilities.

The reduction in government spending means that women will continue to perform large amounts of unpaid labour to substitute for the lack of adequate social services. These responsibilities will continue to limit women's access to alternative economic opportunities. Furthermore, high interest rates will squeeze household resources as payments for bonds on houses and other debts increase. Household resources could be further reduced by the loss of jobs and pressures for wage moderation while prices for necessities such as food continue to increase. Because of their position in the household, women might cut their own consumption or increase their work load in order to compensate for dwindling resources. In many respects, GEAR entrenches the economic oppression women face and increases their risk of poverty.

ECONOMICS AND THE CAUSES OF POVERTY

In order to develop strategies and a vision of how the economic system of South Africa can be transformed so as to eradicate poverty, a theory of how the current economy produces and replicates poverty must be developed. Such an understanding must look more broadly at the distribution of human and material resources – in the workplace, in the household, and in the context of an accumulation of assets and wealth.

The importance of economic theory should not be slighted. In the fight to eliminate poverty, the understanding of the relationship between economics and poverty remains vehemently contested. Orthodox economics – often called mainstream or neo-classical economics – is the dominant theory of economics in western industrialised countries, most notably Britain and the United States. Orthodox economics connects poverty to productivity, economic growth, prices, and individual choice. Such an approach embraces the *status quo* in terms of institutions, patterns of ownership, gender dynamics, and productive relationships. This acceptance of the *status quo,* in terms of the environment in which people make choices, risks entrenching and reproducing conditions of poverty.

The following section briefly outlines – in a somewhat stylised manner – the primary features of the orthodox argument and then proceeds to put forward an alternative framework for beginning to link economics and poverty. Since economic policy often arises from a particular set of theoretical assumptions, different analytical frameworks will produce different understandings of the strategies which will move towards eliminating poverty.

The Orthodox Approach to Poverty

The orthodox theory of income distribution links income received to the productivity of different "factors of production" – these include, labour, land, capital equipment, and human capacities. Therefore, the wages workers receive is a reflection of the productivity of the workers themselves. The profits earned by capitalist firms, farms, and enterprises would be simply a reflection of the assumed productivity of the capital or land used in production. Differences in salaries and wages among workers would reflect a difference in the talents and abilities of the employees – again, income is linked to productivity. Therefore, this theoretical approach would argue that if an individual receives an extremely low income, it is because that person does not produce enough.

Poverty, in the orthodox framework, is tied to low productivity – in an economy, among a group of workers, or within an informal subsistence sector. In order to eliminate poverty and achieve higher standards of living, productivity must improve. The improvements in productivity will spur economic growth and, in turn, economic growth will produce the resources necessary to reduce the level of poverty. Education and training play an important role in this framework. Training will increase the stock of "human capital" – that is, the skills and experience of the workforce, expand the capabilities of workers, and heighten productivity. Higher levels of productivity will subsequently be rewarded with higher levels of income.

The Assumption of Free Choice

Orthodox economic theory emphasises the central role of individual choice and responsibility. For example, the amount that an individual works is described as a free choice between the trade-off of additional income (from working) and enjoying leisure time. Gender dynamics take on an unusual interpretation within this framework. According to this approach, women perform labour in the household because they freely choose to do so. Since women earn less in the formal economy then men, then it is only rational that women should specialise in reproductive work. Why do women earn less then men in the formal economy? The disruptions of raising children and other reproductive duties mean that women are not able to accumulate skills as consistently as men, their productivity suffers, and they are therefore paid a lower wage. Discrimination, women's oppression, and gender dynamics have no place in an orthodox world.

In general, orthodox economics tends to assume a particular distribution of assets, a particular set of power relations, a fixed collection of cultural factors, a given set of institutions, and a specific productive logic in its analysis. All these factors can be called *structural factors* because they cannot be changed through an individual's choices or behaviour. Within this framework, individual choices and capabilities then determine the distribution of income. Poverty is simply an outcome of low productivity, slow economic growth, and lack of education and training. From this analysis, the road to a poverty-free world is clear: improve productivity, boost economic growth, and put in place a training programme. In due time, the mainstream approach promises, poverty will disappear.

GEAR and the Orthodox Approach

The current macroeconomic strategy being followed in South Africa sounds remarkably like an orthodox analysis of the problems of poverty in the country. The medicine proposed by GEAR – economic growth, productivity improvements, and education and training as solutions to wide-spread poverty – falls out very neatly from the conservative approach to economics. The GEAR strategy, as discussed in the previous section, will most likely only entrench, and quite probably increase, the level of poverty in South Africa. Therefore, an alternative approach to economics and poverty is needed.

An Alternative Economic Framework

In order to incorporate many of the factors excluded from, or de-emphasised within, the orthodox approach, an alternative framework for understanding the distribution of economic resources in an economy must be developed. In the analysis suggested below, the flows of economic resources necessary to sustain an individual or a household come from numerous sources and, unlike the orthodox obsession with productivity, are rooted in a particular distribution of assets, productive relationships, gender dynamics, and class distinctions. The economic aspects of poverty are then linked to the inability to command a sufficient flow of resources to avoid growing inequalities and to prevent deprivation – be it nutritional, medical, in terms of shelter, or a lack of full participation in society.

The diagram below is a simple presentation of the different sources of economic flows – primarily, but not exclusively, income flows – to individuals and households. There are five broad categories of economic flows reflecting different economic positions in an economy. These include income derived from owning property, income received in terms of salaries and wages, economic resources mobilised through subsistence and household activities, transfer payments received from private or government sources, and self-employment. Each of these categories is intimately connected to a set of economic relationships which define and structure a modern capitalist economy. Exclusion from, or marginalisation within, these sources of economic resource flows greatly increases the risk of poverty. A brief discussion of each category follows.

INCOME FROM PROPERTY AND ASSET OWNERSHIP

The highly concentrated ownership of property – land, capital, financial holdings, and real estate – inherited from the apartheid era are a primary source of inequality, of both income and wealth, in the country. The skewed ownership of property is clearly one key economic factor in the causes of poverty in South Africa. Not only does the distribution of assets deny the majority of the population access to economic resources, it also facilitates the exploitation of the majority by perpetuating grossly unequal economic power relationships.

Income from property can be divided into three different types – profits, rents, and interest. Profits are the result of productive economic activities in which wage labour is hired to produce commodities, and then those commodities are sold in the marketplace for a price greater than the costs of production. The proceeds from their sale – called sales revenue – are used to pay workers their wages. What is left over after the costs of producing the goods and services is deducted are the profits. In a capitalist economy, the profits belong to the owners of capital and account for an important source of income in an economy.

Rents refer to any income generated, not because an asset is productive, but because it is scarce. The scarcity of the asset – for example, housing in South Africa – allows it to generate an income without producing any additional goods and services. Interest is somewhat similar to a rent – it reflects income earned due to command of a scarce commodity, in this case credit and financial assets. Like rents, interest can be earned without producing additional goods and services.

Property, Income, and Inequality

Orthodox economics would argue that profits, rents, and interest are earned because of the inherent productivity of the assets in question. An alternative explanation would point to the ability of property owners to stake a claim on the income produced in an economy simply because property confers on its owner a high degree of economic power. Such ownership allows an industrialist to stake a claim on output produced by wage labour in the form of profits. Or it allows a landowner to demand rents from the landless. Or it allows a bank to demand interest from those without access to money.

This economic power is derived from a socially constructed scarcity which follows from a highly concentrated asset ownership – in other words, assets are scarce in South Africa precisely because so very few people own so much. If people had access to capital, they would not need to sell their labour in order to generate profits for someone else; if people had access to housing, they would not have to pay rents for shelter; and if people had access to abundant credit, the ability to charge high rates of interest would be compromised.

An unequal asset distribution is an important determinant of the economic attributes of poverty not only because it denies the poor access to factors of production (e.g. land and capital) but also because it allows a distribution of income away from lower income households to other individuals and institutions. For example, lowering wages so as to generate an "adequate" rate of profitability is a redistribution of income which will increase inequalities. Rents can often take the form of payments from poorer segments of society to those who are wealthier because of a lack of access to basic needs. And higher interest rates transfer income away from borrowers, who tend to be low and middle-income households, to lenders. This transfer of income away from households can place pressures on household resources and women often compensate by diminishing their own consumption or increasing their workload. Clearly an analysis of asset distribution must form part of a broader analysis of poverty and policies of *asset redistribution* must be entertained as a core element of a strategy to eliminate poverty.

INCOME FROM WAGES AND SALARIES

With a grossly unequal access to productive and financial assets, wage employment has become a primary source of potential income or many households in South Africa. In a capitalist economy, when people do not own productive assets, they are often forced to sell the one commodity which they do own – their labour power – in order to generate an income to sustain themselves. The ability to sell one's labour, however, is not guaranteed, nor are the conditions under which labour is exchanged always secure. Often an economy is characterised by unemployment, underemployment, and low wages, all of which can contribute to the persistence of poverty. Before moving to a broader discussion of employment, wages, and unemployment, it is helpful to document, insofar as the available data permit, the employment situation in South Africa.

Employment and Unemployment in South Africa

Employment in South Africa is at its lowest point in 16 years. Employment trends in different sectors of the formal economy from June 1996 to June 1997 show that all sectors have lost jobs, with the exception of wholesale/retail trade and financial services. Despite positive levels of growth, 62 000 jobs were lost in the formal, non-agricultural sectors in the first six months of 1997, flying in the face of the targets set out in the government's macroeconomic framework. Historical trends in job destruction from 1990 to 1996 indicate significant losses, with the manufacturing sector suffering a 9,1% loss in jobs, construction 21,3% and mining 27,5%. Due to the recently announced budget cuts, the public services will face job losses in the near future, despite a record of job creation in the past.

Overall, astronomically high unemployment rates prevail, with total unemployment being at 29,3%. Table 7 shows the estimated unemployment rates across gender and geographical categories. Women, people in rural areas, historically disadvantaged groups and youth are particularly hard hit. For example, the unemployment rate among African women is over 50 percent - over half the African women who want to work cannot find jobs. Furthermore, the majority of unemployed people have never worked (69,2%) – creating an "unemployment trap" for a large number of long-term unemployed individuals.

Table 7. Unemployment Rates

	Male	**Female**	**TOTAL**
Urban	19.9	30.8	24.5
Rural	27.3	49.5	37.6
TOTAL	22.5	38.0	29.3

Source: *1995 October Household Survey.* CSS. November 1996

According to the RDP, 53% of the poorest are unemployed. While unemployment is an important aspect of poverty, low wages also play a role. Quite a significant number of people fall within the category of the working poor. The 1994 October

Household Survey reported that one in seven employed or self-employed earn R 500 or less per month.

Labour Market Segmentation

Not only does South Africa have extremely high levels of unemployment, but the jobs which exist are often highly segmented – yet another legacy of the apartheid years. Highly paid professional and managerial positions largely remain the domain of white men. Within this segment of the labour market (often called the primary labour market), unemployment is low and job security is high. Production workers and service employees (often called the secondary labour market), on the other hand, face higher levels of unemployment and far less job security. Wages are lower and benefits are minimal or non-existent. Workers in the informal sector constitute yet another segment of the labour market. Many of these people face greater risks, very unsteady employment, and little legal protection or regulation of employment conditions.

Labour market segments are divided by race and gender. For example, a disproportionate number of women work within the lower paid, less secure labour market segments. A gender division of labour is clearly reflected in the South African economy in which women's work is often under-valued. Perhaps the best example of this under-valuation is domestic work in which women (mostly African) perform household wage labour for relatively wealthy families which would be unpaid labour in lower income households. Likewise, workers from historically disadvantaged groups are often locked into low-paying, unstable jobs and face a much higher likelihood of being unemployed.

Movement between these labour market segments (primary, secondary, and informal) is difficult, if not impossible, in many cases. Workers become trapped in various labour market enclaves with very different access to employment opportunities. Such segmentation and division within the South African labour markets means that these workers in more vulnerable jobs will face heightened risks of poverty.

Causes of Unemployment

The unemployment crisis in South Africa has many causes that underscore the need for an active, interventionist, and comprehensive strategy to address the problem. The problem of unemployment in South Africa is structural – that is, it is characterised by the evolution of the apartheid economy over time and recent policy developments. Some of the key causes of the current high levels of unemployment include:

- The history of apartheid capitalism which depended on a racially marginalised and exploited workforce to secure profits.
- The development of extremely capital intensive production processes in a country with abundant labour resources.
- The dramatic decrease in investment in South Africa in the 1980s and 1990s.
- The decline and labour-shedding practices of important primary industries – agriculture and mining.
- Falling levels of employment in the parastatals during the later years of apartheid.
- The systematic under-development of skills for the vast majority of the labour force.
- The tendency to export low value-added goods using capital intensive technologies and to import high value-added goods.
- The promotion of vast income inequalities which constrained domestic demand and the expansion of productive investments.
- The recent rapid trade liberalisation and reductions in tariffs.
- The marginal economic development of the former homelands and the townships.
- A relatively contractionary monetary environment and the development of a financial sector with uneven

industrial and developmental linkages, as mentioned in the section which discusses GEAR.

Deteriorating Conditions and Underemployment

The growth in the levels of structural unemployment in many countries internationally over the past several decades has raised an important question concerning the nature of employment and jobs. Do modern capitalist economies destroy jobs? The answer to this question is not straight-forward and critically depends on what constitutes a job. Not all jobs are equivalent. For example, in Great Britain, the country with the lowest unemployment rate in the European Union, only a third of the population capable of work is still employed in a classical "good job" - a full-time position with guaranteed long-term benefits. Two decades ago, the same figure was 80 percent. Furthermore, despite Germany's higher level of unemployment than that of the U.S., new, well-paid, and secure jobs are created at the same rate - the OECD estimates 2,3 percent - in both countries.

In countries such as Great Britain and the United States - heralded as models of flexible labour markets and low unemployment - job creation has been achieved by changing the nature of jobs and work. Unemployment is merely disguised and hidden by an erosion of well-paid, secure, meaningful work. One lesson becomes clear - employment flexibility has little impact on the creation of these secure, well-paying jobs. Furthermore, such labour market flexibility has been shown to increase inequalities in many countries. The new dynamics of the global economy has created jobs, but often too few jobs with the result that unemployment rates have been climbing. In those countries which have maintained a low unemployment rate, good jobs have been destroyed and replaced by more marginal forms of work.

A useful concept to extend the discussion of recent international employment trends would be to introduce the concept of underemployment or sub-employment. Underemployment would refer to a situation in which the conditions of employment associated with a job have eroded substantially due to the mechanics of modern capitalist economies.

Underemployment does not just mean accepting part-time work when full-time work is more desirable. It would also refer to all forms of casual, atypical, and contingent labour. Moreover, if we include the failure to pay a living wage as an aspect of underemployment, the scope of discussing the deterioration of employment expands further. Using this concept of underemployment, the extent of the crisis in South Africa and its contribution to sustaining poverty are profound.

Underemployment and casual employment also have a gender dimension. Women are often used by businesses as a reserve supply of labour. They are frequently the last hired and the first fired, and many women work in part-time, casual or unstable jobs. Such employment is sometimes described as a "revolving door" in which women continuously enter and leave employment in accordance to fluctuating demand for labour in the economy.

Jobs and Poverty

Clearly, the South African economy, over its recent history, has a dismal record of job creation. Furthermore, South Africa is facing an employment crisis at the same time the government is pursuing a strategy of rapid integration into the global economy. The drive to stream-line government and capitalist businesses, to improve productivity, to moderate wages, and to introduce a high degree of market competition could further compromised the ability of the South African economy to create jobs and the ability of those jobs to lead to improvements in standards of living. In an economy with such an unequal distribution of assets, in which a majority of people depend on jobs for the economic resources they need to survive, and in which the labour market is highly segmented by race and gender, such trends will only entrench the historical patterns of poverty and deprivation.

ECONOMIC RESOURCES FROM HOUSEHOLD AND SUBSISTENCE ACTIVITIES

Wage labour is not the only category of labour which is important for the functioning of a modern economy and not the only form of work which has an important impact on the magnitude and manifestation of poverty in an economy. Unpaid labour performed in the household is critical in ensuring the integrity and continuity of an economy. The responsibility for unpaid labour – strongly shaped by gender power dynamics – directly influences an individual's involvement in other economic activities (e.g. formal sector employment) and the risk of poverty that person faces.

Gender and Reproductive Labour

Women perform the largest portion of unpaid labour: household production, childcare, care of the sick and elderly, and subsistence activities. Often such work is called reproductive labour because of its central role in ensuring the continuity of society – from day to day, from year to year, and from generation to generation. In addition, women face discrimination and segmentation in the formal labour market, limiting the amount of income women can earn from such activities. Women face much higher levels of unemployment than do men. Property ownership is concentrated among men, further weakening women's economic position. The lack of economic opportunities and the responsibility for reproductive labour, combined with cultural and historical forces which naturalise gender oppression, mean than women are dependent on an outside source of income, often under the control of a man, to sustain the family.

These dynamics place women, and their children, at high risk for poverty in South Africa. Women not only are responsible for unpaid, reproductive labour. They also often must bear the costs of raising children and delivering caring services. These costs tend to increase over time – e.g. the costs of food, housing, education, clothing, etc. Increasing costs combined with ongoing economic marginalisation can rapidly push women and children into poverty. This is particularly crucial in South Africa, where an estimated 26 percent of households are headed by single women.

Economics and the Invisibility of Gender

These economic and gender dynamics must be incorporated into an analysis of income distribution, command of economic resources, and poverty. The forces which maintain traditional household economic relations also contribute to sustained poverty and gender inequalities.

Orthodox economics and mainstream policy analysis often ignore the role of household and subsistence activities in the functioning of an economy. Economics is seen as the science of formal sector activities – industrial wage labour, trade and exchange, banking, investment, and management. During the history and development of modern economic theories, these occupations were men's occupations, and much of the legacy of economics contains strong gender biases. These biases must be explicitly recognised and an alternative framework for understanding the relationships between economics, gender and poverty must be developed.

TRANSFERS OF INCOME

The income which sustains a family might not come from owning assets or from wage labour. An additional source of income must be considered – transfers of income to a household from another source. There are two broad categories of such transfers which must be considered – private transfers and public transfers. Private transfers refer to income earned by a "bread-winner," by relatives, or by a private institution which are then used to maintain one or more households.

Remittances of income in South Africa are a clear example of a private transfer. Public transfers refer to income grant programmes initiated by the government. They include such programmes as pensions for the elderly and family maintenance grants. The role of both public and private transfers must be incorporated into an understanding of poverty in South Africa.

Private Transfers

Private transfers play a critically important role in the South African economy. Because of the high rates of joblessness and lack of economic opportunities, many families depend on such transfers to survive. The income of one individual could support many others. Such payments form part of a private "safety net" which can be instrumental in preventing the economic desolation of many households and which serves as an informal mechanism of income redistribution – ironically, from low-wage workers to poor households. Private income transfers are subject to the dynamics of households and the economy. Control over these transfers often lies in the hands of men, due to greater labour market opportunities and lower rates of unemployment. This can produce a strong dependency within the household which can potentially be threatening for women. For example, women might be forced to remain in an abusive domestic relationship because they do not have alternative economic opportunities. Furthermore, female-headed households are more likely to be poor because of lack of access to this traditional source of income. Single mothers are often blamed for their own poverty because of their perceived inability to sustain a traditional household relationship.

The dependence on this private safety net also puts a large number of people in a very tenuous position in the face of jobless growth, retrenchments, and a drive for wage moderation. The loss of one job places far more than one person at risk. An entire network of people dependent on private transfers can be devastated by the developments in a modern capitalist economy (e.g. jobless growth, downward pressures on wages, and the erosion of conditions of employment).

Public Transfers

Public income transfers could be an alternative to private transfers of income. South Africa has developed a number of public income transfer programmes which, given the widespread lack of economic opportunities and access to assets, can reduce the negative impacts of an economy which generates widespread poverty. Internationally, similar programmes have come under increasing attack, largely from a drive to reduce the level of government spending and to cut back on the size of budget deficits. Public transfer programmes to the poor seem to be a relatively easy target of such macroeconomic policy initiatives. Public transfers are claimed to produce "perverse incentives" (e.g. women choosing to become single parents or individuals choosing to remain unemployed) which compromise economic performance. The elimination of such support measures are supposed to reclaim values of self-sufficiency and support.

Income Support and Poverty

The connections between public transfers, private transfers, and poverty are important. Cutbacks to public support programmes expand the dependency on private support measures. This can be problematic for a number of reasons. First, private income transfers to help sustain low income families come from the poor themselves. Cutbacks to public transfers can be therefore seen as an extremely regressive tax on the poor to fund poverty alleviation. Second, such cutbacks can intensify gender oppression in the context of few economic opportunities for women. If women are not allowed to choose to live independently, then many women could be forced to remain in exploitative relationships. Finally, without a commitment to a broader programme of economic transformation to eliminate poverty, such cutbacks amount to an abdication of responsibility for the inequalities passed down from apartheid and retrenched by a modern economic system.

INCOME FROM SELF-EMPLOYMENT

Self-employment, in the formal and informal sectors, can also generate flows of economic resources to sustain households. Self-employment, however, does not guarantee that sufficient income will be generated so as to fend off conditions of poverty.

In particular, self-employment in the informal sector can be characterised by low incomes, high levels of insecurity, and a lack of regulation and protection by government policies. Informal self-employment must be examined critically, especially given the emphasis on micro-enterprise development – that is, the development of very small-scale informal production – as a strategy for providing economic opportunities to low income households.

Characteristics of Informal Work

The conditions which the self-employed face are often directly linked to other factors which have already been mentioned – access to assets, unemployment, and household dynamics. Lack of access to productive and financial assets can prevent self-employed individuals from improving their standards of living by expanding their activities. High levels of unemployment can push increasing numbers of people into marginal forms of informal self-employment. Larger numbers of informal sector workers – for example, more and more hawkers – can increase competition within the informal sector and lead to deteriorating standards of living, conflict, and, at times, violence. Finally, household responsibilities could limit women's economic opportunities to low-income forms of informal self-employment.

In South Africa, little is actually known about the informal sector – for instance, incomes earned, conditions of employment, economic relationships, and linkages to the formal and to the household economies. This lack of knowledge makes it difficult to recommend specific policies to address poverty among the self-employed. The very fact that the sector is called informal means that government policies meant to regulate the economy and protect individuals largely do not apply to the informally self-employed. Unless the informal sector is incorporated into specific measures to address poverty, these people can remain invisible. In many respects, the informal economy is seen as a residual segment of the economic system – absorbing people who cannot find economic opportunities in the formal sector.

This is not to say that there are no lucrative opportunities in the informal sector; nevertheless, a large number of informal sector activities, however, remain marginal.

As mentioned above, opportunities for workers in the informal sector are constrained by lack of access to economic resources - for example, finances and land. There is much international evidence showing that lack of access to financial resources severely limits informal sector economic opportunities in small and micro enterprises. For example, the operation of the Grameen Bank in Bangladesh demonstrates that if women working in the informal sector gain access to even very small amounts of financial resources, large gains in economic development and welfare can be achieved.

In South Africa, poorer regions have relatively much larger informal sectors than do wealthier regions. Table 8 summarises the estimated size of the informal sector by province. Provinces such as the Eastern Cape and the Northern Cape have a larger percentage of informal sector employment than do Gauteng and the Western Cape – provinces with a history of strong formal sector economic development.

Women in the Informal Sector

The table also shows that a large number of the informally self-employed are women – 70 percent for South Africa as a whole. Women are concentrated into lower-income and subsistence activities in the informal sector. There is an informal gender division of labour which is parallel to the gender segmentation in the formal sector.

Often, policies which aim to expand economic opportunities focus on micro-enterprises and informal sector economic activities. Such an approach to economic empowerment ignores the fact that most informal sector activities are characterised by low incomes, unstable employment, high risk, long hours, and, as mentioned above, a lack of regulation. Promoting micro-enterprises uncritically can mean the continued marginalisation of many workers, particularly women, within the economy and a failure to address the concrete sources of poverty and dislocation in South Africa.

Table 8. The Informal Sector

	Informal workers as % of employed population	**Informal sector. Self-employed women as % of total self-employed.**
Gauteng	14%	58%
Western Cape	12%	67%
Free State	21%	90%
Northern Cape	14%	88%
Eastern Cape	23%	76%
Northern Province	25%	65%
Mpumalanga	17%	78%
North-West Province	18%	67%
KwaZulu/Natal	18%	67%
SOUTH AFRICA	17%	70%

Source: *1995 October Household Survey*. November 1996

DEVELOPING A WAY FORWARD

If poverty is to be successfully addressed in South Africa, an alternative approach to economics must be developed and appropriate policies implemented. Again, it is important to remember that economics is only one aspect of poverty and, while necessary, economic transformation by itself is not sufficient to overcome the crisis in South Africa. Nevertheless, the workings of the economic system and the economic policies which are adopted have far-reaching consequences. These consequences are not only in terms of income distribution; they also influence how health care is provided, the focus and extent of education, how work and workers are valued, and the role of women in society. Therefore, a programme of economic transformation must occupy a central place in a strategy to end poverty.

The idea of economic *transformation* must be stressed. The operations of the current South African economy, if left alone, will entrench and replicate the conditions of poverty inherited from the apartheid era. While poverty relief programmes can mitigate the negative impacts of these outcomes, they will not eradicate the crisis situation. This is the central problem of the orthodox economic approach to poverty – it takes existing economic structures as given. The current macroeconomic policy direction also adopts this general mindset. Higher rates of growth and productivity improvements are assumed to be necessary and sufficient, more fundamental economic changes are not.

Furthermore, the economics of poverty cannot be reduced to a simple essential formula. A wide range of class, racial, gender, historical, and productive relationships influence the manifestation of poverty in South Africa. In order to develop an economic strategy which moves towards the elimination of poverty, an equally textured approach is required. Therefore, job creation alone cannot eliminate poverty, nor can the development of a public social security system. Transforming gender dynamics can form part of the solution, but does not make up the entire picture. A more comprehensive set of strategies which build on the interactions between these different elements is required.

Areas of Focus

Building from the alternative analysis of poverty offered in this discussion document, several areas of focus emerge as forming a possible foundation on which to move forward. These areas could be summarised as follows:

Asset Redistribution – Highly concentrated asset ownership can contribute to the persistence of poverty through unequal access to income, an unequal distribution of economic power, and the persistence of relationships of dependence. A redistribution of assets – through an effective housing policy, land reform, expansion of credit availability, competition policy, and policies to expand community and worker ownership – can form one element of an attack on poverty. Asset redistribution can be linked to alternative ways of organising production, which emphasise participatory and co-operative management.

Job creation, job enhancement, and full-employment – Lack of access to employment opportunities can severely limit a household's ability to mobilise sufficient economic resources. Developing a comprehensive job creation strategy, which aims at creating new jobs without eroding conditions of employment, is critical and can be explicitly linked to other components of a strategy to eliminate poverty. A comprehensive employment creation strategy must address issues of investment, industrial policies, trade reform, state-asset restructuring, public works programmes, and labour market transformation. The ultimate goal would be full voluntary employment with jobs paying a living wage.

Transforming gender relationships in the economy – There is an urgent need to address the gender structures which place women and children at greater risk of poverty. These include discrimination in the formal sector, labour market segmentation, women's responsibility for reproductive labour, dependency on private transfers of income, and marginalisation in the informal sector. At the core of these issues is women's economic oppression. Transforming these structures requires providing women with access to assets, providing public support for unpaid reproductive labour, changing the gender dynamics of the household, lessening the private burden of the costs of childcare, eliminating labour market segmentation and discrimination, and ensuring that informal sector activities generate an adequate, sustainable flow of economic resources.

Creating a public safety net – The dependency on private transfers of income to support households which have, for whatever reason, been excluded from economic opportunities carry with them a myriad of problems which have been mentioned previously. Furthermore, such dependency places female-headed households at a much grave risk of poverty.

While a system of public transfer programmes will not transform the economic dynamics which produce poverty, they can help to alleviate the negative impacts of poverty and to provide a socialised form of insurance against unforeseen circumstances.

Develop strategies for the informal sector – In order to develop effective policies for the informal sector, much better information needs to be collected about the conditions which employees and the self-employed face. From this information, appropriate policy interventions can be constructed so as to ensure that developments within the informal sector do not entrench poverty in the South African economy.

In developing approaches to these issues it is important that much detailed policy work has already been done in South Africa – in the RDP, by NGOs, by trade unions, and by government departments and committees. In many cases, there is no need to re-invent the wheel. It is rather a question of bringing policies together in a single framework and developing strategies for implementation.

There is a set of interventions which have not received adequate attention in this paper, largely because they will be addressed in the other hearings on poverty. These are the areas of public service provision and meeting basic needs. Public provision of basic goods, services, and infrastructure – for instance, water, housing, electricity, education, and health care – must form part of an alternative approach to economics and poverty. It can be argued that a basic level of these goods and services must be publicly provided in order to address poverty and inequalities in society. Such provision reflects an alternative to the dominant mechanics of a capitalist economy – they would not be produced for sale in a market in order to generate profit, but would be provided as an essential human right.

CONCLUSIONS

This paper has attempted to outline the general linkages between poverty and economics. The extent of poverty, as narrowly measured by a household's or individual's control over economic resources, was documented within the confines of existing data. A framework for thinking about basic socio-economic rights within the function of an economy was suggested. Following this background, how economic theory explains poverty was explored – looking briefly at the orthodox approach and then putting forward a more complex alternative. From this alternative analysis, discussions could begin on how to move the economy, and economic policy in particular, in a direction which effectively address the crisis of poverty in South Africa.

Moreover, the document has attempted to link poverty to how an economic system is structured. The analysis is not based on examining "the poor" and "the non-poor" as distinct social groups; rather the approach is to look at the economy as a system which can produce and entrench poverty – a system in which both "the poor" and "the non-poor" play crucial roles.

This document is meant to fuel discussion and debate. It is not meant to be a complete exposition of all the issues and alternatives raised. Nevertheless, it is hoped the ideas suggested here can help frame the difficult analysis of the interaction between the economy and the perpetuation of poverty.

8

Investments to Eliminate Poverty

Investing in the eradication of poverty in America would increase the resources of each non-low-income American household by an average of more than $18,000 a year, equivalent to a wage increase of more than 30 percent. Middle-income supports – such as Medicare, social security, and income tax breaks – cost the average family about four times as much as do low-income supports such as homeless shelters and food. What makes poverty expensive to the rest of us is not those social supports but rather its large but indirect costs, especially in health care, crime, and lost productivity. Poor people who become more productive members of the economy spend all their income, which multiplies through the economy to become savings and thus capital for the rest of us. The new capital generated by eradicating poverty creates more jobs, which multiply even further through the economy to create more capital which creates still more jobs, and so on throughout the economy.

Eliminating the indirect costs of poverty in the simplest way – directly raising incomes to a low but decent level (60% of current median income) – would return almost four times the investment. In other words, the annual cost of eliminating poverty would be no more than about a quarter of the annual savings for the average non-low-income family (households with more than $60,000 annual income). These calculations are conservative and leave out many benefits of eradicating poverty, such as the savings of increased preventive health care and the productivity lost due to underemployment (employment below skill level). So the payoff from eliminating poverty is actually even larger than four-to-one. Earlier studies done by Oppenheim and MacGregor show that targeted investments in high-quality pre-school education and energy efficiency return nine and seven times their investments, respectively. While some direct assistance to the poor such as grants of cash, food, and medicine will remain important during a transition period, other targeted investments to eradicate poverty might have similarly high payoffs. The following areas are rife with investment opportunities.

HEALTH

Studies show the effects of wealth disparities on the health of a population. The health of individuals in society is strongly and inversely correlated with inequality of income. The US is the wealthiest nation on earth – ever – but people live longer in Sweden and Japan, where incomes are more equal although per capita health expenditures are less than half. About a third of Americans under age 65 do not have year-round health insurance. When uninsured people get sick, they are less likely to seek medical attention until they are really sick and it is more expensive to treat them. Then, if they were not poor already, medical bills can push them into poverty. So poverty helps make people sick, and being sick helps make people poor.

CRIME

The cost of judicial, correctional, and security systems could be substantially reduced by removing the desperation that causes a large fraction of crime. In societies where inequality of income prevails, violence is more prevalent than in more equal societies. Half of male prisoners are unemployed when they are arrested, and up to 70 percent are functionally illiterate. Saving one child from a life of crime can save society around $2 million.

EDUCATION

Educating all our people so that all can take jobs at high skill levels would increase the income circulating through the economy. High school graduates earn more than 40% more than high school dropouts. This benefits everyone as the resulting additional savings (America's savings rate is now negative) creates investment capital to create more jobs; the additional income creates economic demand to support businesses that create jobs; and the additional income also spreads the tax burden more broadly to support needed infrastructure maintenance such as for our failing roads and bridges. Education is the primary means by which people can lift themselves out of poverty, yet the amount spent on education targeting low-income children falls far short of the need.

EMPLOYMENT

Joblessness is a primary cause of both absolute and relative poverty in otherwise wealthy societies. About a quarter of Americans try to live on $26,640 or less while the rest live on incomes averaging more than $60,000. For the lower quarter, there is not enough income to heat and/or cool their homes, feed their children, and afford medical care. Providing good jobs at living wages permeates through the economy. A healthy economy means more new cars, air conditioners, home theatres and all the good things that money can buy — which supports automobile manufacturers, department stores, dry cleaners and grocers.

HOMELESSNESS

More than 3.5 million Americans are affected by homelessness for at least part of the year each year. Homelessness contributes to interrupted educations, lack of adequate health care, persistent hunger, and higher crime rates. Yet federal spending on housing is less than half what it was in 1976. If all American families could afford decent housing, it would save the economy nearly $70 billion a year.

HUNGER

An estimated 14 million American children live in homes where there is not enough food. In fact, 28 percent of Americans had to choose between medical care and food in the first half of 2004, and even more had to choose between food and rent. Hungry children can't learn, and hungry people are not healthy. Making sure every American has enough nutritious food to eat will redound throughout the economy in healthier, better educated, more fully employed citizens.

CONCLUSION

Investments in low-income Americans are among the most cost-effective investments we can make. It is time for America to invest in eliminating poverty for the benefit of all Americans.

INSTITUTIONAL ECONOMICS OF POVERTY: AN INQUIRY INTO THE CAUSES AND EFFECTS OF POVERTY

Impoverished parents do not have, and the welfare system does not provide them with, adequate means to make the necessary investment in their children to lift them out of a life of poverty. The types of investments in human capital that are both most important and most likely to be inadequate for impoverished children include nutrition, health care, and education. The inadequacy of these kinds of investment in the human capital represented by impoverished children condemns them to lifelong poverty through succeeding generations. Nobel Laureate Gary Becker has investigated this problem and has concluded that "the case is overwhelming that investments in human capital are one of the most effective ways to raise the poor to decent levels of income and health" [Becker 1995, 7].

More than one-fifth of all American children were impoverished in 1993. The rate of childhood poverty was higher in the United States than in most other Western nations [Bergmann 1996, 1; Duncan and Brooks-Gunn 1997, 1]. "American children are twice as likely to be poor as Canadian children, 3 times as likely to be poor as British children, 4 times as likely to be poor as French children, and 7 to 13 times as likely to be poor as German, Dutch, and Swedish children" [Lavelle 1995, 38]. Welfare does not eliminate poverty. In the early 1990s, the combined benefits from Aid to Families with Dependent Children and Food Stamps amounted to only 72 percent of the poverty line for a mother with two children in a median state [Danziger and Gottschalk 1995, 91]. The children of working poor mothers are more endangered than children on welfare because they are not eligible for Medicaid, and the cost of child care averages more than 25 percent of their mother's income [Chase-Lansdale and Brooks-Gunn 1995, 161-168; Lavelle 1995, 104].

Persistent poverty usually causes chronic malnutrition, which produces extremely detrimental consequences for children. The severity of these detrimental consequences is influenced by the intensity and duration of the poverty and by the age of the impoverished child. Malnutrition during infancy and childhood can damage their immune system and produce a wide variety of negative health outcomes [Sidel 1996, 143-147]. Moreover, chronic malnutrition adversely affects the development of the central nervous system and can cause permanent brain damage and mental retardation. Chronically inadequate nutrition inhibits the development of cognitive ability and social skills. Learning disabilities are an almost inevitable result of chronic malnutrition during infancy and childhood. All of these negative physical and mental outcomes of infant and childhood poverty combine to cause learning failure and to limit academic performance [Duncan and Brooks-Gunn 1997, 70-99; Karp 1993, 13-30; Walker 1994, 117-135]. Impoverished children are two to three times as likely to suffer from physical and mental disabilities as children who are not poor [Sidel 1996, 142-144; Lavelle 1995, 131].

These physical and mental disabilities, which have been caused by malnutrition, are greatly exacerbated by the very low quality and the woefully inadequate quantity of health care that impoverished children receive. Only about half of poor children are eligible for Medicaid, but even these children receive health care that is substantially inferior to the health care that children who are not poor receive. Most Medicaid providers are over worked and under paid. The access of poor children to Medicaid care is frequently limited by the inconvenient location of medical facilities and the long waiting time for service. For these and other reasons, Medicaid health care is likely to be piecemeal, discontinuous, uncoordinated, inefficient, and therefore inadequate. Medicaid providers are especially derelict in their failure to provide adequate preventive care [Rodgers 1996, 69-128; Chase-Lansdale and Brooks 1995, 159-1691.

Although the children who are covered by Medicaid receive inferior health care, they are more fortunate than the children of the working poor who are ineligible for Medicaid. Financial barriers deny these impoverished children access to the health care they need. This medical neglect causes a substantial deterioration in the health of most of these poor children who are not covered by Medicaid. Impoverished children are much more likely to be inadequately immunized than children who are not poor [Chase-Lansdale and Brooks-Gunn 1995, 159-185; Sidel 1996, 146].

Most of these impoverished physically and mentally disabled children attend our very worst schools either in central city ghettos or in impoverished nonmetropolitan school districts with tax bases that are woefully inadequate to finance quality education. The neighborhoods are depressed and dangerous; the infrastructure of buildings and equipment is ancient and decrepit. The faculty, which ranges from inexperienced to incompetent, works with totally inadequate resources in an impossible attempt to teach the unteachable progeny of poverty [Will and Vatter 1970, 9396; Sidel 1996, 141-143; Jargowsky 1997, 110-111]. Because of their physical disabilities, impoverished children are irregular in their attendance; because of their mental disabilities, they fail to learn when they are present in their schools [Sidel 1996, 142-144; Lavelle 1995, 131]. Impoverished parents usually fail to provide adequate support for their children's quest for education; poor parents are more likely to have low expectations for their children and less likely to be involved in their schooling than more affluent parents [Handler 1995, 37].

For all of these reasons, impoverished children are very likely to receive an inferior education. Indeed, the quality of education in schools located in central city ghettos is likely to be so low that it is only marginally better than no education at all. If the compensation that ghetto youths can receive from criminal activity is considered, then additional years of schooling would involve a significant opportunity cost. Adolescents who have lived in poverty for four years are approximately 75 percent less likely to graduate from high school than non-poor adolescents [Duncan and Brooks-Gunn 1997, 388-399]. The probability that an impoverished child will graduate from college is extremely low. Less than 4 percent of the children from the lowest quartile of families by income graduate from college; more than 75 percent of the children from the highest quartile of families graduate from college [Lavelle 1995 691.

Impoverished youths who graduate from high school, but who have no education beyond high school, fare hardly better than dropouts. During the 1950s and 1960s, most male high school graduates found secure and lucrative employment in the manufacturing sector, but more recent changes have affected their employment opportunities in an extremely adverse manner. Manufacturing employment has declined drastically during recent years. Moreover, most manufacturing plants have moved out of the central cities into suburbs that are far beyond the commuting range of ghetto youths [Holzer 1996, 1-44].

Meanwhile, the trend toward increased automation in manufacturing has eliminated many of the jobs of unskilled and semi-skilled laborers and has increased the skill requirements for the remaining jobs beyond the qualifications of high school graduates. Most good jobs in manufacturing require at least the equivalent of an associate's degree from a community college. The most popular method of recruiting laborers is through informal referrals from current employees and other contacts, but this method of recruitment inherently discriminates against disadvantaged minorities. This inherent discrimination is intensified by the screening methods that are used to select the successful candidates from the pool of applicants [Holzer 1996, 45-70].

Most female high school graduates find employment in the service sector where employment has increased rapidly and substantially, but there has been a tendency for employment opportunities to move from the central cities into the suburbs. Moreover, technological progress has increased the skill requirements for the better jobs to a level that is beyond the qualifications of an impoverished high school graduate [Holzer 1996, 71-105].

Even if impoverished youths are fortunate enough to find employment, the wages are likely to be so low that they are condemned to continuing poverty as a members of the working poor. During recent years, the incomes of Americans without college degrees have decreased significantly. Income differentials between whites and minorities have increased, and gender differentials between men and women continue to be large [Holzer 1996, 106-125]. The final result of these trends in employment and wages has been to perpetuate poverty from one generation to the next indefinitely into the future [Holzer 1996, 126-135]. The fundamental cause of perpetual poverty is the failure of the American people to invest adequately in the human capital represented by impoverished children.

A single mother who is a victim of poverty has a choice between two alternatives: she can choose to go on welfare, or she can choose to seek employment in order to support herself and her children. The tragic outcome of her choice is that neither alternative is likely to lift her and her children out of perpetual poverty. If she chooses to go on welfare, she will qualify for benefits worth about $7,500 a year in a typical state. She will also qualify herself and her children for free health care provided by Medicaid, and she can stay at home and care for her children [Bergmann 1996, 12-13; Rodgers 1996, 69-107]. Even these inadequate benefits have been jeopardized by the conservative Republican Congress, which has decentralized control over these programs, reduced federal expenditures on them in real terms, and repealed the legal entitlement of dependent children to aid [Bergmann 1996, 91-95]. It is interesting to note that the Congress that repealed the dependent children's entitlement to aid did nothing to limit or reduce the entitlement of millions of affluent elderly citizens to extremely bountiful Social Security benefits, which they do not need.

If the single mother chooses to seek employment, then she will probably join the ranks of the working poor. Most impoverished single mothers are not qualified for any job that would pay above the minimum wage of $5.15 an hour. If she is fortunate enough to find a full-time minimum-wage job and to hold it for a year, she will earn an annual income of $9,893 after Social Security taxes have been deducted from her wages. Additionally, she would qualify for an earned income tax credit and food stamps worth approximately $3,400, but she would lose the Medicaid benefits for herself and her children. Moreover, the working poor single mother would need to provide care for her children at a cost of more than 25 percent of her income. If all of these benefits and costs of working are considered, then the inevitable conclusion is that working poor mothers are at best only marginally better off than single welfare mothers. At worst, working poor mothers endure a lower level of living than welfare mothers [Bergmann 1996, 12-13].

The structure of the American welfare system, which punishes welfare mothers who seek employment, creates a disincentive for them to leave the system. This disincentive has been exacerbated by the very limited and rapidly deteriorating employment opportunities for unskilled laborers. These circumstances have contributed not only to the perpetuation of poverty, but also to the increase in the childhood poverty rate from 14 percent in 1973 to 19.7 percent in 1991 [Danziger and Gottschalk 1995, 90].

The American welfare system is destroying the lower middle class. The minority of the members of this class who are fortunate enough to acquire skills that can be marketed in the high-technology economy of the twenty-first century will prosper and move up into the upper middle class. The majority of the members of the lower middle class who fail to acquire marketable skills will sink into the lower class and suffer from a lifelong damnation of perpetual poverty. In sharp contrast to the United States, France has developed a system of public assistance that has virtually eliminated poverty. This system encourages, facilitates, and subsidizes investment in the human capital represented by children. Unlike the United States, France maintains a national system of health insurance that provides free health care for all legal residents, including children. Additionally, France has established a special public health service to provide a comprehensive system of free preventive medical care for all pregnant women and their babies. All French working mothers are entitled to maternity leave with pay [Bergmann 1996, 59-61, 7085].

The French government provides very liberally for day care and education for infants, children, and youths. Publically supported centers provide high-quality day care for infants and toddlers from birth to the age of three. The fee for this service is based on the ability of the parents to pay. Impoverished parents make small token payments; parents with an annual income of more than $80,000 pay the full cost of the care [Bergmann 1996, 35-41]. Free nursery schools are provided for all children, regardless of the income of their parents, from the time that they are toilet trained until they enter the free public elementary schools. Free child care before and after school is provided for children of working parents [Bergmann 1996, 2835].

The French government maintains a dual system of free secondary schools: the regular system of secondary schools, open to all students; and a special system of superior secondary schools, called lycees, for especially talented students. Admission to the lycees is based on competitive examinations. Approximately 45 percent of all French students graduate from a lycee. Free tuition at state universities is available to anyone who can qualify for admission [Bergmann 1996, 27-28]. The education of French children is never limited by the ability of their parents to pay for their education. All levels of French schools, from nursery school through universities, provide high-quality educations.

French social programs offer several cash benefits that are paid to parents for the purpose of raising the standard of living for their children. All parents, regardless of their incomes, are entitled to a family allowance that is based on the number of children they have. They are entitled to an additional allowance for each handicapped child they have. All pregnant women are eligible for the new baby allowance of $134 a month from the beginning of the second trimester of their pregnancy until their babies are three-months old. This allowance can be continued beyond the normal termination date for impoverished mothers. Single-parent subsistence is paid to destitute single mothers with small children. These destitute single mothers are eligible for a guaranteed minimum income to assist them when they reenter the labor market. All of these programs provide French parents with supplementary income that they can invest in the human capital represented by their children [Bergmann 1996, 50-69].

The American people have a choice. They can choose to continue the present welfare system, which oppresses dependent children in order to grant very lucrative tax breaks and bountiful Social Security benefits to millions of citizens who range from affluent to obscenely wealthy. The alternative would be to follow the French model of investing in the human capital embodied in our children in order to eliminate poverty in two generations. It is my highest hope and my most fervent prayer that the American people will choose the latter alternative and that the United States will become the land of opportunity, not only in theory, but also in practice.

THE POVERTY OF ECONOMICS

In 1766 the Marquis de Mirabeau, the father of the celebrated revolutionary orator, declared that history was over. "There have been, since the world began," he wrote, "three great inventions which have principally given stability to political societies. The first is the invention of writing, which alone gives human nature the power of transmitting, without alteration, its laws, its contracts, its annals and its discoveries. The second is the invention of money which binds together all the relations between civilised societies."

So far so good. But what could be the third invention to match or combine these two? At a distance of two centuries, one holds one's breath. "The third," the marquis wrote, "is the Oeconomical Table, the result of the other two, which completes them both by perfecting their object." The table in question, a bizarre arrangement of squiggles and zig-zags, has come down to us. A copy was discovered in the marquis's papers in the

French national archives in Paris at the end of the 19th century and published soon afterward to a mystification as deep as it was complete. Devised by Mirabeau's friend, Frané{s de Quesnay, a part-time economist and full-time gynaecologist to Mme de Pompadour, it purported to show the way in which money multiplies in society. In as much as any meaning can be disentangled, it is nonsense. The early economists were entranced by Harvey's picture of the circulation of the blood: they took it over as their metaphor for society until Adam Smith popularised the theatrical image of the invisible hand. The tableau is interesting only as a primitive instance of the economists' intense, almost mystical, yearning for the key to existence; and their love of rapturous conclusions.

A century later, the economists are still at it. In his Principles of Economics, Alfred Marshall, Keynes's master and the founder of the modern British school of economics, announced that he had uncovered the secret of modern society. It was, he said in the accents of a man of the world, money: "... it is this definite and exact money measurement of the steadiest motives in business which has enabled economics far to outrun every other branch of the study of man. Just as the chemist's fine balance has made chemistry more exact than most other physical sciences; so this economist's balance, rough and imperfect as it is, has made economics more exact than any other branch of social science."

Modern economists are not quite so gullible or rash. But common to all the economists I've met-and, who knows, maybe to the hundreds of thousands of tenured and commercial economists in the world-is a placid and ineradicable belief that only economics can provide a coherent picture of society: all else is anecdote or impression. It doesn't matter that no two economists agree on anything except the prestige of their branch of study; that they are ignorant of the world and human nature and proud of it; that they like to sample their own merchandise, speculating in financial markets or binding themselves to narrow commercial interests; and that they devise models and make forecasts which are so maniacally precise that they are never borne out by events except by chance. Economics, they say, is the language in which human beings should describe their activity, and states should describe their affairs.

All intellectual castes try to impose their view of the world, if only to put bread on their own tables. But economists have an advantage over, say, mechanical engineers, because their stock-in-trade-money-has a property not found in applied mathematics: a property which, for want of a better word (and please forgive the impropriety), might be termed psychological. Just as money, because it will gratify all desire, becomes the equivalent of the most intense desire and will crowd out all other goals in life; so economics, the science and gospel of money, will tend to displace other intellectual activity. Economics, which has always claimed to reason on the basis of the rational pursuit of money, actually prospers because of money's irrational cult.

The result is that governments and public are happy to consume economics in much greater doses than physics or ethics or Homer or even an honest, properly labelled religion. As a child in England in the 1960s, I was delivered nightly to the economic obsessions of British television. A profound gloom, appropriate to that prosperous epoch, lowered over my early schooldays. In the 1970s, the economists told me that the world was running out of fuel and I prepared for a Malthusian catastrophe which, however, was postponed. In the 1980s, I learned that inflation was always and invariably a monetary phenomenon, except when it wasn't. In the 1990s, the economists told me that I had to import the German deflation through semi-fixed currency rates of exchange and when that didn't work, that I shouldn't. Now, the national history of Europe is drawing to a close. We hear, faintly through the temple door, the economists mumbling obsequies for it in their dead liturgical language: budget deficit, GNP, inflation and so on; but it is not a ceremony to which the public is invited. Economics, which is supposed to have had a hand in restoring democracy to Europe in the 17th century, has now abolished it.

At the heart of economics are notions that seem to me ludicrously antiquated-old-fashioned even in the 17th century. The most important of these is that reality must only be described in categories of quantity, the chief of which is money. Money is not simply the common denominator by which the costs and gains of technically rational conduct can be measured, explained and predicted. For the economists, money is a synonym of happiness: sums of money embody the welfare of the nation and the happiness of the individual. Admittedly, national welfare is no longer measured by holdings of bullion (as in the 16th century) or as an Overplus in Foreign Trade (as in the 17th) but as GDP or, an even greater refinement, GDP divided by the number of people sharing in it. But the hero of economics, its Achilles or Roland, is still the person who pursues money tenaciously till his last breath. The heir of antiquity and the age of faith, the culmination of 50 centuries of social evolution, is Cedric Brown of British Gas.

As a picture of both the individual and society, economics is almost unbelievably crude. To select something as measure simply because it can be measured, and not because it is particularly suitable, puts the economist in the position of the drunkard who has lost his house keys, and searches not where he thought he dropped them, but under a street light, because there is light. The economists do not tell you what people are doing, let alone why, only what they would do in various imaginary situations if they were perfectly wise and compulsively avaricious. As for nations, GDP does not begin to describe a nation's welfare even at starvation levels and certainly does not measure the condition of a society, such as ours, which has been well-to-do since the voyage of The Golden Hind. And anyway money is the worst of all measures because it will not hold its value from month to month, let alone over centuries: imagine using a tape-measure that was forever expanding and contracting. That is why economists cannot understand the past or imagine a future: they are imprisoned in an ideal present. Keynes's excursions into history, in the later sections of the General Theory, are deeply embarrassing. On October 16th 1929, Irving Fisher declared that "stock prices have reached what looks like a permanently high plateau."

Does it matter? Aren't the economists, to develop an idea of Dr Samuel Johnson, harmlessly employed? If they weren't tinkering with their competitive equilibrium models in the shed, might they not be doing something horrible in the basement? Even economists, it seems, have alternative uses.

I am not sure. The economists are happy to claim for themselves or their profession the credit for gains of quantity such as expanded product, rising populations, and more houses, medicines, automobiles, televisions and things in general. For the sake of consistency, they should also take credit for the deteriorating quality of existence. For it is their philistine notions of personal and national welfare that have helped to ruin the natural world; confused technology with culture; reduced art to money, time to interest, sexual relations to pornography, friendship to advantage, charity to the charity ball and liberty to shopping, and wasted whole generations, who because they have been taught to think only in categories of money have, in Schopenhauer's phrase, "missed the purpose of existence." All these aspects of modernity, which are quite striking, are ignored by the economists to a degree that can only be termed pathological. The economists seem to be petrified of human nature: Sir Samuel Brittan wrote recently in the Financial Times that he had not read much of The Theory of Moral Sentiments (by Adam Smith) because it looked as if it might have some "armchair psychology" in it. (It hasn't). In all the corpus of economic literature, I am aware of only three locations-a shy footnote in Marshall's Principles of Economics, short paragraphs in Keynes's Economic Possibilities for our Grandchildren, and Book V of The Wealth of Nations-that attempt to describe the world you and I live in.

Where did economics go wrong? The short answer is that it never went right. In a passage in the Politics, Aristotle breaks off from a discussion of lending at interest to say that such discussions were all very well but not really a proper occupation for a philosopher. In that he was quite right, not for reasons of social propriety or Standesw2de but of the proper allocation of resources: "economic" preoccupations distract a person from the much more important studies of ethics and politics. Joseph Schumpeter, in a commentary of blissful ignorance, accuses Aristotle of being a bad economist: to which

Aristotle would no doubt have replied that Schumpeter was a bad philosopher.

In the middle ages, the integrity of thought and character that we associate with antiquity begins to break up under the pressure of mercantile self-interest. New questions come rushing in. What is prosperity? How does it relate to national power? What is trade? And how does it relate to agriculture and money? What is money, anyway? And why is Holland, though it only makes cheese, so rich and powerful, while Spain, with all its American silver, is so poor and weak? What is the best form of government? The merchants need a new language in which to pose and answer these questions, a language which will derive its authority not from the stale old world of church or court but the new certainties of natural science. It will be Newtonian science carried over into society, and will aim, in the ominous words of Sir Wiiliam Petty, "to express itself in terms of number, weight or measure, to use only arguments of sense and to consider only such causes as have visible foundations in nature; leaving those that depend upon the mutable minds, opinions, appetites and passions of particular men to the consideration of others." This process culminates 100 years later in the pseudo-Newtonian system of Adam Smith, in which the role of gravity is taken by self-interest.

Smith ignored the warnings of Aristotle and compartmentalised his thoughts on ethics, the law and political economy. I suppose he was practising a crude division of philosophical labour. The trouble is that nobody reads The Theory of Moral Sentiments or the Lectures on Jurisprudence, but large numbers of people have heard of the argument of The Wealth of Nations. I understand that even some economists have read it, though not to the end. If, as Adam Smith does here, you dispense with all human psychology except its self-regarding tendencies, and all social experience except mercenary exchange mediated by money, you can still have a view of society of sorts; but it ain't likely to be very accurate or edifying. And then to suggest that it's all for the best, in the best of all possible worlds, presided over by a benign mechanical deity or invisible hand. How soothing to bad commercial consciences!

The whole production is shot through with an intense, and very Scottish, mystical fervour: "It is the produce of the land which draws the fish from the waters; and it is the produce of the surface of the earth which extracts the minerals from its bowels." Just Isaiah, really, but about Mammon, not God.

The book has some very witty passages, but it has no new thoughts. I confess that I have not read all the 17th century English and Scottish economic pamphlets in the British Library, or indeed more than a fraction of them; but from my reading of these and the 18th century writers, it is clear that Adam Smith is a compendium of existing notions. The most important thoughts-that the merchants should be left alone to make money, that self-interest is the engine of history and that it is all for the good-were self-serving commonplaces in England (and, presumably, Holland) by the middle of the previous century; so is the distinction between real and nominal wealth; the theory of specie-flow (in which trade imbalances are adjusted by exports and imports of precious metals) and so on. The division of labour was well understood in antiquity. Other passages are taken from Diderot's encyclopaedia-for example the famous description of the making of a pin-John Law, Hutcheson, Hume or Mandeville.

In truth, all the interesting thinking in economics had been done by the 1720s. The Wealth of Nations, far from inaugurating economics as a science, is actually its swansong. The life has all gone out of it. Though Smith seems to have been a nice enough man in an absent-minded sort of way, how one misses the raffish brilliance of his predecessors. I am not saying that you need to be a duellist, or murdered by your cook, or be excluded by name from a general amnesty, or start a revolution, to be a good economist, merely that the greatest economists-William Petty, John Law, Richard Cantillon, James Steuart, Alexander Hamilton-did all those things. They experienced the world, not a model of it. That is what Sir Walter Scott had in mind when, in Rob Roy, he blamed the division of labour (that is, Adam Smith) for the departed glory of the world. For economics was not the only or even the best intellectual response to the changes of the 16th and 17th centuries. At the same time as the first economic pamphlets are being written, the novel is invented in prose, the language of commerce. At no point does Cervantes tell us that he is trying to portray the revolution in prices in 16th century Spain; but he does, he does. A hundred years before Cantillon cracks the Spanish conundrum (in a passage of such brilliance that but for him the economists might still be worrying at it today), we have the Knight of the Doleful Countenance wandering, violent, heart-broken and deranged, through a land of money. The best novelists cover the same social ground as the economists, but take on the frightening questions of ethics and psychology. While Smith, Mill and Jevons intone their litanies about money being a means of exchange, token, counter, wholly insignificant, a "Meer Conveniency," George Eliot and Balzac show us the true face of modernity: the face of the compulsive miser. Dickens jeers at the economists' quantitative approach when he describes an industrial process in Hard Times: "So many hundred Hands in this Mill; so many hundred horse Steam Power. It is known, to the force of a single pound weight, what the engine will do; but, not all the calculators of the National Debt can tell me the capacity for good or evil, for love or hatred, for patriotism or discontent, for the decomposition of virtue into vice, or the reverse, at any single moment in the soul of one of these its quiet servants, with the composed faces and the regulated actions."

The good novelists are superior to the economists not just in their awareness of the breadth and variety of human life and the distinction between right and wrong; nor even in their analytical precision; but in their very fallibility. Both economists and imaginative artists make fictions: but the economists don't realise it. And it is the sense of fallibility, as Socrates used to argue, that distinguishes the philosopher from the charlatan.

Bibliography

Ahuja, V.: *Everyone's Miracle?,* Washington, DC: World Bank, 1997.

Balchin, P., & Kieve, L.: *Urban Land Economics,* London, MacMillan Press, 1977.

Barro, Robert J., : *Economic Growth.* McGraw-Hill, 1995.

Bhagwati, Jagdish: *India in Transition: Freeing the Economy,* Oxford, Clarendon Press, 1993.

Chandhok, H.L.: *The Economy: Annual Time Series Data,* New Delhi, Living Media India, 1990.

Dahiya, L.N.: *Dynamics of Economic Life in Rural India,* Delhi, Gian, 1991.

Ehrenberg, Ronald: *Modern Labor Economics,* Harper Collins, 1994.

Greene, William H.: *Econometric Analysis,* MacMillan Publishing Company, 1993.

J.H. Dully, and R. Jolly: *Redistribution with Growth,* London, Oxford University Press, 2001.

Kelly, F. P.: *Charging and Accounting for Bursty Connections,* Massachusetts, MIT Press, 1997.

Little, I.M.D.: *India: Macroeconomics and Political Economy, 1964-1991,* Washington, World Bank, 1994.

Mongia, J.N.: *India's Economic Development Strategies, 1951-2000 A.D..* New Delhi, Allied, 1986.

Petre, D., & Harrington, D.: *The Clever Country? Australia's Digital Future,* Sydney, Lansdowne Publishing Ltd, 1996.

Ray, S.K.: *Indian Economy,* New Delhi, Prentice-Hall, 1987.

Varian, H. R.: *Intermediate Microeconomics,* New York, W W Norton and Company, 1987.

Index

❑❑❑